SOCIOLOGY OF TEACHING AND CURRICULUM

Sociology of Teaching and Curriculum

V.K. KAUSHIK
RAVI PRAKASH

KANISHKA PUBLISHERS, DISTRIBUTORS
NEW DELHI-110 002

KANISHKA PUBLISHERS, DISTRIBUTORS
4697/5-21 A, Ansari Road, Daryaganj,
New Delhi -110 002
Phones : 2327 0497, 2328 8285
Fax : 011-2328 8285
E-mail : kanishka_publishing@yahoo.co.in

Sociology of Teaching and Curriculum
Edition–2010

PRINTED IN INDIA

Published by Madan Sachdeva for Kanishka Publishers, Distributors, 4697/5-21A, Ansari Road, Daryaganj, New Delhi-110 002, Typeset by Sunshine Graphics, Delhi, and Printed at Rajdhani Printers, Delhi.

Preface

Education has been defined many times by many persons. Each definition reflects either the personal point of view of the individual or that of the field of knowledge of which he is an exponent. To the biologist, education is largely adaptation, to the psychologist, it is synonymous with learning, to the philosopher and especially to the educator, it reflects the school of thought to which he belongs. Definitions vary from that of the extreme conservative, who views education as a protective process of the state to preserve the status quo to the extreme progressive to whom education is self expression to assist the individual to do better the things he would do any way.

One basic characteristic of social change is that it does not take place at the same rate in the various aspects of the total culture. A second characteristic is that changes in a single artefact or in an institution have their impact upon other aspects of both material and non-material culture. The unprecedented development of television has had tremendous influence not only upon other media of communication, but also upon the family, the school and the religion. Changes in the family have influenced the school as education has likewise influenced life with in the family.

Sociology of teaching and curriculum is the recent trend in studying the influence of various groups in the educational field and how it influences the behaviour development and modification in the development of the learner.

The editor is grateful to various sociologist and educational sociology experts whose books and articles have been referred and at places used in the preparation of this book.

The editor is grateful to American Studies Research Centre, Hyderabad and the British Council Library, New Delhi for allowing the use of their distinguished libraries and the Shri S.P. Tyagi, Department of Education, University of Delhi for giving expert advice in the preparation of this book.

V.K. KAUSHIK
RAVI PRAKASH

Contents

1

The Social Nature of Education

Interaction of culture and education. Educational needs resulting from changing cultural patterns. The meaning of education. The three-fold function of education. The agencies of education.

Education has been defined many times by many persons. Each definition reflects either the personal point of view of the individual or that of the field of knowledge of which he is an exponent. To the biologist, education is largely adaptation; to the psychologist, it is synonymous with learning; to the philosopher, and especially to the educator, it reflects the school of thought to which he belongs. Definitions vary from that of the extreme conservative, who views education as a protective process of the State to preserve the *status quo,* to the extreme progressive to whom education is self-expression—to assist the individual to do better the things he would do anyway.

Interaction of Culture and Education

Interaction is described in terms of persons and groups. It is equally applicable in the interplay of changes that occur in one institution and in the total social milieu. One basic characteristic of social change is that it does not take place at the same rate in the various aspects of the total culture. A second characteristic is that changes in a single artifact or in an institution have their impact upon other aspects of both material and non-material culture. The unprecedented development of television has had tremendous influence not only upon other media of communication but also upon the family, the school, and the church. Changes in the family have influenced the, school as education has likewise influenced life within the family.

Conflicting Concepts of Relationships

The basis of conflicting concepts of education lies primarily in the varying points of view regarding the interaction of the school and other aspects of culture. There are those who believe that the function of education is to reflect the existing cultural pattern of the community or the nation; that the dominant culture of the community should dictate the objectives, the curricula, and the activities of the school. They emphasize the "Three R's" and assert that only such knowledge and skills should be taught as will aid the individual in adjusting to current needs. Education is basically indoctrination.

Others, with equal sincerity, believe that a basic function of education is to be the directive agent in social change. They emphasize academic freedom and assert that the school should develop in children and youth the ability to weigh issues and to think critically. Two sharply contrasting means are advanced to achieve this objective:

1. letting children play their own school programme and activities with a minimum of guidance from the teacher; and
2. planning of curricula and activities by professional educators to encourage critical appraisal of the existing cultural pattern with the aim of improving it.

The varying interpretations of the role of education in its relation to culture, started above in their more extreme forms, have led to widely publicized conflicts in a number of communities. There will always be honest and sincere differences in points of view as to the role of education in our modern complex society. This is inevitable as individual values are themselves shaped by the varying cultural environment. It is inherent in democracy and, *to the degree that it is based on other than ulterior motives,* it may be beneficial. Unfortunately, the present world situation includes ulterior motives disguised as anti-communism, in addition to those of communism itself.

After briefly analyzing the criticisms of education, Paul Woodring in "An Open Letter to Teachers" makes the following proposals:

> If we are to stem this rising tide of criticism, we must, first of all, make it clear to everyone interested that we fully understand that basic policy in all our institutions is, in the final analysis, to be determined by all the people through their elected representatives. Let us try to make clear the difference between professional problems and matters of policy which have broader import. Let us insist on our right as citizens to take our full part in the establishment of policy, but not upon a right to be the sole determiners of such policy. We must invite and encourage our critics and all other interested people to sit down with us to discuss the policies of the schools, and then listen carefully to what they have to say, without pre-determined judgments on our part. . . .
>
> Let us re-examine with or critics the question of determining the proper range of experiences to be dealt with in public education. Let us discuss with them the problem of the extent to which the school is responsible for vocational training, for training for leisure-time activities, for moral training; and let them help us to decide which of these are the proper functions of the school, the home, the church, or the shop. Let us quit using the argument that the school must do all these things because other agencies have failed. The same argument can be used as well by any other agency.
>
> Let us discuss with our critics the problem of values in education in its relation to the confused status of values throughout our society. If they can suggest solutions acceptable to the majority we should listen eagerly.
>
> With the representatives of all the people let us examine our textbooks for political bias. The selection of textbooks ought to be a professional matter to be determined by professionals, but if we have erred to the extent that

> widespread criticisms have developed it is best that we discuss the problem frankly with our critics. Let us make it clear that we do not, as a profession, assume that we have the right to determine a policy of social change unacceptable to the majority.

This sharing of points of view is social interaction. It frankly recognizes that in a democracy the school cannot develop independently of the cultural pattern of which it is an integral part; nor can any group in society compel the school to reflect only its own values—or prejudices. Education must be dynamic; it must accept or eliminate functions in relation to the adequacy of other institutions; it must modify its curricula in the light of changes in cultural values and social needs. If the schools is to meet wisely the tremendous responsibility which society has placed in its hands, it must recognize its partnership relationship with other institutions and with the total culture.

The issues briefly indicated above will be discussed in detail later and will be related not only to the school but to the other educational institutions of society as well. The importance of the problem is forcefully stated by Counts:

> We know today, if we have learned the lesson to the immediate past, that organized education may or may not serve the cause of human progress. In fact, we know that it may serve any cause, that it may serve tyranny as well as freedom, ignorance as well as enlightenment, falsehood as well as truth, war as well as peace, death as well as life. It may led men and women to think that they are free even as it rivets upon them the chains of bondage. Education is indeed a force of great power, but whether it is good or bad depends, not on the laws of learning, but on the conception of life or civilization which is expresses.

Educational Needs Resulting from Changing Cultural Patterns

Thus far the interaction of the school with the society of which it is a part has been discussed largely in terms of interpersonal and intergroup relations. The same basic principle applies in the relationship of education to fundamental changes in the larger patterns of culture. Only four have been selected though there is hardly an aspect of cultural change that does not in some way touch upon education.

Population Trends

The data on gross population of the United States are shown in Figure 1.1. In 1790, when the first census was taken, the total population was a little less than 4,000,000; in 1950, it was a little more than 150,000,000 and by July 1, 1953, it was approximately 160,000,000. In April, 1952, the Bureau of the Census made three projections as to probable population in 1970, varying from a low estimate of 165,174,000 to a possible high of 179,812,000. If the increase from 1950 to 1953 continues through the remainder of the decade, the high estimate may prove too low.

In the Department of Commerce Building in Washington is a huge clock which ticks off the time and automatically computes and registers the net change in our total population, considering the excess of births over deaths and of immigration over emigration. With the passing of each thirteen seconds, one person is added to our population, or 277 every hour. This represents the equivalent of a town with a population of 6,648 each passing day, or of a city of more than 200,000 each month. In a single year, the increase in population will equal that of the combined 1950 population of Philadelphia and Denver.

Another approach to the study of gross population is that of the per cent of change be decades. As shown in Figure 1.1, from 1790 to 1860 the total population of the United States increased each decade approximately 35 per cent. However, with the 1870 census and continuing through that of 1940, the percentage of increase diminished rapidly and reached a low of 7.4 per cent during the 1930 decade. On the basis of this trend, indicated by the diagonal line in Figure 1.1 it appeared that by 1970 we would have a stable or perhaps a declining population. Beginning in 1936, but especially since 1940, these predictions were proven wrong; total population rose sharply and the 1950 census showed an increased more than twice that of the 1930 decade. The graph indicates the three directions which the increase to 1960 may take based on the 1950 projections of the Bureau of the Census.

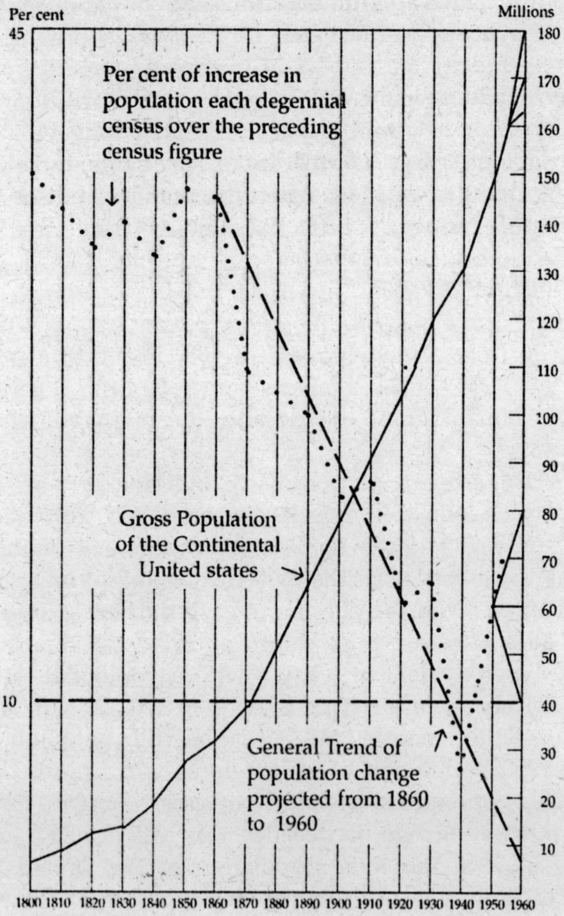

Figure 1.1 : Trends in Gross Population of the United States, 1800 to 1960. (Data from U.S. Census; estimates for 1960, Current Population Reports, Population Estimates, U.S. Bureau of the Census, April 17, 1952.)

When these percentages are translated into the number of persons they represent, their tremendous significance for our entire national life becomes more apparent. The increase in population during the 1930's was only 8,894,229. During the 1940 decade, it was 19,028,082, and sampling surveys made in

1952 indicate that population increase is continuing at the accelerated rate of the last half of the 1940 decade.

Gross figures are important in their implications, but they have even greater significance when broken down into the three causal factors : net immigration, increased longevity, and the number of live births. A fourth factor may be the more complete coverage being procured by census-takers, but this is an immeasurable influence and now of relatively little consequence.

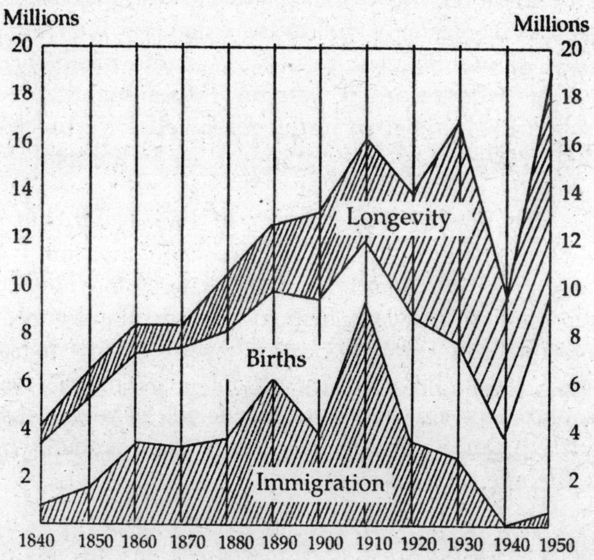

Figure 1.2 : Increase in the Total Population of the United States by Decade and Proportion Accounted for by Increased Longevity, Births, and Immigration. (Data from the Census and the Immigration and Naturalization Service).

In Figure 1.2, these three factors are shown in their relationship to the total increase in population. Since figures were not kept for emigration prior to 1920, net immigration, that is, the number of persons entering the United States in excess of those who returned to their homeland, is shown only after 1920, but the total rather closely parallels the curve of increase of the entire population until the establishment of the quota system in 1924. During the decade 1930-40, the net immigration was less than 50,000; due to special legislation such as the Brides Act and Displaced Persons Act, it rose to 650,000 in 1940-50.

Vital statistics in the United States have been kept only since 1915 but the census figures for the number of persons five years of age and under is a rough measure of the relative importance of the number of births in the population increase. As shown in Figure 1.2, the sustained increase until 1940 not due to immigration was decreasingly the result of the number of births and increasingly due to the extending life span of the individual. This relationship, in spite of the relatively recent discovery of "wonder drugs" was reversed in the decade of the 1940's when the number of births accounted for a much larger proportion of the sharp and significant rise in the total increase in population.

The meaning of these data to the school and to all educational agencies is evident and especially the shift in trends which began in 1936 and has accelerated since 1940. The emphasis upon teaching English to foreigners and concern for first-generation minority groups are rapidly decreasing importance. But the need for schools—classrooms, teachers, and supplies—for children is unparalleled, as is also the need for adult education for the ever-increasing number who live beyond the age of retirement.

Mobility of Population

It would appear that the advice of Horace Greeley, "Go West, young man, go West" has been consistently heeded; the centre of population has moves steadily westward from central Maryland in 1790 to Southeastern Illinois in 1950. A more complete picture to inter-regional mobility is given in Figure 1.3. Every section of the nation is involved. During the seven years from 1940-1947, the emigration from the Southeastern section was a little more than 1,500,000 in excess of immigration while the number of persons moving into the Rocky Mountain and Western states was approximately 2,000,000 in excess of those who moved out of the region. Figure 1.3 also shows the per cent of the population in each section that had not migrated

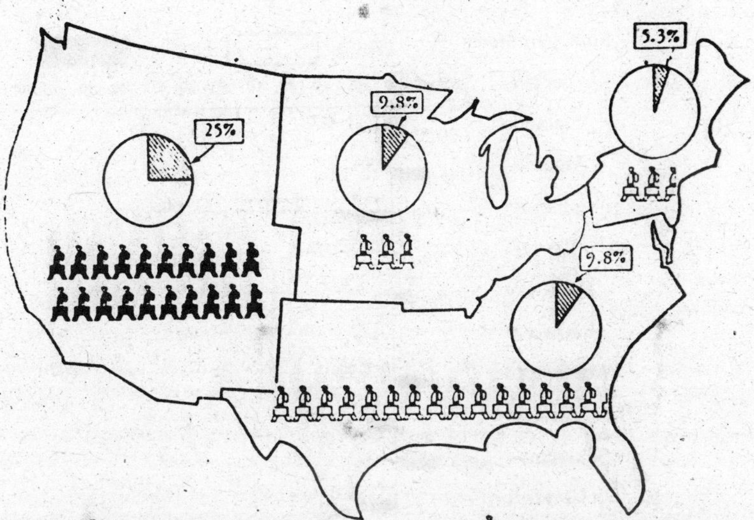

Each [figure] represents a net gain from interregional migration of 1,00,000 persons

Each [figure] represents a net loss from interregional migration of 1,00,000 persons

Shaded portions of circles show the per cent that the total number of migrants was of the 1940 population.

Figure 1.3 : Interregional Migration, April 1940 to April 1947, "Schools and the 1950 Census," *Research Bulletin*, Vol. XXIX, No. 4, p. 152. (Reproduced by permission of the Research Division, National Education Association).

during the seven years and the per cent of the total population which had moved into the region from each of the other three areas of the United States. The trend shown for the seven years has continued since 1947.

As would be expected, the 18-44 age-group shows the highest per cent of mobility. The proportion of Negroes who moved either to another state or into another region was twice that of the white migrant population.

The change in population by states, shown graphically in Figure 1.4, indicates extremely significant trends. Although all three factors—differentials in longevity, in the number of births, and mobility—are involved in the changes, the most important factor is mobility. The small increase, or actual decline, in the Negro population as compared with the white population in the Southern states, and the much larger increase in the number

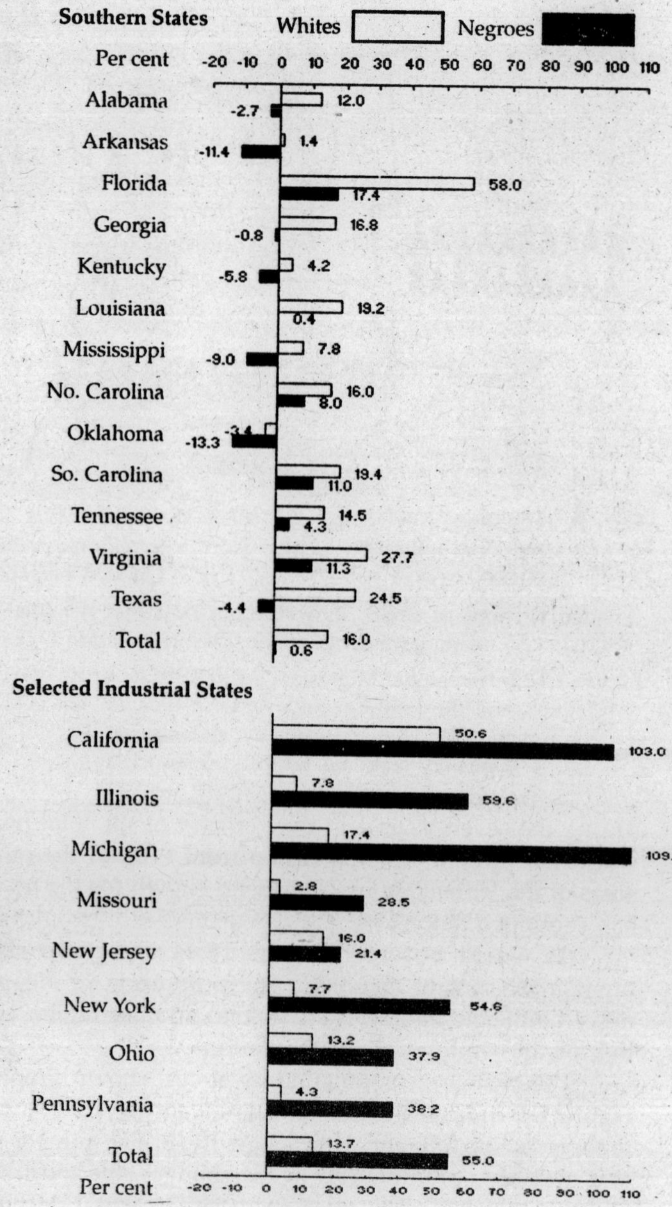

Figure 1.4: Per Cent of Population Changes, Whites and Negroes in Selected States, 1940 to 1950. (Data from U.S. Bureau of Census).

of Negroes than in that of whites in all of the industrial Northern states are especially important since they occurred within a single decade.

Another measure of mobility is the shift of population from rural to urban life. The United States Census for 1950 defines the urban population as persons living in incorporated places of 2,500 or more population plus those in fringe areas of larger cities with a population of 50,000 or more. The consistent shift from rural to urban population from the time of the first census in 1790 to 1950 is shown in Figure 1.5.

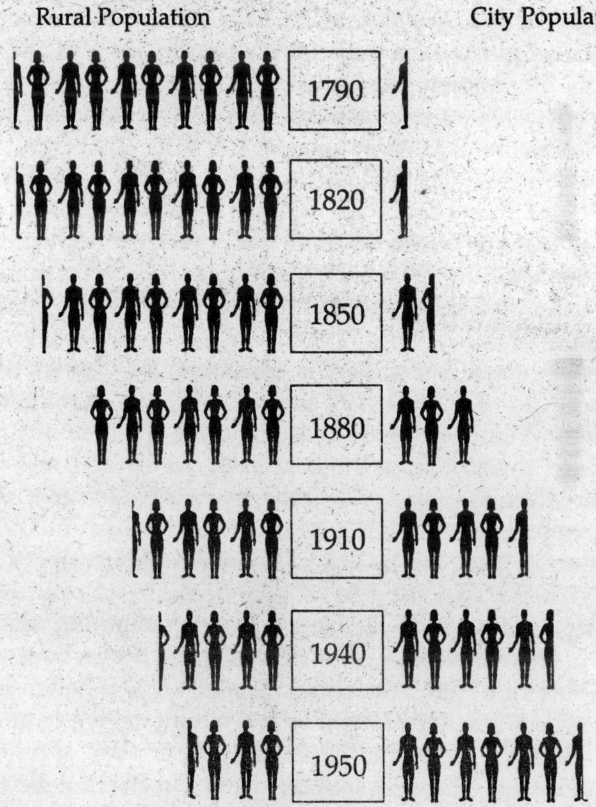

Figure 1.5 : Changes in Per Cent Rural and Urban Population in United States for Selected Decades, 1790 to 1950. (Data from U.S. Bureau of the Census).

For two centuries, America was predominately rural, with scattered towns that were little more than trading areas. In 1800, only five cities had a population of 10,000 or more. A century later, the number had increased to 447, and in 1950, five cities had a population of over 1,000,000; 101, between 100,000 and 1,000,000; 371, between 25,000 and 100,000; and 3793, between 2,500 and 25,000. Even more significant than these gross figures are those in terms of the percentage of the total population classified as urban. The five cities with a population of 10,000 or more in 1800 contained only about 4 per cent of the total population. The 447 cities in 1900 accounted for almost 32 per cent of the total population. In 1950, 47.4 per cent of the population lived in cities of 10,000 or larger. Figure 1.5 presents this change graphically on the basis of census definition of rural (living in towns of less than 2,500 population) and urban for selected decades from 1790 to 1950. Urbanization data are even more significant when it is pointed out that it has continued despite the fact that the net reproduction rate, based on the average number of daughters born per 100 families, is almost twice as high in rural areas as in cities of 100,000 or more population.

The shift of population is illustrated by the growth of New York City. Not until 175 years from the date of its founding, did it attain a population of 33,000. During the next fifty years, it increased to 280,000; in the next thirty, to 630,000; and in the following twenty years, to approximately 850,000 or a rate of gain more than 200 times that of its first 175 years. In 1870, the population of New York City had reached almost one million; it was 5,620,000 in 1920; and in 1950 it was 7,815,099. If New York City is thought of in relation to its commuting area, one twelfth of the entire population of the United States lives within a 45-minute ride from Washington Square on Manhattan Island.

Urbanization has brought with it a high degree of mobility, both in the daily life of the community and in place of residence. New York City's busses, subways, and streetcars collect over 8,000,000 fares every weekday. The average number of cars entering central Manhattan is approximately 300,000 per day. Over a million persons commute in and out of New York City every day. More than 70,000 persons cross 7th Avenue and 40th Street every hour during the day, and an average evening crowd in the theatre district is estimated at 150,000. If the moving vans of New York City in 1940 had moved a different family every time they transferred household goods, each family would be in a different residence approximately every year! One in four would move either in or out of the city each decade.

Patterns of behaviour, well adapted to a predominantly rural and relatively stable population, are not adequate to modern life. Old controls are no longer effective in a highly mobile population, when the world at large is brought to the community and to the home; when a few minutes' ride frees one from all social controls except the minimum of law and one's own standard of values.

Technological Development

The vast developments in technology have been briefly discussed. They are so much a part of our lives that they are taken for granted, yet too little attention has been given to their effect upon the educational process. In later, their effect on employment opportunities and communication and their impact on education will be shown in some detail. Only one illustration can be given here, the effect of hard-surface roads and the automobile.

This writer began his teaching in a one-room rural school not unlike that shown in Plates V and VI. He boarded in a farm home and walked the mile and a half to and from the school. He arrived there in time to build the fire in a metal-jacketed stove which at that time was considered the last word in heating as it was designed to distribute the warm air. The children arrived frequently with wet feet and often thoroughly chilled from wading through mud or snow. Attendance was irregular, especially of the smaller children, who were kept home on days when the weather was bad. Since the grade-range of the children was from the first through the eighth grade, it was necessary to have 28 separate class periods, although it was an unusual day when all classes were "heard."

Today in this same district, concrete or macadam roads pass within a few yards of the door of every farm home. A heated school bus stops for the children and they are transferred to a modern, well heated and lighted building. The teachers are specialists in the grade level and subjects they are teaching and many opportunities are provided for student activities entirely impossible in the "little red school house".

Interdependence of Peoples and Nations

The growing interdependence of the people of the world is obvious in meeting man's physical needs. An examination of the food placed on the dinner table in a modern home is abundant evidence that no man "liveth unto himself." The production of bread, once made by the housewife with flour ground in the local gristmill and with yeast preserved from one baking to the next, now involves a whole chain of commercial activities. From the far-distant farm where it was grown, the grain is hauled by truck and train to a mill and then to a bakery. The final product is again transported to the local grocery. Meat requires an equally complex organization and even the price is dependent upon factors largely beyond the control of either the producer or the purchaser! Fresh vegetables are flown in from distant places or frozen foods are prepared months before they reach the table. When World War II cut off trade with the Far East, pepper became a scarce commodity.

This dependence upon others is obvious, but the same inter-dependence is equally true in the realm of ideas. The unprecedented expansion of the media of communication is described the printed word, newspapers, periodicals and books; and oral and visual communication, telephone, movies, radio, and television. Cultural isolation is no longer possible. Communication, that has provided the vast network of thought transmission throughout the United States, is becoming increasingly world-wide. Even now, the rich tones of Big Ben can be heard around the world. Events occurring in the United Nations Assembly in New York City can be instantaneously seen and heard in more than half of our homes.

In the light of these facts, education takes on new significance. Its goals must be conceived in different terms than if it were only providing the means for living in a stable and relatively immobile population, in a civilization dependent more upon natural resources rather than upon technological developments, and in a culture isolated from an adjacent community and even from the far places of the earth. These changes modify the meaning of education in the modern world.

The Meaning of Education

As previously pointed out, the continual emphasis upon social interaction gives the key to education as conceived by the educational sociologist. *Education is the consciously controlled process whereby changes in behaviour are produced in the person and through the person within the group.* From this point of view, education is a process that begins at birth and continues throughout life.

The phrase "consciously controlled" requires elaboration. Some have maintained that all experience of the person has some, although varying, influence on his behaviours, and hence on his education. From this point of view, education is life and all of life is education. The root meaning of the word "education"—"to lead out"—implies a degree of awareness of the goals to be achieved. This does not imply that education is limited to the school and the Church, the two institutions whose primary purpose is to influence human behaviour. The mother and other members of the family exercise sometimes more sometimes less conscious control than does the school. While economic motives may prompt the development of commercial recreation, such as the movies, their importance in influencing behaviour is evidenced by legal censorship in a few states and voluntary censorship by the producers themselves. Conversely, the term "education," as here defined, does not include modification of behaviour which results from the mere fact of growth or the purely incidental or accidental learning in the usual course of the day. No definite lines can be drawn between such incidental learning and that which is consciously controlled, but the fundamental distinction differentiates education and life.

As Learning

Another term that requires further consideration is "behaviour changes." Here, too, a dual precaution is necessary:

not all changes in behaviour are the result of education, and not all learning produces social interaction; hence these are not social learning and cannot be "education" in a sociological sense. Language may be used as an illustration. The infant develops vocalization in the normal process of growth. Parents and others in the family group call objects by their names and, at the first sound that is even remotely similar to a word equivalent, the response is highly pleasing to the infant. Through such responses, repeated when the sound is made, together with imitation of the sounds continually made by those associated with the child, a one-word vocabulary gradually increases, becomes short sentences, and then emerges into normal word usage. Thenceforth, until the child goes to school, the further development of his language is usually due to incidental learning. One of the first and primary functions of the school is the improvement of pupils in both oral and written expression. In every grade, through at least the first year of college, English is a required subject. All too often, language becomes disassociated from its original function of producing behaviour changes to become rote learning. Studies of reading habits of adolescents and adults are abundant testimony that, for many, the classroom fails to influences the persons choice of free-time reading.

As Behaviour

One other fundamental distinction between educational sociology and the common approach to education is the relation between individual learning and changes in group-behaviour patterns through social interaction. Except for material culture and the formalized social organization, all changes in group behaviour are changes in the behaviour of the individual members of the group. But changes in behaviour that are solely in terms of individual learning and have little social context cannot be considered as education by the educational sociologist. This is a fundamental distinction between educational psychology and educational sociology—the former is chiefly concerned with the *learning* process, the latter, with the *educative* process.

A further differentiation is clearly drawn by Payne. "Education has been frequently conceived as growth or development. And rightly so, for all education implies growth or development. Education involves changes in behaviour, and all such changes imply growth, whether the changes take place in a desirable or undesirable direction. The boy in the predatory gang that learns to outwit the policemen, steals wares from the corner groceryman, sells bootleg whiskey and escapes the clutches of the law, or commits successful burglary is growing in one direction and is thus being educated. The process of education taking place in these instances is as definite as those that occur when the school or the family creates or provides situations that result is desirable behaviour changes. The distinction, then, between mere learning and education or the learning process and the educational process hinges upon the character of the situation in which the growth or learning takes place."

This emphasis upon social interaction should not be construed to imply that the educational sociologist is interested only in resultant changes in social behaviour as such. In social behaviour is included that whole field of human values and resulting attitudes. Education in its highest sense has taken place when external controls have been accepted as convictions by the person and have thus become internal controls. Nor is it to be assumed that education must be functional, if conceived in the narrow meaning of the term. It can be related to life without being vocational, for, again, the development of appreciations, of desire for more information, of ability to weigh and judge relative values is just as functional—perhaps, for many, more so—as knowledge or skill that can be turned to vocational use. The development of common elements of courtesy and a deep sense of human relationships is a vital element of the educative process. In terms of social interaction, no lines of distinction can be drawn paralleling the artificial and unrealistic division between vocational and general education. That which makes for more effective participation in the total process of social interaction whether in terms of social, economic, health, or any other socially desirable human value is education.

The Threefold Function of Education

Educational literature contains numerous statements regarding the function of education. Such statements reflect the economic, political, social, and religious values of the period or country in which they are made. The present rapid changes in the cultural pattern of the world, the meteoric development of our material world of man-made commodities, the breakdown of traditional modes of behaviour, and the resulting emphasis upon social structure and social processes dictate the objectives of education in our time. These objectives from the viewpoint of educational sociology are stated by Payne as

1. assimilation of traditions,
2. the development of new social patterns, and
3. the creative or constructive role in education.

Transmitting the Cultural Heritage

The descriptions of culture patterns in earlier chapter indicate the importance of *assimilation of tradition* as a basic function of education. The biological counterpart of education is inheritance; its sociological aspect is the social process—processes through which the folkways and mores, together with the institutional patterns in social organization, are transmitted to each new generation. Payne describes the process of assimilation of tradition as "imitation" and "inculcation" which he distinguished on the basis of "whether the initiative is taken by the giving or receiving party. When the receiving party adapts himself to social situation consciously or unconsciously, the process of adaptation is imitation; when the receiving party, through social pressure, propaganda, or other instruction, is led to change his behaviour or to make adaptation in conformity with the social group, the process is inculcation." Although such a distinction is valid, it represents but two aspects of social interaction which have been previously described as the social processes of adjustment and social control.

Many agencies contribute to achieve this function of education, beginning with the family and carrying through the formal agencies of the school and the Church, and the constant interaction through the informal agencies of the community and the State. In social organization, they are more or less separate and autonomous institutions and agencies. But the persons in his total social interaction, is only usually aware, and then only when two or more are in conflict, of their distinctive impingement upon his development.

Partly as a result of our artificial divisions of education, partly because of the complexity of our cultural pattern, the transmission of the cultural heritage is a difficult task. What aspects of the cultural heritage will be of value to the person in the mature years of his life? Whose cultural pattern shall be transmitted—that of the Church, of the State, of capital or labour, of the local community or the nation?

For long, the Church held a dominant influence in both the informal and the formal agencies of education, but with the re-establishment of the State, as the supreme organ of society, many of the values that were of prime importance to the Church have become of less importance—some have said even hostile—to the State. "Secular and religious education," "private and public education" are terms that, in juxtaposition, are the bases of long and sometimes bitter struggles in education. They are illustrated by the controversy, which has now continued for more than three decades, over the establishment of general Federal aid to education. Although textbooks presumably have been impartial in their treatment of the problems of the relationship of capital and labour, many have believed that the influence of capital has been dominant, and labour organizations are now actively seeking to have additional courses on labour problems taught by those who are thoroughly familiar with the problems of labour. Another controversy in education is over whether the cultural heritage shall be that of the adult world or that of the child's world.

These few illustrations indicate the concern that must be given to the whole problem of cultural transmission. In Its extreme form, cultural transmission leads to totalitarianism, wherein all of the agencies of education are utilized only to suppress individual judgment and to bring all citizens into conformity with the doctrines of the State. Total absence of conscious efforts to provide for the transmission of culture can lead only to anarchy and social disorganization. To permit the control of the agencies for cultural transmission to fall into the hands of a single group results in the perpetuation of caste and class.

The greater the degree of cultural isolation, the simpler are the problems of education. In the world of today, with its rapidly changing culture and in which isolation is impossible even within the home, the problem becomes acute. In a democracy in which the right of freedom of expression and of individual judgment is inherent, the earnest, co-ordinated efforts of all are required. Only by constant reappraisal of the agencies of education can social stability and security be retained.

Enriching Experience for Development of New Social Patterns

Assimilation of tradition is but one, though perhaps the most important, function of education. The second is the development of new social patterns. As Payne has emphasized; "Social progress depends as much upon the modifications of social heritages as it does upon the incorporation of the past culture and traditions, from group to group and from the old to the young. The development of scientific knowledge requires a transformation of the practices of agriculture and industry, a reconstruction of our modes of living in the fields of health, leisure, vocation and home life. The scientific development requires new behaviour patterns in which induction or planned education plays an almost exclusive role."

The high mobility of our own and the world's population, and its changing trends; rapid development of technology which brings continually changing methods of production, both agricultural and industrial; the multiplicity of institutions and agencies; new types of housing and of household utilities; the development of commercial and non-commercial recreation and the extension of leisure; and the rapidly growing interdependence of peoples and nations both for the artifacts of life and in the realm of ideas make nineteenth-century patterns of social behaviour inadequate to equip the person with the necessary knowledge and basic attitudes essential in the years ahead. Maladjustments had already been on the increase; World War II and the post-war wears have brought a sharp rise. New social patterns are necessary and the agencies of education must take the lead in giving them direction.

Providing Situations to Stimulate Creative Abilities

The third function of education—its creative or constructive role—is less tangible but equally important. It entails providing for the development of open-mindedness to meet the changes which have already begun and will inevitably increase in our dynamic world. Too often education has assumed its purpose has been fulfilled with the transmission of cultural heritage and with assistance to the individual in adjusting to the changes of the moment. The importance of this third function is pointed out by Payne as follows:

> We can, therefore say that one of the great problems of modern education is to develop a programme that creates greater flexibility in the practices of the individual and leads him to make changes in conformity with social changes. Furthermore, we may hope to so educate that at least the leaders in various lines of endeavour will not merely follow the great social changes that are taking place but will also serve a creative function in bringing about change essential to the greatest social progress. Writers have variously designated this function of education as that of developing open-mindedness, of logical mindedness, and the like. We conceive the educational function to be primarily creative or constructive.

This function is in a sense, idealistic in that it can be only approximately achieved. The first step in its realization is the development of an awareness of difference between what is and what can be. It entails a rich background of pertinent information on basic issues and an attitude of appraisal of such data, not in terms of prejudice and fixed opinion, but with a mind ready and willing to draw new conclusions and formulate new policies. The individual and the nation that no longer "dream dreams" cannot move forward to make and possess the new Heaven and the new earth that are within their grasp.

Mead has beautifully and forcefully expressed this point of view: "There has grown up in America a touching belief that it is possible by education to build a new world—a world that no man had yet dreamed and that no man, bred as we have been bred, can dream. They argue that if we can bring up our children to be freer than we have been—freer from anxiety, freer from guilt and fear, freer from economic constraint and the dictates of expediency—to be equipped as we never were equipped, trained to think and enjoy thinking, trained to feel and enjoy feeling, then we shall produce a new king of human being, one not known upon the earth before.... Phrased without any of our blueprints, with an insistence that it is the children themselves who will some day, when they are grown, make blueprints on the basis of their better upbringing, the idea is a bold and beautiful one, an essentially democratic and American idea. Instead of attempting to bind and limit the future and to compromise the inhabitants of the next century by a long process of indoctrination which will make them unable to follow any path but that which we have laid down, it suggests that we devise and practice a system of education which sets the future free. We must concentrate upon teaching our children to walk so steadily that we need not hew too straight and narrow paths for them but can trust them to make new paths through difficulties we never encountered to a future of which we have no inkling today."

It may appear that these three functions of education are internally inconsistent because the educational agency which seeks to inculcate the cultural heritage cannot also aid in the development of new social patterns or exercise a creative role. This is true only if an institution accepts one function to the exclusion of the others, but therein lies the greatest challenge to all education—the need of keeping a balance, of retaining enough of our heritage to assure social stability in the person and in our social structure; of continual adjustment to new social pattern in which recent developments in research and invention have accelerated the tempo of change beyond any that we had previously known; of continuing to envision the world that the labour and the genius of man can transform into a living reality—a world in which the person willingly gives up an element of his own freedom in order that, together with others, he may be more free—free from ignorance and superstition, free from insecurity and unemployment, free from prejudice and discrimination, free from the hideous fear of another World War!

The Agencies of Education

In Part II, the dominant role of the culture pattern has been described both in its impersonal or non-material aspects, including folkways and mores, and in its personal factors through group behaviour patterns, including institutions. The processes of social interaction were analyzed by which the individual, in contact from birth to death with the cultural world around him, becomes a person. The process of social adjustment, dominant in early years, shifts, through conflict and co-operation, to social control. Such processes must, in the interest both of the person and of society, be constantly directed. The alternative of such social planning, or telesis, is insecurity and instability; for the person, maladjustment; for society, chaos.

Society, across the span of centuries, has created an increasing number and variety of specialized agencies to carry out such planning. In Part III, the educational agencies will be studied to determine the extent to which they are achieving their purpose and maintaining a balance among the processes of social interaction. Specific recommendations for changes will be pointed out in order that they may more nearly fulfil their functions.

Educational agencies fall into four major groups:

1. The formal institutions set up more or less deliberately by society as educational agencies : the school, the Church, museums, libraries, organized recreation centres, and others,
2. Groups organized to meet other societal needs but which have a vital educational function, such as the family, the playgroup, and the community,
3. Commercial organizations operating for profit but whose purpose is that of appeal to the interests of people, such as the movies, the press, the radio and television, the theatre, and other agencies of commercialized recreation, and
4. Commercial and industrial organizations that, through the situations within the plant or store, or on the farm, are factors in determining the total cultural patterns for the

person. An increasing number of the last group of agencies are conducting programmes of education and organized recreation.

The person is hardly aware of these distinctions since the above classification is structural rather than functional. But as Payne has stated : "Each of these groups of educative institutions and agencies is constantly operative in society and exerts a definite influence in social adjustment. Each contributes to the development of social controls. They are determining the habits knowledges and attitudes, in a word, the practices of the population." This being true, it is necessary to study the whole educative process rather than the learning process alone. It is necessary also to appraise varying forces in the total community and throughout the world.

To assume, as has been too often done, that the school is the sole or even the primary agency of education of the person, is to lose sight of some of the most important agencies in society for personality development and for societal welfare.

Summary

Education, whether conceived of as the formal agency of the school or in its broader aspects as all of the consciously controlled processes that produce bahaviour changes in persons and groups, is an integral part of the total cultural pattern. It can neither be the direct reflection of the *status quo* nor be divorced from its cultural environment.

The concept of educational sociology which seeks to resolve this conflict is that education takes place in the interaction of individuals, groups, and entire cultures. Education is the process of interaction; changes in behaviour occur in both the individual and the culture.

Viewed in its larger concepts, some of the basic cultural factors which have broad implications for education are : population trends, and its mobility, changes resulting from technological developments and the rapidly growing interdependence of persons and nations upon each other not only for the material things of life but also for information and opinions.

When education is conceived in this context, it is learning, but it is also more than learning. It is the means through which changes in behaviour are brought about. Its function is the transmission of the cultural heritage, but this is not its sole or perhaps even its primary purpose; it is also the enrichment of experience as a basis for the development of new social patterns adapted to and modifying the changing cultural patterns. But were education to consider its task complete when these two functions were realized, it would still fall short of its role in a dynamic society. Education must also provide situations, at all age levels but within the maturity and ability of the individual, to stimulate a creativeness of mind which can explore new horizons and bring the vision of the future into a living reality.

2

The School as a Social System

The Teacher in the Classroom

'The school', Waller has pointed out in his pioneering study in the sociology of teaching, 'is a closed system of social interaction which exists wherever and whenever teachers and students meet for the purpose of giving and receiving instruction.' Yet, since Waller's study, originally published in 1932, the teaching process has been neglected by sociologists, who have preferred to study the role of the teacher in the community or in the school instead of in the classroom. Studies of pupil—teacher relationships have been undertaken mainly by educationists who have attempted to describe the characteristics of the 'effective' teacher. In their earliest form such studies used rating scales and questionnaires based on traits or qualities which superintendents and supervisors considered desirable, and the criterion of teacher effectiveness was whether or not the teacher retained his job. It soon became evident, however, that 'superintendents, principals, supervisors and board members' ratings of teachers showed very little reliability and little relationship to one another's assessments', and researchers turned instead to the collection of pupils' ratings of teacher behaviour. Such ratings however show little relationship with those of administrators, who appear to approach the task of rating with quite different frames of reference. There is evidence both that administrators tend to stress poor discipline as the most important cause of teacher failure and that they tend to favour the 'more rigid conforming personalities among their teachers'. Pupils, on the other hand, appear to prefer teachers whose attitudes are 'receptive and permissive.' Brookover, for example, in a study of the pupils of 66 male high-school history teachers, found that teachers 'who were more friendly, who most frequently joined in the recreational activities, whom the students like to have join in such activities, in whom the students frequently confided, whom they admired personally, and who were helpful to students in their work were rated more favourably as teachers by their pupils. In the same group, teachers who frequently scolded or used sarcasm when speaking to students and those whom the pupils considered peculiar or "sissies" were rated less favourably.'

The fact that pupils appear to like teachers to be friendly does not, however, mean that such teachers are the most effective. Indeed some of the evidence we have suggests that the reverse may be true. Brookover, for example, found that the teachers rated as friendly by the pupils were less successful in imparting information as measured by the pupils' gains in history.

Bush, studying primary-school pupils, found that teacher liking for pupils was seldom reciprocated by the pupils themselves. On the other hand, a study by Davidson and Lang found that primary-school children's perceptions of their teachers' feeling towards them could be very important indeed. The more positive the children's perception of their teachers' feelings, the higher the child's own self-image, the better the child's academic achievement, and the more desirable his or her classroom behaviour as rated by the teacher. These findings at least suggest a complex process of interaction in which the child's achievement, the teacher's approval, and the child's self-image act to reinforce one another.

An alternative to the rating method is the attempt to use observers to assess the leadership styles of teachers in the actual classroom situation. H.H. Anderson, for example, developed 26 categories for the classification of teacher behaviour, involving two main types of teacher style which he calls 'dominative' and 'integrative.' Observers in the classroom recorded the contacts of the teacher with the pupils either individually, or as a group, and the teachers were differentiated on the basis of the number of their contacts in each category. Dominative contacts, as the name implied, are those involving orders, threats, reminders and punishments. Integrative contacts, on the other hand, include approving, commanding, accepting, and helpful contacts. The studies of Anderson showed that teachers who used dominative techniques tended to produce in their pupils 'aggressive and antagonistic behaviours which were expressed toward both their teachers and their fellows. On the other hand, teachers who used socially integrative behaviours appeared to facilitate friendly, co-operative and self-directive behaviour in the children.'

Closely related to Anderson's conceptual scheme are the many studied of authoritarian and democratic leadership styles and their effect on pupil morale and pupil performance which have developed out of Lippitt's original work with youth clubs on Iowa in 1939 and 1940. This famous study utilized experimental groups of 11-years-old boys, who met for six weeks under a leader who employed either a democratic, an autocratic, or a laissez-faire leadership style. Each group was exposed to each of these leadership styles in turn, the same leaders adopting different styles. Two sets of observers kept detailed records of the behaviour of the boys in the groups. Lippitt concluded that different leadership styles produced different group and individual behaviours. Group members in a democratic social climate were more friendly to each other and showed greater initiative than they did under either authoritarian or laissez-faire leadership. Output, however, was highest under authoritarian leadership so long as the leader remained in the room.

Research on autocratic and democratic leadership in school situations has tended to make use of the concepts of teacher-centred and learner-centred teaching styles, and a large number of studies have been made within this general frame of reference, attempting to relate teaching style to cognitive achievement. Unfortunately the general conclusion to be drawn from them is inconclusive. Thus, while a number of studies have reported greater learning in teacher-centred groups, others have found learner-centred groups superior, and many have found no significant differences at all. Several reasons have been put forward to explain the inconclusive and indeed contradictory results of research in this field. It has been pointed out, for example, that most of the studies show a lack of methodological rigour and inadequate research design. Where, for example, students are introduced to a new method, the break from routine or 'Hawthorne effect' may in itself produce a temporary improvement in learning irrespective of the merits of the new method. This 'Hawthorne effect', as McKeachie points out, may also affect the teachers as well as the pupils. 'How many new curricula, new courses, or new teaching methods have flowered briefly and then faded as the innovator's enthusiasm waned or as new staff members replaced the originators? Unfortunately relatively few studies have made comparisons over a period longer than one semester.' Other methodological problems arise in establishing a suitable control group, and in avoiding biased sampling.

Yet another problem is posed by variations in the criteria to be used in judging the effectiveness of a particular teaching style. There are many ways of measuring cognitive achievement, and the criteria in use vary from the transmission of factual knowledge to the development of problem-solving skills. There is some evidence that the techniques most suitable for transmitting knowledge may not be those most effective for developing motivation, the critical use of concepts, and skill in solving problems.

At the same time the distinction between authoritarian and democratic teaching methods not only lacks precision but is an oversimplified view of leadership style. 'To say that a style of leadership is authoritarian', Anderson argues, 'does not adequately describe the behaviour which the leader actually exhibited.' He suggests that the effective style of the leader should be separated from the amount and kind of control exercised over the group. 'For example, because we have grown used to thinking of the authoritarian leader as impersonal, cool and sometimes hostile, the possibility of a leader who maintains complete control of the decisions of the group and yet is friendly and personal does not seem very real to us.' As we have seen in an earlier chapter it has also been found necessary to keep these two areas distinct in studies of parental control.

It should also be noted that Waller's analysis of the pupil-teacher relationship presents it as one of inevitable conflict. The teacher is seen as struggling to maintain order and discipline in the classroom. The reason for this antagonism, Waller suggests, arises because teachers need to force pupils to learn. 'If students could be allowed to learn only what interested them to learn in their own way, and to learn no more and no better than it pleased them to do, if good order were not considered a necessary condition of learning, if teachers did not have to be taskmasters but merely helpers and friends, then life would be sweet in the classroom. These however are all conditions contrary to fact.' If Waller's analysis is correct it may explain why the teachers students like best are not necessarily those who teach them most, and why in school as in industry morale does not appear to be related or productivity.

In line with his particular definition of the teaching situation much of Waller's discussion on pupil—teacher relationship is concerned with such issues as the maintenance of social distance between teacher and pupil and the methods by which the teacher retains the respect of the class. Although he recognizes the place of warmth and affection in the relationship between pupil and teacher, especially in the primary school, and the use of praise as well as punishment as a means of control, the general picture he draws is of a type of leadership by the teacher which is primarily dominative or authoritarian. Because of the antagonism which is always latent in the classroom, if the teacher lays down control the initiative passes to the class itself, and the fact that this sometime happens, and the fear of at the teacher that it will happen, is amusingly and tellingly illustrated by Waller's entertaining case-studies.

Evidence of another kind is also forthcoming in the study made by Gordon of Walbash High School in 1955. Although primarily concerned with the student subculture it also contains a valuable analysis of the impact of the subculture on student-teacher relationships. The status system of the pupils gave much greater weight to extra-curricular activities than it did to academic achievement, and there was evidence of considerable conflict as the teachers sought from the pupils a level of performance higher than they were prepared to set for themselves. There was, however, also evidence that the pupils learned how to manipulate the teachers to improve their grades. This was made easier of the pupils by the acceptance by the teachers of occupational values emphasizing nurturance and warmth. On the other hand, Henry, using an extensive programme of observation in primary-school classrooms, has shown convincingly how the use of techniques relying mainly on affective interaction between teacher and pupil can act as a powerful instrument of control, when the children, fearful of loss of love, are anxious to give the teacher what she wants.

So far in this chapter the focus has been on the behaviour or characteristics of teachers. More recently research has focused upon the differentiation amongst the pupils and its consequences for effective teaching. Several studies have shown that student attitudes to particular teaching styles and teaching methods vary according to the students' own personality. Student-centered instruction tends to be preferred by those students who 'reject traditional sources of authority, have strong needs for demonstrating their personal independence, and are characterized by a high drive for academic achievement.' The type of student with high authoritarian needs is likely to be unhappy in the student-centred class. It is not altogether clear how far these student preferences are related to achievement but there is some evidence to suggest that teaching is more effective if it is geared to the needs of the pupil.

There has also been considerable attention paid to the differentiation of pupils in terms of social status, and it has frequently been suggested that teachers exhibit a good deal of unconscious discrimination against working-class and especially lower-working-class children. This bias against the working-class child is assumed to arise from the adherence to middle-class values which characterizes the school teacher by virtue of his own social-class position. Teachers are, it can be argued, middle class either by virtue of their social origin in the middle classes or, in the case of those who have been socially mobile, because they have adopted middle-class values in their successful passage through school and college. In fact, however, there is little evidence to support the assumption that a teacher's middle-class values leads to discrimination against the working-class child; not because the evidence is contrary but because the assumption is still virtually untested. It has of course frequently been demonstrated that working-classes children are less likely to succeed at school than middle-class children, but this is not in itself a reason to blame either conscious or unconscious discrimination on the part of the teacher. There are, however, some studies which offer indirect evidence that teachers may discriminate against such children. Becker, for example, in interviews with Chicago school teachers found that lower-class children were, on the whole, considered unrewarding to teach. This was particularly true of children in slum schools. Comments were made by the teachers on such characteristics as the low level of motivation of such children, and the difficulty of maintaining control over the classroom. There were also criticisms of the habits of such children including their aggression, and their lack of cleanliness and indifference to hygiene. However while some of these attitudes appear to reflect middle-class values, others are just as likely to be a reflection of the teachers' occupational needs. It is, for example, much easier to teach children who are highly motivated to learn, and who respond to the teachers' efforts.

A larger study by Kaplan into the types of pupil behaviour found disturbing or annoying by teachers reached much the same conclusions as Becker. Teachers reported that they were disturbed by such behaviour as stealing, lying, cheating, aggression and destruction of property. They also disliked inattentiveness, indifference to school work and nonconformity.

There is also evidence that the career patterns of teachers in the United States are away from schools with a high proportion of working-class pupils. Becker found this to be so in Chicago in the 1950s, and his findings have recently been reinforced by a much wider study by Herriott and St. John. According to their survey, not only do schools with pupils of low socio-economic status contain proportionately more young and inexperienced teachers, but teachers in these schools are the least satisfied with their teaching situation. Moreover, '42 per cent of the teachers in these schools, as compared with 18 per cent in schools of highest socio-economic status aspire to a school in a better neighbourhood.'

Although findings such as these suggest quite strongly that teachers prefer the child who is easy to teach and so, unwittingly perhaps, discriminate in favour of the middle-class child, who is more likely to be hard-working and well behaved, we still have almost no studies of actual classroom behaviour in these terms, and especially no studies of the rewards and punishments, deprivation, and privileges accorded to the pupils. There is, however, one relevant study by Hoehn which attempts to measure the amount and kind of classroom contact the teacher has with high- and low-status pupils. Using a modified form of the Anderson Brewer observation scheme already described, the author attempted to measure not only the number of contacts made, but whether they were predominantly dominative or integrative. He found that teachers had in fact no more contacts with high-status than with low-status pupils, but argues that this is because the teachers studied tended, on the whole, to concentrate on the low achievers. They were, however more likely to have integrative contacts with high- rather than with low-status pupils and with high rather that low achievers. Hoehn's study, therefore, can be taken as evidence that teachers do sometimes discriminate against lower-class children, not by giving them less attention but by giving them less approval. More research is, however, clearly needed not only to substantiate Hoehn's findings in other schools but also to discover whether the lower achievement of working-class children is reinforced by teacher attitudes and particularly by teacher disapproval.

On the whole there has been little research into how pupils from different social classes perceive and react to teacher behaviours, although the study by Davidson and Lang already referred to found that working-class children tended to perceive their teachers as less approving than middle-class children. Brookover has drawn attention to the extent to which the teacher acts as a model of behaviour with which the child may or may not identify, and this may be influenced by the discrepancy between the teacher as model and the parents, neighbours and often adults in the local community. The middle-class teacher may therefore appear as a more acceptable model to the middle-class child. Bernstein has also drawn attention to the problem of communication between middle-class teachers and working-class pupils. Little research has been done in this field either, but a recent study by Piesach found that when children were asked to restore words deleted from sample of teachers' speech, middle-class children performed better than working-class children, and these differences were more marked in the fifth than in the first grade. Performance was also related to I.Q., although whether as a course of a consequence is not clear from the study.

The need for genuine interaction studies would therefore appear inescapable if any progress is to be made in studies of teacher effectiveness. Moreover, it is clear that the attempt to view effective teaching in terms of relatively permanent characteristics of the teacher must give way to a concept of classroom interaction as a dynamic process. So far, however, studies which actually focus upon the interaction process within the classroom are extremely rare. Nevertheless, there have recently been some important developments in the techniques of the systematic observation of classroom behaviour. For example, Flanders has introduced a matrix technique which attempts to provide a picture of the total interaction occurring in a classroom. It is possible, therefore, that considerable advances in knowledge may come in the near future.

The Peer Group and the Student Sub-Culture

Although the interaction between pupil and teacher is, perhaps, the most important set of relationships within a school, the pupils themselves form significant social groupings such as cliques, gangs and the like, which are in part a reflection of the community, in part related to the structure of the school itself. These social groupings, moreover, are characterized by a distinctive youth culture which is to a large extent distinct from, and can even be in opposition to, the adult world of the teacher and the school.

Waller was one of the first to draw attention to the existence of this separate student culture, but its more systematic analysis has not been undertaken until more recently. Gordon, in the study already referred to of Wabash High School, reported that, for boys, athletics and, for girls, popularity were the chief determinants of status, rather than academic achievement, which appeared to be considerably less important as a source of prestige. Coleman's findings, a few years later, and using 10 high schools varying in size and type of community, was in substantial agreement with Gordon. The student subculture for both boys and girls was centred upon predominantly non-academic issues, in which athletics for boys and looks and personality for the girls were the most important ingredients. Good grades and academic achievement had relatively low status in all the schools, although it is interesting to notice that the 'leading crowd' tended to get better grades than the student body as a whole. On the other hand, Coleman was also able to show that the achievement of students of high I.Q. varied according to the value climate of the school. Where it supported achievement the students of high I.Q. were more likely to perform at a high level. Indeed in the schools with the strongest anti-intellectual bias, the students showing the highest performance were not the most intellectually able students, but those with motivation to stand out against the prevailing value climate.

Interesting as Coleman's findings are, they appear to raise as many problems as they solve. Why for example should the 'leading crowd' consistently get higher grades than other students ? It would appear that value climate is at most only one factor in achieving behaviour. Other studies, moreover, have come to rather different conclusions. Turner, for example, in a larger questionnaire study of high-school seniors in the Los Angeles area found little evidence in most schools of 'an effective youth conspiracy against academic excellence.' There was, for example, no general relationship between endorsement of youth-culture items on a questionnaire and either level of ambition or lower-class background. Moreover, there was a 'higher degree of conformity to youth-culture values in response to a question asking for the kind of person one preferred to have as a friend than in response to questions asking for personal goals or admiration.' Similar findings are also reported by Riley, Riley and Moore. These contradictions suggest 'that the query concerning the relative impact of the adult and the peer group and the amount of conflict between these influence agents has not yet been satisfactorily answered.'

An interesting and unusual approach to the problem of peer-group influence is to be found in the comparative studies carried out by Bronfenbrenner and his associates at Cornell University. In a small cross-national attempt to evaluate the part played by peers *vis-à-vis* adults in the socialization process, and using an ingenious experimental design, they found important differences between the United States and the U.S.S.R. In order to measure reaction to peers, the children were asked to respond to questionnaire items dealing with a series of conflict situations under three different conditions : a neutral condition in which they were told that no-one except the researches would see their replies; an adult condition in which they were informed that their responses would be shown to parents and teachers; and a peer condition in which the children were told that the responses would be shown to the class itself. In both countries children gave more socially approved responses under the adult than under the neutral conditions, although the shift was more pronounced for Soviet children. When told that their classmates whould see their answers there was a national difference in direction as well as degree. 'American pupils indicated greater readiness to engage in socially disapproved behaviour, whereas Soviet children exhibited increased adherence to adult standards. In other words, in the U.S.S.R., as against the United States, the influence of peers operated in the same direction as that of adults.' In England, on the other hand, the peer group seems to operate in the same direction as in the United States, although the evidence suggests that the influence is even stronger.

At the college level, studies of Vassar College students under the general direction of Nevitt Sanford have also found evidence of a student value climate. Although this climate is certainly not anti-intellectual and high marks and generally respected, 'the one reservation voiced by most students is that scholastic excellence should not be the sole virtue. If there is an ideal Vassar girl, she is the one who receives consistently high grades without devoting her whole time to the endeavour.' Similarly, studies of student society in a medical school show vividly the extent of which the students themselves reinterpret the demands made on them by their teachers. For example, the students believed that 'the patients whom it is really important to study thoroughly are those who have common diseases—whether simple or complicated—for which there are available treatments a general practitioner could utilize.' They regarded anything they did not expect to do as general practitioners as a waste of time. Moreover, 'matters of this kind are widely discussed among the students and have important consequences for the way they interpret their experience in school and distribute their effort and time among their many competing interests.' This is not to assert, however, that student values are always in opposition to those of their teachers, or that college-going has no effect on values. The influence of college on values is indeed a complex and difficult area of study, which is discussed in some detail in the following chapter, and where evidence is presented that under certain conditions important changes in attitude do occur. There is, however, sufficient evidence of the importance of distinctive student cultures to justify the attention the subject is now beginning to receive.

An alternative and perhaps more fruitful approach to college value climates is to consider them in terms of sub-cultures within a single institution. Not all students necessarily go along with the values of the 'leading crowd', and these students may not be isolates, but may instead form their own well-integrated group. Martin Trow, for example, has suggested that there are at least four types of college culture or climate : the collegiate, the vocational, the academic and the nonconformist or bohemian. The collegiate culture is anti-academic and anti-achievement oriented; it stresses football, dates, drinking and campus fun. In this sense it resembles the high-school climate described by Gordon and Coleman. The vocational climate is also anti-academic although not anti-achieving. It is clearly the predominant climate in the medical school described above. Trow believes that the vocational culture is gaining ground in American colleges, largely because of the expansion of higher education and its role in social mobility.

The typology suggested by Trow is obviously useful for classifying both schools and colleges, and for describing differences between institutions as well as differences within them. Moreover, as interest grows in this field, it is likely that our knowledge of value climates is likely to expand quite quickly. At the moment, however, we still need to know much more, not simply at the descriptive or classificatory level, but on the consequences of different value climates on individual behaviour, and—of even greater interest to the sociologist—the reasons for the differences we find. So far, evidence on this point remains fragmentary. Nevertheless it is worth considering the few studies we have, and making an attempt to assess the significance of their findings.

There have been several attempts to relate pupil aspirations and pupil achievement to school milieu, defined in terms not of value climate but of the social-class composition of the school. Wilson, for example, showed not only, as we might expect, that the level of educational and occupational aspirations varied with the class composition of the school but that, within each social class, educational and occupational aspirations varied according to the social composition or social-class milieu of the school. For example, in the predominantly working-class schools, only a third of the sons of working-class parents wished to go to college, whereas in predominantly middle-class schools half of the working-class boys had college aspirations. Moreover, the social-class milieu of the school also affected middle-class children. In predominantly middle-class schools as many as 93 per cent of the sons of professional workers aspired to college, but this proportion dropped to below two-thirds in predominantly working-class schools. Academic achievement, as well as aspirations, was affected by the school milieu, so that it was lower for both working-class and middle-class boys in predominantly working-class schools. Indeed the achievement of the middle-class boys was affected even more than their aspirations. High achievers were also found to be less likely to want to go to college if they had attended a predominantly working-class school, and low achievers had higher aspirations in a predominantly middle-class school.

Wilson's study does not tell us which aspect of the school milieu was the operative one, and clearly a number of factors might have been responsible, not just highly but in interaction. These factors include more effective teaching, higher expectations on the part of the teacher leading to greater pressure on the pupils to achieve, the imposition of higher standards by the teacher, and the operation of the value climate and the pressure of peer-group norms. There is of course the possibility that working-class parents who live in predominantly middle-class areas differ in terms of their own values and aspirations from other working-class parents. Wilson, however, was able to show that, in his area of study at least, the working-class parent living in middle-class areas was not likely to be better educated or more highly skilled than other working-class parents.

A later study by Michael, using a national sample of schools, came to very much the same conclusion as Wilson. Indeed, in Michael's study the differences in achievement according to the school milieu are very great indeed. The achievement scores of those from a high-status background in a predominantly working-class school were lower than those of a low-status background in predominantly middle-class schools. Moreover school milieu has more effect on attainment than on aspirations.

Studies in Britain are less easy to interpret because of the complication introduced by the selective system of secondary education, which appears to act as an independent and highly important factor in determining aspiration levels. A study by Himmelweit and her associates showed that working-class boys in grammar schools have vocational aspirations above middle-class boys in secondary modern schools. Moreover, these middle-class boys are likely to see themselves as downwardly mobile. Other writers have drawn attention to the very 'realistic' ambitions of the secondary modern pupil. Although part of these differences almost certainly arises out of factors in the home background of the pupils, it is likely that 11-plus success or failure and the school milieu itself also play their part both in reinforcing and sustaining previous aspirations, and also in raising and lowering them.

It is clear, however, that such studies of schools milieu can in themselves throw no light on the actual processes by which the school society influences the aspirations or the achievement of its pupils. Genuine interaction studies are as necessary at this level as at the level of pupil-teacher relationships. Some attempts have however been made to fill this gap by means of peer-group studies which focus on the level of the friendship group, or clique, rather than on the school climate or school culture as a whole.

Peer Groups, Reference Groups and Social Mobility

Implicit in the concept of the reference group is the idea that the individual will employ the perceived, or possibly imagined, behaviour of his group of reference as a criterion for his own behaviour. In certain cases he may also attempt to be accepted as a member of the group. Parsons has suggested that within the schools class 'the individual headed for higher occupational status will choose peer groups that tend on the whole to facilitate his progress in this direction.' In these groups he will not only have the opportunity to learn the appropriate values and behaviour but will actually be required to do so in order to gain acceptance. The acceptance by the achievement orientated peer group of the candidate for higher status, can also Parsons argues, 'be a major factor in reinforcing the child's predispositions in terms of his own ability and its encouragement in the school, to transcend the expectations of his class origin.'

It is, however, necessary to consider how far Parson's largely theoretical formulations are supported by empirical evidence. A large number of studies have pointed out that potentially mobile working-class boys are more likely to have middle-class friends. Simpson, for example, in a questionnaire study of high-school boys, found that ambitious working-class boys tended to have more middle-class friends than unambitious boys from both the middle and the working class. They were also more likely than the unambitious boys to be members of extra-curricular clubs. Similarly, Ellis and Lane, in a four-year panel study of working-class boys entering a high-status university found that these boys had close associations with middle-class boys while they were at high school.

Parsons' position is also in line with the findings reported by Turner in the Los Angeles study which has already been described. He found that, amongst high-school seniors, stratification in terms of aspirations, or stratification by destination as Turner calls it, was more important than stratification by parental background, that is to say there was no tendency for cliques to form on the basis of a class background. There was, however, a 'marked cleavage according to ambition. In more that two-thirds of the classrooms there is an apparent tendency for students to select as friends others with ambitions like their own.' At the same time, 'some of the classic "middle class" values were uncorrected with stratification of origin but were correlated with stratification of destination.'

A study by McDill and Coleman also found that, by the end of the senior year at high school, status in the social system of the school contributed more to variation in college plans than father's or mother's education. The authors suggest that a plausible explanation for this finding lies in the influence of the cliques themselves, which are differentiated not only by status but by attitude to college. Consequently, those in high-status cliques who had not, in their freshman year, planned to attend college are orientated towards college by the rest of the clique. In the low-status cliques on the other hand, 'there is socialization away from college plans.' The plausibility of this explanation is reinforced by the finding that 'in those high schools where college attendance is highly valued, social status in school is a more important source of variation in such plans than in those schools in which college going is not highly valued.'

In should be noted that because neither McDill and Coleman, nor Turner, are able to include high-school drop-outs, it is possible that they have under-estimated the total effect of parental background. This is not, however, to deny the importance of their findings for the understanding of the role of the peer group in the anticipatory socialization of the mobile working-class boy.

In Britain, too, such studies as we have, then to suggest that peer-group or friendship cliques are associated with both attitudes and behaviour. An early study by Hallworth, using sociometric techniques in a study of grammar-school pupils, found that cliques were bifurcated, as Parsons has suggested, in terms of their agreement with or their opposition to the values of the school staff. Those cliques with opposing values contained a higher proportion of both absentees and early leaves.

Sugarman, in a more recent study, administered questionnaires to fourth-year pupils in two secondary modern one grammar and one comprehensive school. The pupils in all the schools, but particularly in the grammar school, contained a relatively high proportion from non-manual homes. He found that high teenage commitment, as measured by such criteria as smoking, going out with girls, wearing teenage fashions, etc., was associated with unfavourable attitudes to school, to poor conduct according to teachers' ratings, and to 'under' achievement relative to I.Q. as measured at the age of 11.

Hargreaves has successfully combined the approach of both Hallworth and Sugarman in an intensive study of the fourth-year pupils at a secondary modern school using participant observation, questionnaires and sociometric data. An analysis of the friendships and status systems of the boys revealed two value climates, the academic and what Hargreaves calls the delinquescent. The academic subculture as Hargreaves describes it is characterized by hard work, a high standard of physical hygiene and dress, the avoidance of 'messing' in class, and of copying work from another pupil. The delinquescent subculture is its exact counterpart. Dress is deliberately nonconformist, ties are taboo, and long hair and jeans, both of which are against the schools rules, are encouraged. At the same time 'messing' in class becomes a substitute for work, truancy is frequent and copying is the rule. Smoking in the school yard and fighting are signs of status. Moreover, a number of factors such as staff allocation, the structure of the time-table and the schools promotion/demotion system combine to associate these two subcultures with the system of school streams. As Hargreaves points out, 'the higher the stream, the greater degree of pupil commitment to school, satisfaction with school life, and conformity to the expectations of the teachers.' At the same time the higher the stream, the greater is the tendency for high status within the peer group to be associated with academic values. In the lower streams by contrast, the academically orientated boys are deviants from group norms, and the boys of high status are those who conform to the delinquescent culture.

These studies taken together provide fairly impressive evidence that both in Britain and in the United States, it is more fruitful to consider differences within the student culture rather than to postulate an all-inclusive student society. Moreover these differences within the student culture appear to be associated, in some school settings at least, not only with student values but also with several aspects of behaviour. At the same time it is still not clear how far this bifurcation is itself a causal factor or how far it is a reflection of student values and student friendship choices. It is true that Turner shows that social origin is of less importance in student clique formation than ambition or stratification by destination, but he presents no evidence to show either that the peer group is itself a factor in changing values, or that the values of these students needed to be changed. It may be that the potentially mobile child from a working-class family comes to high school with middle-class values already acquired from the pressures of the family itself, and finds in the high-status clique a congenial because familiar frame of reference. It is true that both experimental studies in the formation of group norms and industrial studies of group pressures on output, suggest that peer groups can and do influence both aspirations and performance, but the process itself has yet to be adequately demonstrated in the school setting. Although the methodological difficulties in the way of such a demonstration are considerable, interest in the topic is high at present and it seems likely that this will prove to be one of the growth-points of the subject in the future.

The Teacher in the Staff-room

So far in this chapter we have considered the teacher only in terms of the pupil-teacher relationship. Yet the concept of the school as a social system implies that the teacher is enmeshed in a whole system of social relationships which include not only his pupils but also his colleagues on the schools staff. Yet curiously enough very little attempt has been made to study informal colleague relationships. Brookover has, however, suggested a number of factors which underlie clique formation amongst teachers. These include age, length of service, sex, values and interests both inside and outside school. Corwin points out that 'segregation between sexes, and between college and non-college graduates is nearly complete in many school faculties. In some schools coaches who teach social studies part-time are excluded from the informal activities of the social studies department because their primary identification is with the physical education department. The structure of these cliques and their cohesiveness is influenced by the school's physical structure, by considerations such as whether there are segregated smoking lounges for male and female teachers, whether there is a place for coffee, and whether or not smoking is permitted in the building.'

Informal cliques of this kind will often compete with each other for power within the school system and influence with administrators, parents or pupils. Frequently conflict will arise between older and younger teachers, or senior and junior teachers, over the introduction of new methods, or new organizational forms or procedures. Other controversial areas include the allocation of funds to particular departments or for particular subjects or activities; the relative importance of subjects within the time-table; 'poaching' of students; the allocation of particular duties or responsibilities amongst the staff; and so on.

Teacher colleagues may also be expected to play a significant part in the socialization of the teacher into the organization. This will include the transfer not only of official values and objectives but informal goals, ideologies and procedures. Newcomers may learn, for example, that even though it is officially outlawed, corporal punishment is customarily used in some schools. Webb has described some of the methods used to bring a new colleague in line with the dominant ideology in the school. 'If a teacher lets playground chaos into his class, it may spill over into a colleague's, so threatening him with increased fatigue. Ridicule is used to stop this threat. (Hell of a row from your room this morning, Mr. Penguin. Thought you'd let them for a minute, and the little blighters were taking advantage. Just going to go in and step on them, when I saw you were there.)'

A study by Finalyson and Cohen suggests that this process of socialization may begin while the teacher is still a student. In a comparison of student and head-teacher expectations for teachers' behaviour in four role sectors, they found that a consistent pattern of change towards less authoritarian classroom behaviour was found to reach its peak in the second-year students' responses. The third-year students were closer to the head teachers and more authoritarian in expectations than the second-year teachers. The authors suggest that it is during the second year that students are most detached from the everyday workings of school, and more likely therefore to come under the influence of the liberal views of college of education lecturers. During the third year of training, however, the student teachers are in closer contact with the schools and in consequence they seek 'to narrow the gap in the conception of what is thought to be desirable teacher behaviour by the college and what they see will be expected of them in schools.'

An interesting approach to informal relationships in the school is made by Corwin in a study of staff conflict in seven high schools, ranging from 'jealousies over promotions to concern about the side of the typewriter on which the typing book should be left after class. In such a setting certain face-saving devices or strategies are commonly utilized in order to preserve the face-to-face formalities and prevent incipient interpersonal breakdowns from crystallizing.' These strategies include the avoidance of the individuals involved, the use of inter-mediaries and what Corwin calls polite rituals, discretion, or the art of ignoring an embarrassing situation, secrecy and joking relationships. Corwin argues that, although his discussion of these strategies is only illustrative, 'the basic relevance of this type of analysis to understanding the vocation of the public school teacher is undeniable. It is at the level of day to day personal relations that teachers actually function. It is therefore, at this level that the teaching roles and expectations are forged out and compromised.'

We are left, therefore, with the same conclusion that was reached from the survey of research into pupil-teacher relationships. In both cases the immediate necessity is for research into the actual relations within a school, whether these occur within the classroom, the head-master's office, or the staff common rooms. Only when these studies have been successfully carried out can we expect to have an adequate sociology of the school. At the same time there is enough evidence to show that informal relationships between staff and student, colleagues and peer groups, are as important in their way to the functioning of the school as the more formal relationships.

3

The School as a Formal Organisation

The Concept of Bureaucracy

Organizations have been defined as 'social units that pursue specific goals which they are structured to serve.' Typical organizations include hospitals, prisons, armies and churches as well as schools and universities. The distinctive characteristic of an organization, which distinguishes it from social structures like the family, is that it has been formally established for the *explicit* purpose of achieving certain goals. Every organization has a formally instituted pattern of authority and an official body of rules and procedures which are intended to achieve its specific goals. Alongside this formal aspect of the organization, however, are networks of informal relations and unofficial norms which arise out of the social interaction of individuals and groups working together within the formal structure. In practice the informal and formal aspect of the organization are inextricably intertwined, but for the purpose of analysis it is possible and customary to distinguish between them and this practice has been followed here. The present chapter therefore considers the school as a formal organization, and the subsequent chapter is concerned primarily with informal relationships.

One of the most important aspects of the formal structure of an organization is its system of administration, and in a modern society the typical administrative system is the bureaucracy. 'Complex organizations in American society are bureaucratized,' Corwin argues, 'and schools are no exception.' It is necessary, therefore, to consider the concept of bureaucracy and its meanings for the functioning of educational institutions. Weber is still the foremost authority on bureaucracy and, in spite of criticisms of particular aspects of his analysis, all discussions of the concept are derived from his treatment of the subject. According to Weber a bureaucracy is characterized by a high degree of specialization; a hierarchical system of authority; explicit rules which define the responsibility of each member of the organization and the co-ordination of different tasks; the exclusion of personal considerations from official business, and impartiality in the treatment of subordinates and clients; recruitment of experts; the existence of a career.

Clearly, all of these characteristics are present to some degree in education, just as they are in political and military organizations, churches and industry. Schools, for example, increasingly employ specialized personnel recruited on the basis of expert qualifications. They have, to varying degrees, a hierachical system of authority involving specific lines of command from the school superintendent or Director of Education downwards. At the same time there is considerable standardization with respect to such matters as textbooks, courses and examinations, although the extent to which the teachers' behaviour in the classroom is routinized varies considerably from one educational system to another and between different parts of the same system. Moreover, wherever rules exist the teacher is expected to apply them with strict impartiality.

Corwin has suggested some of the conditions favourable to the development of bureaucracy in education. These include population expansion, urbanization, increasing mobility, the knowledge explosion and the growing economic importance of education. The professionalization of teaching has also done much to encourage bureaucratic tendencies by its promotion of policies with respect to qualified entrants, security of tenure, career opportunities and the pressure for control by the expert rather than the layman or amateur. Yet the process of bureaucratization also carries with it consequences that run counter to the conceptions of the teacher role held not only by the teachers themselves but by many other educators. For example, the standardization inherent in a bureaucratic system comes into inevitable conflict with the ideal of individual attention to students and pupils which is basic to most current educational thinking. The hierarchical authority structure typical of bureaucracy also conflicts with the teachers' demand for professional autonomy in the classroom and a share in the decision-making process. Consequently there are strong pressures within the educational system working for what Bidwell has called de-bureaucratization. It is necessary therefore to look more closely at research on the school as an organization in order to determine the effect of these conflicting pressures on the teacher's role and the teacher's performance.

The Teacher in the Authority Structure of the School

Many writers on organizational theory have pointed to the different ways in which authority is legitimated from a bureaucratic as distinct from a professional basis. In a bureaucratic system the legitimation is in terms of rank and deference, and obedience is due from those of lower to those of higher status in the organization. In professional terms, however, deference is due only to competence or expert knowledge. Consequently, the loyalty of the professional is to his professional standards, whereas that of the bureaucrat is to his superiors and to the organization itself. Moreover, whereas the bureaucrat obeys orders and carries out the tasks allotted to him, the professional fulfils his professional duties according to his own or his profession's decisions. The role of the professional in a bureaucratic organization is, therefore, of particular interest to the sociologist, involving, as it is almost certain to do, diverging role expectations and the possibilities of role conflict. It is, accordingly, of some importance to consider to what extent the teacher is in this position, and it is unfortunate that research on this topic is so limited. Bidwell has argued that 'there is no existing study of the prevalence or incidence either of bureaucratic structures or processes in school systems or of their consequences for school-systems operation.' Moreover, although the study of administrative behaviour is increasingly attracting the attention of educational sociologists, the studies that have been made so far are not only small in scope but are more likely to be concerned with the setting up of a theoretical framework than with either the frequency of different administrative styles in education or their consequences for the teacher.

In general, what information we have about the authority structures in schools suggests that teachers have very little control over important decisions. Corwin, for example, argues that the participation of teachers in the decision-making process 'is usually limited to either:

1. interpretation of established policy,
2. advice, or
3. the execution of established policy.

The actual policy decisions are usually reserved for the chief executive.' Corwin is describing the American teacher but his conclusions apply in some degree to the English situation as well. Nor are bureaucratic tendencies confined to the schools. 'In higher education the increasing specialization of work and differentiation of roles extend the need for bureaucratic co-ordination, and there is a pronounced trend toward formal codification of rules, accompanied by a weaker trend toward the fixing of responsibility in a higher and wider hierarchy of administrative positions.'

A number of studies have also explored the extent to which teachers actually perceive a conflict between their positions as employees and their professional standards. Washburne, for example, interviewed 20 teachers who were graduate students in education and found that 'the status of teachers is given one role by the teacher and another by the bureaucracy in which he works.' Sharma also found that the percentage of teachers desiring teacher participation in decision-making was greater than the percentage reporting such participation. Getzels and Guba also found evidence in interviews with teachers of a conflict between their professional role and the expectancy that they will submit to others. On the other hand, a study by Seeman found many teachers reluctant to participate in decision-making.

Undoubtedly, too, teachers vary in the extent to which they adhere to professional values. A number of studies have found that women teachers are less professionally orientated than men teachers, and there is also some evidence that teachers of higher social origin are more likely to be committed to professional norms. Other factors which may well be important are the place of teacher training and the commitment of the individual to a professional organization. The raising of the educational level of teachers may also mean that younger teachers are more professionally orientated than older teachers, and the more highly qualified more so than the less-qualified. The relationship of the teacher to the community may also be of great importance. The teacher in the small town may well see himself or herself in traditional terms as a servant of the community, especially if he or she is well integrated into local life. Yet another factor of some significance is the commitment of the teacher to a professional organization and the attitude of the organization itself to professional autonomy. The National Union of Teachers, for example, has shown more interest than the teachers' organizations in the United States.

On the other hand, there is no evidence that schools and colleges are organized on rigidly bureaucratic lines. In practice, as Corwin points out, there are certain areas in which authority must be delegated, especially when the knowledge of an individual teacher in a particular field is greater than that of the school principal or head. Similarly Bidwell argues that 'the organizational arrangements of schools appear to be unusual in the degree of autonomy characterizing the operations of school and classroom units'. In higher education particularly, the administrative hierarchy is countered by the tradition of academic self-rule, which still persists to a varying but wide extent. Moreover, there may well be important national differences, both in schools and universities, as well as differences between areas and even individual schools. As Bidwell has implied, this is an area in which more research is badly needed.

It must also be noticed that the growth of bureaucratic elements in education is not the only hindrance to the development of professional autonomy. Traditionally, elementary school teaching has had a very low status in the eyes of the community, and in spite of improvements in qualifications and education in recent years there is strong resistance to the idea that teachers are true professionals. Consequently we find that school teachers are frequently subjected to a degree of community control that is quite incompatible with professional status but which has nothing to do with bureaucratic organization. In the United States in particular, the authority of the teacher is still severely restricted by community pressures. Clark, for example, has described the system of elementary and secondary education as 'characterized by a vulnerable bureaucracy'. This vulnerability, he suggests, 'stems in part from the decentralization of control to local lay boards, with job security of administrators closely dependent on lay approval. The vulnerability is extended by the correlated ideology of local lay control that has been a sacred component of the American conception of education governance. In addition, the ideologies of public school administration have adjusted to the vulnerability, with administration often guided by conceptions of service to lay demands, and efficient operation of the schools in line with community dictates.' Under such circumstances the decline of lay influence and the growing significance of a professionally orientated administration could well have the effect of raising rather than lowering the professional status of teaching.

Administrative Styles and Teacher Performance

An alternative approach to administrative leadership in education is to consider its consequences for the educational process, and a number of studies have attempted to relate administrative styles to teacher morale. For example, there have been several attempts to show that staff participation in decision-making is related to teacher satisfaction, although most such studies are limited in scope and tend in any case to rely on teacher perceptions of administrative behaviour. The general findings appear however to indicate, as we might expect, that teacher morale or job satisfaction is influenced not by the actual extent of the participation in decision-making but by the teachers' conception of its significance.

The concept of authoritarian or democratic leadership is, however, only one aspect of administrative behaviour and a number of investigations have attempted to develop more sophisticated theories of administrative styles, one of the most interesting being that developed by Halpin and his associates, although deriving initially from the work of Hemphill and Coons. This approach based upon a series of detailed descriptions of the behaviour of leaders and factor analyses of these descriptions, leading to the isolation of two principal dimensions of administrative behaviour—initiation of structure and consideration. These two empirical dimensions are related by Halpin to the social psychological concepts of goal achievement and group maintenance; concepts which are in fact found very generally in both sociological and social psychological literature under different names. According to Halpin, measures of the frequency with which an administrator emphasized either goal achievement or group maintenance or both, lead to a profile of his administrative style. It is also Halpin's belief that effective leadership requires high performance on both dimensions of leadership behaviour. 'In short', he writes, 'the effective leader is one who delineates clearly the relationship between himself and the members of the group and establishes well defined patterns of organization, channels of communication and ways of getting the job done, and whose behaviour at the same time reflects friendship, mutual trust, respect and warmth in the relationships between himself and the group.'

An attempt by Halpin to describe the behaviour of school superintendents by means of descriptions of their behaviour collected from both their staff and their boards of education showed that, although the two sets of respondents tended to agree amongst themselves, they did not agree with each other. Staff members were more likely than board members to perceive their superintendent as low an consideration or group maintenance. Nor did board members and staff members agree when asked to give their expectation of how a superintendent should behave. Staff members were more likely to stress consideration or group maintenance, and board members initiation of structure or goal achievement, Bidwell has argued that these differences 'reveal certain essential variations in their normative orientation, which differentially legitimize and thus differentially limit the administrative actions of the superintendent. These variations can be viewed as, in part, an outcome of the different tasks of board members and professionals and of variations in their background, and types of training.' Differences in perceptions of actual behaviour while interesting in their suggestion of differential perception in the light of expectations do, however, make it dangerous to use the material as an objective description of administrative behaviour.

More recently Halpin has turned his attention to the construction of a typology to measure the organizational climate of schools. This typology was arrived at inductively by factor analysis of respondents' answers to a set of questionnaires. The statements in the questionnaire covered eight dimensions, four on the principals' behaviour and four on teachers' response to this behaviour. The respondents were asked to what extent each statement characterized his school. The dimensions were chosen to include behaviour directed towards goal achievement or initiation of structure as well as group maintenance or consideration. The six organizational climates that form his typology vary primarily in the way in which the school principal is seen to handle these two aspects of his leadership function. The Open Climate, for example, is characterized by a principal who is perceived as having high consideration for his staff, a high level of what Halpin calls thrust, i.e., motivations through example, and an absence of close supervision. From the point of view of the staff we have high esprit and high intimacy between staff members, who also perceive the school organization as helping in the performance of their task. At the other extreme, the Closed Climate is characterized by high aloofness, close supervision, and low consideration on the part of the principal, and a high level of disengagement on the part of the staff, who also perceive the organization of the school as hindering their task. The other organizational climates show various alternative combinations of these factors. Nevertheless, interesting as Halpin's typology is, much more needs to be done before it will be possible to relate his measurements either to the actual behaviour of superintendents or to objective measures of teacher of pupil performance. An alternative but strikingly similar conceptualization of administrative style has been developed by Getzels and his associates, who have used a theoretical framework derived from Talcott Parsons. They describe three types of leader; the nomethic leader who is orientated towards the organization and its task at the expense of the satisfaction of the personal needs of his staff; the ideographic leader who, in contrast, tends to minimize the organizational requirements and is oriented towards personal relationships; and the transactional leader who can reconcile the fundamental conflict between the requirements of the system and the needs of the individual within it.

Guba and Bidwell used this framework in a study of administrative style based on the expectations held by the principal of his teachers, and teacher reports on what they believed their principals expected of them. This study showed that teachers' perceptions of their principals as transactional leaders was positively related to their level of confidence in their principal and in themselves, and in their satisfaction with the teaching situation. This supports the hypothesis that transactional leadership is the most effective. When, however, the measure of administrative style was based on the principals' own reports, no such correlations were found. It is difficult, therefore, to be sure that it is the behaviour of the principal which is the causal factor in the teachers' confidence and job satisfaction.

In the main, Getzels and his associates have used their conception of leadership style mainly in order to study, not the consequences of variations in administrative style in itself, but the consequences of divergences in perceived style from desired style. Their studies show consistently that convergence of teachers' role expectations of the administrator with their perception of his behaviour was related to satisfaction, and divergence to dissatisfaction with the total teaching situation. Again, however, it is difficult to disentangle the causal chain in these studies. As Charters has pointed out, 'since most of the studies are correlational we can turn the findings around to say that subjects who report high levels of satisfaction are inclined to perceive agreement in role expectation.' The main problem is that is customary in these studies to use the subjects' own perceptions of role agreement rather than indices of agreement furnished by methodologically independent sources. When this is done, as Charters points out, 'correlations are inclined to vanish.' Consequently, in spite of the plausibility of the assumption, it has not been shown empirically that divergence of role expectation between teachers and principals causes job dissatisfaction. Nor is such divergence clearly related to types of administrative style.

Yet a further weakness of much research in this area is the tendency to assume that teachers' job performance is related to their job satisfaction or morale, rather than to subject it to empirical verification. Since industrial studies have shown that workers' morale is not necessarily related to productivity it is at least conceivable that this is also true of teachers. It is therefore of particular interest to look at Gross's recent attempt to study leadership in education, which tries to relate administrative style both to teacher morale and to teacher performance.

The context in which Gross places his study is the problem of leadership in an organization staffed by professional workers, and who therefore may be expected to demand a certain level of autonomy in their work. In such a context the executive will meet with special difficulties, especially if he attempts to conform to a role definition that 'stresses his obligation to improve the quality of staff performance.' Gross calls such effort Executive Professional Leadership (E.P.L.) and puts forward the hypotheses not only that formal leaders will vary in the amount of E.P.L. they show, but that the amount will be related to the performance and morale of teachers and the behaviour of pupils.

The study itself was undertaken as part of a large-scale enquiry which involved a study of stratified random-cluster sample of school principals in large American cities. Apart from the school principals, data were collected from immediate supervisors of the principals in the study, and a sample of teachers randomly selected from each of the schools. For the purposes of this particular study, however, only elementary schools and their principals were included. In order to measure the E.P.L. of a particular principal, the sample of teachers in his school were contacted by means of postal questionnaire and asked to describe how frequently their principal engaged in types of behaviour believed to represent executive professional leadership. The 18 items used were drawn up after a review of the literature on the potentiality of the principalship for professional leadership. They cover such aspects of the principal's role as his contribution to the morale of the teachers ('Gives teachers the feeling that their work is an important activity'); his effect on teachers' task performance ('Gets teachers to upgrade their performance standards in their classrooms'); the assistance he gives to teachers ('Helps teachers to understand the sources of important problems they are facing'); and the extent of his support for the professional aspirations of teachers ('Takes a strong interest in my professional development'). The use of reports of teachers rather than of higher administrators of outside observers is justified because the definition of E.P.L. refers to the principal's attempts to influence his teachers. The reports of teachers on a particular principal did not necessarily agree, and the actual E.P.L. score for each principal was averaged from scale scores developed from the reports of each teacher in each of the schools.

The teacher-observers were also used to assess the behaviour of the principal towards his teachers. The areas of behaviour investigated included the extent to which teachers were permitted to share in decisions, the extent of his equalitarian relationships with teachers and the amount of support teachers were given in a number of different areas. Scores on all these items were cross-tabulated with the E.P.L. score, and in each case a positive relationship was found. These may all be viewed as further aspects of the principal's leadership style.

The effects of E.P.L. were also studied by means of the teacher observers. They were asked to report on teacher morale in their school, on the classroom performance of the teachers in their school, and the academic progress of their pupils. All of these were found to be positively related to E.P.L. Finally an attempt was made to assess some of the determinants of E.P.L. It was found for example that the stronger the professional leadership offered by the principal's immediate superiors, the greater his own E.P.L.

The authors of the study are well aware of the problems involved in attempting causal inferences, using this kind of data. Nevertheless they argue, on the basis of a very sophisticated and complex statistical procedure, including amongst other methods the use of the split sample, that 'both teachers' professional performance and morale may serve as links in a causal chain between the E.P.L. of principals and the performance of their pupils.'

Clearly the study has a number of important shortcomings, some arising out of the techniques of measurement, some out of the limited theoretical analysis of its most important variable, E.P.L. It is, for example, hard to justify the use of teacher-observers to assess teacher and pupil performance. Nevertheless, in its attempt to assess the effects of leadership style and in its attempts to relate teacher morale and teacher performance, it is an important step forward in the sociology of education, and it is to be hoped that it will encourage others to pursue this important but neglected aspect of the organization of the school.

The Organization of Learning

The concept of the school as an organization is, however, much wider than the study of administrative styles. In particular there are a number of aspects which related primarily to administrative aspects of the teaching situation itself, and one of the most important of these is the organization of the teaching group. There are many ways of grouping pupils within a school, and only the most important of them can be described here. One of the most common is the system known as grading, which is customary both in the United States and in many European countries, including the U.S.S.R. It is a grouping system based upon the pupil's level of attainment and rate of progress. Under such a system pupils who fail to complete the work satisfactorily are made to repeat the grade. The teaching group in a graded school is, therefore, relatively heterogeneous since it will include pupils of widely different abilities and of different ages.

The main alternative to the graded school is the system known usually as streaming. This involves classifying children of the same age into two or more groups on the basis of some measure of ability. These groups are then used as the teaching unit, for all or most subjects, the rate of progress and the curriculum often being varied according to the level of ability of the group or class. A system of this kind, especially in a school with a selected intake, is often very homogeneous, both in age and in ability.

Setting, on the other hand, is the system of grouping pupils by ability for individual subjects and can be combined either with a system of grades or other forms of heterogeneous grouping, or with a system of streaming. It has, for example, long been common in British Grammar schools for such subjects as languages or mathematics. Comprehensive schools, too, usually combine streaming and setting to produce homogeneous teaching groups, and heterogeneous or 'mixed ability' groups are restricted mainly to non-academic subjects, if they are used at all.

Finally there is the system known as tracking, in which pupils are allocated to particular 'sides' or 'courses'. Examples of tracking are the allocation of pupils to science are art sides in the English grammar school or to the college preparatory course in the American High School. Many comprehensive schools in Britain also organize their senior or upper school in the forms of 'sides.'

A recent survey on grouping in schools concluded that research so far has been abundant but inconclusive. 'For example, some investigations into the effect of grouping pupils in accordance with their abilities and attainments have yielded results favourable to homogeneous grouping, some have indicated that heterogeneous grouping leads to superior attainments; others shown that there is no significant difference between the two.' At the same time the survey is highly critical of much of the research that has so far been carried out. In particular it points to the small samples frequently used and the short periods of time which have been included in the studies. There is a tendency, too, to ignore many important variables, including the attitudes of the teachers towards the method they are using and their ability to exploit its potentialities. The method of instruction is another important variable which is often neglected, and so is the material to be taught. The effects of streaming may also vary as between primary and secondary schools.

On the other hand, there is, the survey concludes, a growing body of evidence that the gap which separates 'able and less able children appears to widen if they are assigned to separate schools or to separate streams or tracks within a school.' The reasons for this are not entirely clear, but there is no doubt that the causes are extremely complex, and include the attitude and expectations of the teachers are well as of the pupils themselves. Those in the top class quickly perceive that a great deal is expected of them, just as those in the bottom class learn fairly soon that they are the failures and the dunces. Another reason may be the tendency in some at least of the streamed schools to give the lower streams the worst teachers and the worst accommodation.

In recent years there has been considerable controversy over the merits of heterogeneous versus homogeneous groupings both in Britain and in the United States. On the whole the use of homogeneous groups, and especially the more rigid forms of streaming, tend to be associated with the system of sponsored mobility. Consequently its opponents in Britain tend to be those who oppose early selection and a selective secondary system. It is all the more surprising therefore to find so many comprehensive schools continuing to stream. Pedley found in the early 1960s that out of 102 schools he questioned on the subejct 'eighty-eight "stream" the children on entry, 11 during or at the end of the first year. The remaining three do so after two years.' The streaming, however, is often in blocks, involving perhaps three parallel classes. Fifteen of the 102 schools had some mixed ability classes but 'only four carry such "unstreamed" classes beyond the third year, and these only in such subjects as crafts, art, music religion and physical education.'

Part of the reason for this is undoubtedly the strong pressure placed upon the schools to compete in academic terms with the grammar schools. In their anxiety to prove that the comprehensive school does not lower standards, the heads are loth to experiment and possibly risk the academic progress of the abler pupils. At the same time mixed-ability groups are undoubtedly unpopular with teachers, and this is so even at the primary level. Several studies have shown that the great majority of primary school teachers favour streaming, believing it to benefit the backward as well as the more able pupils. The Headmistress of Woodberry Down, one of the London comprehensive schools, has recorded the dislike of teachers for the idea of the mixed-ability group, and indeed London's inspectorate, reporting on progress in London's comprehensive schools, dismissed the idea of 'teaching groups covering the whole range of ability' as impracticable.

In the United States, on the other hand, the common practice of grouping relatively heterogeneous teaching groups has recently come under fire for its neglect of the needs of the able child, and there are pressures upon the schools to experiment with homogeneous groupings within the framework of the American comprehensive high school. The experiments that have been carried out include so-called acceleration programmes which enable the academically talented pupil either to move faster through the grades, or enrichment courses which aim to provide the talented student with additional work. The advanced placement programmes which are now being introduced into many high schools enable the preparatory college students to pursue courses of college level in the high school and so earn college credits while still at school. Such programmes, however, fall very far short of streaming at it is practised in the English context.

The tendencies working towards the bureaucratization of education have also, in general, worked towards an increase in school size. One of the main influences in this direction has been the growth in specialized knowledge, with its accompanying demand for specialized teaching and equipment. Consequently, as Conant has pointed out, it has become difficult for the small high school to meet the needs of its pupils for advanced courses in mathematics, science and foreign languages, on the one hand, and non-academic training, on the other. In the British setting this problem has been less serious, since the highly selective nature of the grammar schools has meant that they could concentrate their resources on the academic needs of the abler pupils. However, the development of comprehensive schools has raised the issue in an acute form, since the schools have been expected to satisfy their critics that they could provide advanced courses to the same level as the more specialized grammar schools. In consequence there has been very strong pressure to ensure that all comprehensive schools are large enough to provide advanced teaching especially at sixth-form level.

If however a school can be too small to run efficiently it can conceivably also be too large, and there has been some anxiety expressed that the large school will be an impersonal, unfriendly place for teacher and pupil alike. Some evidence of an indirect kind is provided for this view by the researches at University of Kansas under the guidance of Barker and his associates. Thirteen Kansas high schools varying in size were studied intensively, and the results were seen in some respects at least to favour the small school. It was found, for example, that the pupils in the small school were more likely to participate in extracurricular activities and more likely to take a leading part in them in spite of the fact that the larger schools provided a greater number and variety of such activities. The authors suggest that part of the reason for this lies in the greater opportunity to participate, and especially to lead, in a small school. For example, the same size of school orchestra will involve a higher proportion of pupils in a small school than in a large school, and so will the school football team and the school play. On the other hand, the study also suggests that in strictly academic terms the small school is at a disadvantage, especially in terms of the number of subjects it is able to offer. There is, however, little evidence directly relating school size to such measures as achievement test scores, drop-out rate and college grouping. Clearly this is another area in which the amount of research is inadequate to support the conclusions that are drawn.

Size of class has aroused much less controversy than size of school. Indeed it has been regarded as almost axiomatic that small classes are more effective than large classes. Teachers' organizations in particular have worked hard to reduce the size of classes, and any success is widely regarded as a significant educational reform. It is surprising, therefore, to find that research in this field does little to support the general belief in the superiority of small classes at either the school or the college level. Nevertheless, it is possible that a relationship does in fact exist but is masked by other factors in the situation. It is extremely difficult in this kind of research to set up a true experimental situation in which all but one variable is controlled. Classes which differ in size will therefore differ in other respects, some of which may be related to academic achievement. For example, rural schools may have smaller classes than urban schools, but for other reasons may also have lower academic achievement. It is also very probable that the effect of class size will vary according to the teaching method in use, so that 'one would expect class size to be of minimal relevance in television teaching, of slight importance in lecturing, but of considerable importance in discussion teaching.' It may also be of less relevance when the method is by rote learning rather than pupil participation.

The very firm belief in the greater efficiency of the small class as a teaching unit may also have something to do with teacher preferences. A small class may well be both more interesting to teach and easier to handle. This is particularly likely to be true for the teacher who has been trained in the child-centred approach and who tries to approach the children as individuals.

Finally, it is of interest to consider the development of what Corwin has called the bureaucratization of the search for talent. 'In the face of growing shortages of trained technicians and professionals', he argues, 'there is a natural impulse to search for misused and unused talent', an impulse which is powerfully reinforced by a concern for the underprivileged, and the demand for equality of opportunity. Consequently the education system has been expected to take on the identification as well as the training of the gifted child; and the development of selection mechanisms within the educational system is a feature of modern industrial society. The function of these mechanisms is the same, but the form that they take varies considerably according to the dominant mode of mobility characterizing the society.

In Britain, where sponsored mobility is the dominant form, and where early selection and segregation of the elite has dominated secondary and higher education, the process of selection for secondary education has long been bureaucratized. At the beginning of the century the awarding of scholarships was the almost exclusive prerogative of the head of the secondary or grammar school. The methods of selection most favoured were the interview and the essay type of examination, both of which allowed maximum scope for the free play of subjective impressions and the personal choice or even idiosyncrasy of individual heads. Increasingly, however, the responsibility for selection was taken over by the local education authorities, who introduced standardized procedures in order to ensure that the system operated with the maximum of objectivity. The result, known as the 11-plus, has exerted a profound influence on the primary schools.

Entry to higher education is also virtually controlled by the system of external examinations which characterizes secondary education in Britain and which, because it is also used by employers as a qualification for various types of employment, has exerted considerable influence on the curriculum in the secondary schools. For example the old School Certificate with matriculation exemption became, in the years between the wars, the goal of many pupils who had no intention of entering a university, largely because it was so widely demanded for entrance to employment; and it was this, more than anything else, which stereotyped grammar-school teaching and the grammar-school curriculum into a predominantly academic mould.

There have been several attempts to free the grammar schools from the domination of external examinations, the most important being the attempts during and after the Second World War to substitute an internal examination for the General School Certificate. A Committee of the Secondary Schools Examinations Council, the Norwood Committee, suggested that, since an external examination taken at the age of 16 was difficult to reconcile with the freedom of the schools, it should be replaced, after an interval of seven years, by a wholly internal examination. An external school-leaving certificate, it was argued, should be reserved for those leaving school at 18-plus, with separate examinations for those wishing to try for a university award. In the event this idea proved unworkable and the General Certificate of Education, or G.C.E., at both the Ordinary and the Advanced level, have become the entrance requirements for many types of employment, including apprenticeship, as well as servicing as a qualification for higher education. The fact that it is a subject examination does, however, leave the schools more freedom than with the group system of the School Certificate. Nevertheless it is undeniable that the G.C.E. syllabuses are the dominating influence on the grammar-school curriculum, a consequence of the demand by employers and universities for a standardized assessment of the attainment of school-leavers.

Perhaps, however, the most dramatic evidence of the demand for formal educational qualifications is the spread of external examinations into the secondary modern schools in direct opposition to official policy and educational opinion. Fundamental to official thinking about the secondary modern school in the years after 1944 was its freedom to experiment, and this implied that secondary modern pupils were not to be entered for external examinations. 'Free from the pressures of any external examination these schools can work out the best and liveliest forms of secondary education suited to their pupils', argued a Ministry of Education pamphlet in 1945. Unfortunately, as Taylor points out, this movement of opinion against examinations in both secondary grammar and secondary modern schools 'ran counter to social and economic forces which were, and are, tending to make examinations and "paper qualifications" of more rather than less importance, and the strength of these factors has succeeded in turning the tide of much educational practice in favour of the extension of the examination system to fields previously unaffected by it.' Consequently, the years since 1945 have seen the gradual but relentless spread not only of the G.C.E. but many other external examinations into the secondary modern school, until finally the Ministry of Education was forced to yield and a new lower level examination, the Certificate of Secondary Education, was designed specifically for secondary modern and comprehensive schools.

In the United States, in contrast, the ideology of context mobility and the dislike of centralization have worked to ensure that the 'talent-hunt' is far less bureaucratized. Individual schools and colleges are less standardized in terms of curriculum, organization and academic climate, and there is far more variation in college entrance requirements than is customary in Britain. Nor is there anything even approximating to the British 11-plus. Consequently it is necessary to look at the school itself and the way in which it acts as an agency of selection. Parsons has argued that 'the primary selective process occurs through differential school performance in elementary school, and that the "seal" is put on it in junior high school.' This differentiation, which is made in terms of a fusion of cognitive and moral elements, 'leads up through high school to a bifurcation into college goers and non-college goers according to whether or not the pupils are enrolled in the college preparatory course in high school.' Moreover, this differentiation is made on the basis of a relatively systematic evaluation of the pupil's performance. 'From the point of view of a pupil, this evaluation particularly (though not exclusively) in the form of report card marks, constitutes reward and/or punishment for past performance; from the view point of the school system acting as an allocating agency, it is a basis of selection for future status in society.' Within this general picture there are of course considerable variations between schools according to the background of the pupils and the social and intellectual climate of the schools. Nevertheless the important point that Parsons is making stands; the evaluation of the pupils' performance by teachers and principals becomes the basis for his future status in society.

Further information on the allocation of pupils to courses within the school is provided by a recent case study of the school-counselling service in an upper-middle-class suburb. The authors suggest that because of his control over the programming of courses and his letter of recommendation in support of college and of job applications, the school counsellor has assumed an increasing amount of authority and responsibility for the student's career within the school and his vocation choice. They found, in their case study, that students who were considered by counsellors to have low ability were automatically excluded from the college preparatory course. However, ability was not judged simply on test scores or grade point averages, but included such criteria as belonging to the in-group and not getting into trouble; the result is a system of sponsored mobility with the counsellors acting as sponsors.

On the other hand, although it is possible to contrast the two systems in this way, there is much that they have in common. In Britain teachers' assessments play an important part in the allocation of primary-school children to different streams, and even enter into the 11-plus procedure in many areas. In secondary schools, too, it is the teachers' assessment which will decide the course the pupil is to follow and the examinations for which he is to be prepared. Moreover it is very probable that, with the extension of the comprehensive school system and the gradual abolition of the 11-plus, these assessments by teachers will become more, rather than less, important. It is urgent, therefore, that research should be focused on the selection procedures as they operate within the schools, as for example in streaming, setting and promotion, as well as on the more obvious selection procedures such as the 11-plus.

In order to develop a sociology of the school it has been necessary to consider the school as an organization, and this chapter has explored, as far as possible, both administrative leadership and methods of structuring the learning process within the school. Yet clearly a school is much more than its formal structure; like all organizations it is also a social system involving a complex pattern of interaction both on the level of roles and on the level of individual personalities, and including relationships not only between teacher and pupil, but between teachers and between pupils. It is, therefore, to a consideration of the school as a social system that we now turn.

4

Education and Social Change

The Problem Stated

In the past education has had primarily a conservative function, transmitting a relatively unchanging culture and traditional skills to the new generation. Only in a changing society, or one seeking to change, does it make sense to enquire into the part that educational institutions play in the introduction of change. Yet this question has proved to be extremely difficult to answer. Of considerable practical as well as theoretical interest, it has aroused considerable and often passionate controversy, yet we are still far from any real agreement as to the answer. One reason for this is undoubtedly the complexity of the relationship between education and social change in modern industrial societies.

In the first place, the education system is still expected to play a part in the preservation of the cultural heritage by means of its transmission to the next generation. Consequently schools are expected to teach the dominant value system of the society. Schools in the United States, Brookover has argued, are expected 'to preserve the capitalist system, to demonstrate that the enemy is always to blame for war, to prevent the intervention of government in business, to maintain permanent patterns of family relations, to teach respect for private property, and to protect the middle class by perpetuating the belief that the poor are inherently lazy "no-count" people for whom nothing can be done."

At the same time, schools may also be expected to serve as agencies of social reform or social improvement, to build, that is to say, a new social order rather than perpetuate the old. In post-revolutionary Russia, for example, the schools were given the task of destroying the old bourgeois values and creating new values appropriate to a socialist society.

Finally the educational system may be charged with the task of encouraging innovation in the material and technological sphere. This may involve the process of innovation itself, or the training of the labour force in the new skills required by an expanding technology. Education may also be required to smooth the path of innovation by breaking down traditional attitudes, and so lessening the resistance to change. It may also be encouraged to promote social mobility and to allow new elites to threaten and overcome the old.

Clearly these expectations are, to a large extent, contradictory. The radical or innovatory functions of education are hard to reconcile with its role in the transmission of culture. For example, schools may be expected to teach traditional values alongside a belief in the inevitability and desirability of technical change, as well as the skills and knowledge which make such change possible.

Further and more serious complications arise from the fact that schools and universities are themselves a part of society, subject to pressures from other parts of the social system. In a highly stratified society, for example, it is unrealistic to expect the schools to inculcate strongly equalitarian principles. Those controlling the school system are likely in such a society to hold strongly to elitist principles, and to ensure that these principles are taught in the schools, so that teachers who seek to challenge them may be silenced or dismissed. Moreover the schools themselves are likely to function as important agencies within the stratification system, training the young for adult status, and, accordingly, elitist principles will be built into the educational system itself. Only where equalitarianism is accepted as part of the dominant value system of a society is it likely either to influence the organization of education or to be part of the moral and social training given by the school.

Developments within education are also influenced considerably by economic and technological factors. The extreme economic determinist position would deny education any but a purely adaptive role, but there is no need to go as far as this to admit that the economic and technological systems set often quite severe limits on the type of educational provision. Education may, however, influence social and economic change directly as a consequence of its role in the discovery and dissemination of new knowledge.

Finally, we must draw a distinction between planned and unplanned change. The spread of education, and changes in its content, the organization of schools and the training of teachers may have important social and economic consequences. Planned social or economic change is another and far more complex issue.• It is necessary, however, to consider how far social reform can be brought about by changes in the educational system.

Although many of these issues have been raised in previously by they have not, so far, been given more than a passing mention. Nor, in the present state of the subject, is any really systematic treatment possible. All that the present chapter can attempt to do is to delineate certain areas which have received attention in recent years and discuss them in terms of the most relevant research findings.

Education and Economic Development

There has long been a widespread faith in both academic and government circles that education is the main determinant of economic growth. This belief is reflected, for example, in the increasing proportion of the United States Technical Co-operation Programme devoted to educational assistance. In fact, however, planning policies which have given priority to investment in educational expansion have often had disastrous consequences, and increasingly the simple view of the primacy of educational institutions in economic development has lost ground. Moreover, a closer look at the empirical data available suggest that in its relationship to the occupational structure, education is likely to be dependent rather than in independent variable. It is interesting, therefore, to consider why education has been deemed to be of such overriding importance.

One of the reasons, undoubtedly, is the misleading analogy with highly developed and rapidly growing economies. 'It should be noted', Hoselitz has pointed out, 'that those who have stressed the productive aspects of education have, on the whole, drawn their examples and their empirical evidence from such countries as the United States or Western European nations.' These are all countries with, amongst other relevant factors, 'a high degree of specialization in many occupations and hence with a substantial need for elaborate training programmes for many of the skilled occupations.' Hoselitz goes on to point out that these conditions apply only to a limited extent, if at all, in many developing countries. Nor did they apply during the initial stages of industrialization in Europe. Consequently, although some returns from investment in education may be expected at all stages of economic development, investment in educational facilities may produce much lower returns at certain earlier stages of economic growth than the application of equal amounts of investment in other forms of capital. For example, the development of roads and power stations may yield higher returns in terms of economic development than an equal investment in education.

A further problem relates to what economists call the optimal mix for a particular economy, in terms of the proportion spent on widespread or universal primary education as against highly selective secondary or higher education. This issue is still largely a controversial one. Moreover the decision in any particular case will depend not only upon economic consideration but upon various social and political pressures, and the spread of populist ideologies.

All this is not to suggest that the failure of an educational system to meet the needs of its labour market will be anything other than harmful to the economy, generally, and to the possibilities of economic development. Indeed there is some evidence to suggest that an educated population is an asset of considerable importance to the country anxious to 'catch up' with a more advanced economy. In Germany, for example, the educational system was developed as a tool of political control, which from the start 'was seen as providing educated men for the upper levels of the labour force. It was not difficult to build on this ideal after the industrial revolution came to Germany and to see the educational system as a whole as serving all levels of the labour force.' Musgrave has suggested that the efficiency of her educational system enabled Germany to catch up with Britain after an initially late 'take-off' into industrialization. Dore, too, has claimed that a high literacy rate in the 1870s was an important factor in the swift development of Japan as a highly industrialized nation. Moreover both Musgrave and Dore rest their case mainly on the greater efficiency and adaptability of an educated labour force. This applies not only at the managerial and higher technical levels, but at all levels of the economy. The literate factory operative, for example, is not only better able of follow instructions and undertake new tasks, but has been trained in the school in habits of order and discipline.

On the other hand, educational expansion which outstrips occupational need results in educational 'devaluation.' This has happened, and is continuing to happen, in a very striking way in the United States where high-school graduation is now the norm, and college graduation has itself ceased to be linked to elite states. This process of devaluation can also be shown to have occurred in a number of developing countries where investment in education has outstripped the comparatively limited growth in the economy. 'The result, now a commonplace, is a vast and nearly uncontrollable increase in the number of unemployed and under-employed school leaves, whose political orientation toward the policy is marked by disaffection and alienation.' This discontent arises primarily because education has become linked with the expectation of elite status. This is particularly likely to occur in ex-colonial territories where education has been given an exaggerated importance, and where social advancement has been closely tied to educational achievement. At the same time the speed of the educational expansion has undoubtedly made the adjustment harder to make.

The content of education is also seen as relevant to economic growth, and the traditional literary education inherited from colonial days is contrasted sharply with a more practical and scientific approach. In higher education in particular, but also at the secondary level, there has been an emphasis on the humanities, law and arts subjects rather than on science and engineering. A number of reasons have been put forward to explain this, including the lower cost of a liberal education, the continuing influence of the European tradition, and the attraction of the civil service. In Africa, for example, 'not only did the civil service continue to enjoy the high prestige it had in the colonial period, but independence meant that many new posts were opened up to young Africans. For ten years or more, the new universities were able to look forward to a period during which abundant employment opportunities were available to their liberal arts graduates.' A number of developing societies have accordingly, attempted to move towards a more practical education and African educational schemes in particular are 'full of provisions for manual work, especially agricultural, for all, and specialized technical education for as many as can be afforded.'

To a large extent this move away from traditional arts subjects is necessary, particularly if secondary and higher education is to be expanded. In Egypt, for example, 'about 70 per cent of the university enrolment is in the Faculties of Art, Law and Commerce, and for the vast majority of these graduated there is no demand; there is meanwhile a pressing need for scientists, doctors and engineers and the 20 per cent enrolment in these fields absorbs the best student talent.' On the other hand, the swing towards science and technology carries its own dangers. It is just as easy to over-estimate the demand for scientists and technologists as it is for lawyers, and it is even more expensive. Foster, for example, has suggested, taking Ghana as his example, that there is a real danger that technicians will be produced before they can be made use of by the economy. Nor is it enough to provide training programmes it students do not choose to undertake the training, or if they do not make use of it afterwards. Whether or not they do so will depend ultimately upon their perception of the opportunities provided by different types of career. Only if technical and scientific employment can compete with law and administration in terms of social and economic rewards is it likely to appeal to the college graduate.

Moreover, as Hurd and Johnson point out, the same argument applies at lower levels of the educational ladder.

'School graduates, whether prepared as general farmers or as agricultural technicians have proved unwilling to return, so equipped, to the land of their fathers, or to the land of anyone else's fathers for that matter. It is argued that this unwillingness stems from the content of education in many under-developed societies, which stresses an elitist attitude towards manual work of all kinds, thus prejudicing students against farming life. It is true that a prejudice against manual work may exist, but in a number of societies it has been observed that such school graduates are more willing to face urban unemployment or accept labouring jobs in the city than return to the villages.' This was, indeed, very much the situation prevailing in England between the wars, when grammar schools were tied, so it was asserted, to a bookish and irrelevant curriculum which served to divert the best brains of the country into clerical occupations. In fact, however, it is probable that it was the organization of industry rather than the curriculum of the school which was the decisive factor in turning boys away from industrial employment. Not only was industry largely organized to recruit elementary school boys at the age of 14, but prospects within industry were uncertain and haphazard. Clerical work not only had higher status in the eyes of pupils and their parents, but offered, or appeared to offer, greater opportunities for advancement.

It would seem, therefore, that however imperative it is for the educational process to keep pace with the demands made by economic and technical development on the labour force, there is a very real sense in which educational expansion is a consequence rather than a cause of economic development. On the other hand it may also be argued that to concentrate upon the relationships between education and occupation is to overlook the possible significance of changes in attitudes and values. From this point of view education is seen as introducing the developing society to new needs, and new expectations and even to the idea of change itself. In short, education helps to wean the developing society away from the old, and towards the new; it inspires a belief in progress, in efficiency, in achievement and in rationality. At the same time education may be seen as creating the conditions for political as well as economic development by laying the foundations of a democratic form of government. Since a belief in the power of education to change attitudes and values is found in developed as well as developing societies, it is of great interest to consider how far the evidence we have available justifies this faith.

Education and Democracy

It may be appropriate to begin this section with a review of the findings on the relationship between education and democracy. It can be shown, for example, that the higher the education level of a country, the more likely is it to be a democracy. Within countries, moreover, there is an even stronger relationship between education and democratic attitudes. In a summary of the main research findings Lipset argues that 'data gathered by public opinion research agencies which have questioned people in different countries about their beliefs on tolerance for the opposition, their attitudes toward ethnic or racial minorities, and their feelings for multi-party as against one-party systems have showed that the most important single factor differentiating those giving democratic responses from the others has been education. The higher one's education, the more likely one is to believe in democratic values and support democratic practices. All the relevant studies indicate that education is more significant than either income or occupation'. Particularly impressive in this connection is Lipset's evidence that the working classes, and the less-educated, tend to be more authoritarian in their attitudes, and to be more likely to favour extremist political and religious groups. There is also some, although by no means conclusive, evidence that students at college become more liberal 'in the sense of being more sophisticated and independent in their thinking, and placing greater value upon individual freedom and well-being.'

Lipset's picture of the working class as authoritarian has however been criticized as over-drawn. It has been pointed out for example that another characteristic of the working-class respondents is the tendency to give uncertain or no opinion responses, and that in fact the proportion holding extremist or anti-democratic views in the working classes is probably fairly low. Nor is a tendency towards authoritarian views found only amongst the working classes. As Lipset himself has pointed out, 'data from numbers of countries demonstrate that classic

Fascism is a movement of the propertied middle classes.'

At the same time there is evidence to suggest that there is no necessary connection between education and democracy, and both Germany and Japan are examples of nations which have combined a high level of literacy with a totalitarian form of government. Moreover Coleman has argued that the content of education is itself a factor of considerable importance, and suggests that there may be something of an affinity between a predominantly scientific and technological emphasis in education and totalitarian government. He points, for example, to the 'comparatively slight attention given to the humanities, law, the arts, and the social sciences in Communist totalitarian countries.' Jacob, however, found that the 'values and outlook of students do not vary greatly whether they have pursued a conventional liberal arts programme, an integrated general education curriculum or one of the strictly professional-vocational options. The more liberally educated student may take a somewhat more active interest in community responsibilities and keep better informed about public affairs. But the distinction is not striking and by no means does it occur consistently among students at all colleges.' Nor, according to Jacob, do social science courses appear to exert influence on students' beliefs and values. These findings, on the other hand, relate only to the United States.

The contents of education may however be important in another way. Most totalitarian regimes attempt to use their schools to inculcate conformity, submissiveness and uncritical loyalty to the state. In Japan, for example, before the war the schools were expected to encourage submissive acceptance of the existing order. The principal instrument for the inculcation of these principles was the teaching of morals. 'A minimum of one hour per week of morals was mandatory in all schools, from elementary through the secondary schools. But apart from the formal morals course, the ideas were worked into the curriculum and into school life in any way the ingenuity of the educators could devise.' Moreover inside the classroom, 'self-expression was discouraged and disagreement with teachers and elders severely frowned on.'

In Russia, too, emphasis in the schools has been on the indoctrination of the pupil in conformity and obedience as well as in love for the Soviet system. In the school itself, 'the atmosphere was pervaded by a spirit of discipline and hierarchy,' and teachers were warned 'not to coax students but rather to demand obedience, for only in this way would students develop the desired moral qualities.'

Moreover in considering the developing countries of Asia, Africa and South America, we cannot overlook the possibility that democratic government is, as Max Weber suggested, unique to the countries of North America, Western Europe and their English-speaking offspring. According to this explanation both democracy and capitalism were the products of historically unique development in which Protestantism and its emphasis on individual responsibility played a major role. Indeed, in his more pessimistic moments Weber seems to have doubted whether democracy would continue in the future. Instead, he suggested that the 'dictatorial potential implicit in mass appeals added to the desire for a secure subsistence would result in a centralized bureaucracy under a dictator.'

We must conclude, therefore, that the influence of education upon political attitudes is very much more complex than has sometimes been supposed and that although it may be correct to argue that a high level of education is necessary for effective participation in democratic government, there is no guarantee that education and democratic attitudes are necessarily related.

Education, Value Transmission and Value Change

On the other hand if, as we have seen, totalitarian governments can use the educational system to attempt to inculcate a docile and submissive belief in authority it is relevant to ask how far it is also possible to educate for democracy. It is useful, therefore, to look more closely at the education process as a means of value transmission, and to consider not only the extent to which such indoctrination is possible, but also the conditions under which it is likely to operate most effectively.

There is every indication that the educational system of the U.S.S.R. has not only transformed a largely illiterate and traditionally orientated population into both a literate and industrialized work force, but it has also managed to produce a generation who are in the main ideologically committed to the social order. At the same time observers have noted some signs that the process of indoctrination is by no means complete. There is evidence of a small number of young people who are disenchanted with the system, and a much larger number who are not only politically apathetic but to some extent oppurtunist as well. Students in particular have been accused of a dislike of manual labour, of elitist attitudes, and of putting their own career before service to the state. The 1958 school reforms with their introduction of the concept of 'polytechnical education' were designed to teach the dignity of labour, and to prevent the development of a new upper class. Khurushchev, for example, spoke bitterly of the distinction that still exists in the Soviet Union between mental and manual work. 'This is fundamentally wrong and runs counter to our teaching and aspirations. As a rule, boys and girls in secondary school consider that the only acceptable path in life for them is to continue their education at higher schools. Some of them even consider (work) beneath their dignity. This scornful and lordly attitude is to be found in some families. If a boy or girl does not study well and fails to get into college, the parents frighten him by saying that if he does not study well and fails to get into college he will have to work in a factory as a common labourer.'

Moreover, it should not be overlooked that the schools, as such, have only been expected to play a small part in the total process of indoctrination. Indeed, the aim of a totalitarian system is to ensure that every agency of socialization is involved in the process. Directly and indirectly, Grant points out, 'the communist viewpoint is put over at every stage of schooling, and reinforced by other media of communication outside the schools, such as the theatre, films, radio, television and the Press, while the youth organizations act as a link between the school and the world outside.' This is in striking contrast to most democratic systems where the various media of socialization are only loosely controlled. This is not to suggest that democratic societies do not attempt to indoctrinate their children in the religious, moral and political values dominant in the society. The process, however, is normally less conscious and less thorough, partly because there is less emphasis on the production of new values, and concern instead is with the maintenance of traditional religious and moral beliefs and attitudes, partly because democratic societies are usually pluralistic and different and even opposing value systems may be transmitted by different institutions. An exception, however, is the deliberate and largely successful 'Americanization' of immigrant children which has been an important function of the American school.

It is, therefore, important to consider some of the possible reasons for the partial failure of the Soviet system's indoctrination programme. One of the most important handicaps would appear to be the failure to indoctrinate the parents, who are, in consequence, unwilling to accept the consequence of Soviet policy as it affects their children. Even more significant, however, are the contradiction which have clearly arisen between the official ideology and actual experiences and observations in everyday life. The existence of a privileged elite group, and income and status differences between manual and non-manual worker, are the source of parental and student anxieties as well as of their ambitions, and are likely to serve as a serious handicap to the full acceptance of the official doctrine of the equality of all forms of service to the state.

Indeed it would appear that indoctrinating through the educational system is by no means a simple process, and that propaganda, even in the conditions of a totalitarian system, is limited in its scope. For this reason it would appear unreasonable to expect a school system alone to achieve major changes in attitudes, especially when the changes expected cut across strongly entrenched interests, traditional values or everyday experience.

For the same reason we may be somewhat sceptical of the more optimistic claims to reform society by somewhat limited changes in school reorganization. It is unlikely, for example, that either the changeover to the comprehensive system in secondary education, or the abolition of the independent schools, will succeed, on their own, in introducing any radical change in the nature of British society.

This somewhat pessimistic conclusion should not, however, lead us to suppose that education can have no effect on values. In his now classic study of Bennington, Newcomb showed that, given the right conditions, the experience of college could change student values. The students concerned, who came in the main from upper-middle-class conservative families, became more radical in their attitudes as a result of their stay at Bennington. According to Newcomb's analysis, the teachers' interest in and attitude to social and political issues appears to have been the crucial factor. Because the student leaders were strongly influenced by their teachers, liberal opinions enjoyed popularity and prestige, and incoming students were consequently exposed to such opinions not only from the teachers but as part of the student culture. Significantly, it was the students who were most involved in peer-group activities who were the least conservative.

The situation at Bennington does not appear to be typical and it seems that a great many students, in the United States at least, pass through college 'without experiencing significant changes in basic values, or without becoming much involved in problems that interest teachers.' There is evidence, however, that certain colleges, at least, appear to have what Jacob calls a 'peculiar potency' that seems to be the result of a combination of factors, which produce a distinctive institutional atmosphere or a 'climate of values' in which students are decisively influenced. Although the precise combination of factors is not known, Jacob suggests that it is more likely to be found in the 'liberal arts' private college with a sense of special educational mission.

On the other hand there is some evidence that different types of institution attract different kinds of students, and that the effectiveness of certain colleges in changing values may in part be due to the greater readiness of the students to be influenced. It has been found, for expample, that the highly productive colleges in terms of future scholars and scientists, 'attract highly motivated students who are more inner-directed, socially independent, receptive to learning, non-authoritarian, theoretical, aesthetic, unconventional and creative.'

We are left, therefore, with very little direct evidence on the part played by education in changing values. Nevertheless, our greater awareness of the problems of research in this area, including the difficulties of measuring values themselves, and the greater interest taken in such issues as the school and college 'climate' may well offer some hope for the future. It is, however, unlikely what we will make any major progress until we know much more about the effect of the peer group on the learning situation and the consequences for different pupils of variations in the teacher-pupil relationships. The study of the effect of education on values is therefore very much a part of the still undeveloped general sociology of learning.

Education and the Under–Privileged

One of the dominant themes in educational reform in both the nineteenth and the twentieth century has been the extension of educational opportunities to wider sections of the community. In general this has taken the form of free schooling, scholarships, and maintenance grants for needy students, all with the objective of providing equal educational opportunity for all classes in the community. Increasingly, however, we have come to realize that the provision of formal equality does surprisingly little to eliminate educational privilege. Whatever changes we make in our selection mechanisms, or in the scope of our educational provision, many children, because of their home background, are still unable to take advantage of the opportunities opened up to them. Accordingly, attention is now being turned, not simply to the removal of formal barriers to equality, but to the provision of special privileges for those who would otherwise be handicapped in terms of educational achievement.

Such provision is not, of course, new. The fact that a hungry child cannot learn was officially recognized at the beginning of the present century, and provision of school milk and meals and the school health services early became established features of the British education scene. Yet it has taken a long time to see beyond the purely physical needs, and to grasp the concept of what has come, perhaps misleadingly, to be called 'cultural deprivation.' Moreover although the idea of equal educational provision for all classes in the community is now accepted, it has by no means been translated into everyday practice. Even today, children from slum homes are all too often educated in slum schools quite untypical of schools elsewhere. The Plowden Report has described the gaunt-looking buildings, the cramped and often overcrowded conditions inside them, the inadequate and old-fashioned lavatories, the lack of staff rooms and similar facilities, and 'sometimes, all round the ingrained grime of generations.'

Yet, increasingly, it is being recognized that, for these children, even equality is not enough, and the Plowden Report has emphasized the need for 'positive discrimination' in favour of slum schools. It is argued that 'schools in deprived areas should be given priority in many respects. The first step must be to raise the schools with low standards to the national average, and second quite deliberately to make them better. The justification is that the homes and neighbourhoods from which many of their children come provide little support and stimulus for learning. The schools must supply a compensating environment.'

In the United States, where slum areas face problems certainly as severe as anything in Britain, the idea of providing compensatory education for the culturally deprived child is further advanced. In New York City an experiment known originally as the Demonstration Guidance Project was started in 1956. Originally involving one junior high school and one senior high school the intention was to 'identify and stimulate able students from a culturally deprived area, and from generally low income families without any educational tradition, to reach higher educational and vocational goals.'

The success of the original experiment led to its extension in a less intensive form to 65 schools, and it became known at this stage as the Higher Horizons Programme. The scheme involved remedial teaching, an intensive counselling service, and trips to museums, theatres, libraries and laboratories. In 1960 the Great Cities School Improvement Programme, sponsored by the Ford Foundation, extended the experiment into other cities, and into the elementary school. Apart from the intensive work with the children inside and outside the school, there are also attempts to bring the parents into the scheme. At the same time, New York has started to experiment with pre-school education for Harlem children.

Some of these experiments has been highly successful. Academic grades have improved, more children have gone on from school to college, school attendance figures have improved and parents have become more closely involved with the school. On the other hand, there are some critics of the scheme, who doubt whether it is in fact radical enough. Riessman, for example, points out that in the early years of the Project enormous resources of money and energy were poured into a relatively small area, and consequently in view of the previous neglect of these schools, it was not surprising that the results were positive. He argues that what we really need is to 'develop approaches that will be effective on a large scale in the everyday school setting, where teachers are not working day and night and 14 Sundays per term. We need techniques that can be applied by the average teacher, hopefully with a fair amount of devotion, but not necessarily the short-lived zeal fostered by a unique experiment.' His own suggestions involve a more radical change in teaching methods to bridge the gap between the teacher and the deprived child and, in particular, a broadening of the curriculum based on an understanding and respect for the culture of the under-privileged.

Gordon in a recent review of special programmes of compensatory education is also critical of the absence of a really radical approach. He blames the failure of the behavioural scientists to provide sufficiently convincing theories on which the educator can act. Wolf and Wolf have also warned against expecting more from the schools than they can be expected to achieve. They argue that compensatory education cannot in itself solve problems of health, housing and discrimination, and that these must be tackled by agencies outside the school. None of these criticisms, however, is an argument against some form of compensatory education, and they all acknowledge that formal equality of opportunity is an inadequate basis for an equalitarian policy. They do, however, underline the interdependence of education with other aspects of the social structure.

Finally, in this same context, it is necessary to pay some attention to the issue of school integration, since this has proved to be a particularly intractable aspect of the problem, especially in the United States. Since the Supreme Court of the United States declared that equality in education could not be attained in segregated schools, desegregation has proceeded gradually, although often slowly, and not by any means always peacefully. It is useful, therefore, to consider some of the consequences of desegregation particularly as they affect the school system and the under-privileged child. There is already, for example, evidence of the extent to which white pupils leave schools where desegregation has brought in a high proportion of Negro students. This has occurred more particularly in the big cities, and many examples can be found in Detroit, Chicago, New York and Los Angles. In these areas, desegregation often means an influx of pupils whose educational standards are extremely low, in part because of the poverty of their home surroundings, in part because of the inadequacy of their previous schools; and this situation is particularly acute in areas where there has been much recent immigration from the South, from Puerto Rico and from Mexico. In such circumstances parents may move house, or they may move their children to a parochial or other non-public school. The result is an increase in the racial and ethnic imbalance in the schools, with consequences not only for the policy of integration, but on the standards in the schools themselves. Attempts have been made to overcome the problems of residential segregation by means of a transfer programme between schools, by rezoning, or by reclassifying schools to handle fewer grades and thus serve larger areas, but none of these solutions can be effective on anything but a small scale. The development of compensatory education programmes becomes, therefore, one of increased urgency.

Conclusion

The precise relationship of the educational systems to social and economic change can therefore be seen to be one of extreme complexity, and it is almost impossible to draw any conclusions that are not misleading. It is possible, however, that at least part of the problem lies in the way the question is framed. The concept of education as producing or impeding social change is enormously complicated by the fact that the educational system is itself a part of the society which is changing. Consequently the real issue is one of the actual inter-relationship between educational institutions and other aspects of society. Moreover it is this inter-relationship which makes it so difficult to use the educational system to produce conscious or planned social change. The present chapter contains numerous examples of such efforts which have come to grief just because the educational system has been seen in isolation from its social context. This is not to suggest, on the other hand, that change in education is never important or necessary. An educational system that fails to adapt to the needs of the economy can, for example, seriously handicap economic development, and an elitist ideology can restrict educational development and waste a very considerable amount of working-class ability. Moreover education, in so far as it increases knowledge and understanding, both of man himself and of his environment, creates the conditions necessary of the development of both the individual and society. The discovery that educational reform is not a universal panacea should not therefore lead us to minimize the importance of knowledge about the educational institutions in society. The very complexity of the issues involved suggests rather that we need not only more but better and more sophisticated research into the inter-relationship between education and society.

5

The Teaching Profession

Development of the Profession

In any attempt to construct a sociology of the school, a study of the teacher must at all times have a central place. The crucial position of the teacher in the educational process has indeed been widely recognized, and studies of teachers as a group have been fairly widespread, so that we now have a fair amount of knowledge of the characteristics of teachers in Britain and, to some extent, elsewhere. First, however, it is necessary to look briefly at the structure of teaching as an occupation, since, although it is customary nowadays to think of teaching as a unified profession, in reality teachers form a very diversified group. As Brookover and Gottlieb have pointed out, 'The range of teachers is very great. They teach in everything from kindergarten to graduate school; in schools supported by churches, by private corporations, by foundations, by taxpayers; on assignments ranging all the way from the entire first eight grades in one to private sessions with a student in deed of individual attention. A roll call would include those engaged in such diverse activities as driver education, training prison inmates, rehabilitation of veterans, and work with the physically and emotionally handicapped, in addition to the countless specialities usually identified with the traditional teacher role.' Brookover and Gottlieb are writing about the USA but the point they make is equally valid in Europe. Moreover these different types of teacher not only perform different roles; there are also frequently differences in remuneration, status, qualifications, sex, social-class background, and many other characteristics.

One of the most usual ways to categorize teachers is in terms of the age-range of the pupils. Those teaching younger pupils in primary or elementary schools are distinguished in this way from those who teach in secondary schools, while those working in higher education form another and quite distinct category. An alternative system of classifications is in terms of the subjects taught. The broad differentiation here is between academic and practical subjects. When this is combined with the age-level of the pupils, it gives up important subdivisions between teachers in different types of secondary school, or between various kinds of higher education. Yet a further distinction which has been of great importance historically is made in terms of the social origin of the pupils. This is particularly important where middle- or upper-class children are educated in separate schools. In addition, wherever State education has been provided, mainly for the children of the poor, there may be important distinctions between teachers in State and in independent schools.

Tropp has described the development in Britain during the nineteenth century of the new profession of elementary school teacher. Faced with the need to give the rudiments of education to the children of the poor, the demand was for a whole new army of teachers who could be provided at little cost. As Tropp puts it, 'in the 1830s and 1840s the great question was whether education could mitigate the dangers inherent in an ignorant industrial population or whether it would, by teaching the poor to read and write, make them a still greater danger to society. An important but secondary question was—who was to provide the education and what should be its nature? Once it was conceded that education should be extended to the poor through the medium of voluntary religious societies and that this education should be suffused with morality and religion, it became obvious that the main need was for a supply of efficient, religious and humble teachers.'

The answer was found in the pupil-teacher system, a method of teacher training already practised on the continent. Under the pupil-teacher system the most intelligent and moral pupils of the elementary schools were apprenticed as pupil-teachers to the headmaster at the age of 13. During their five years' apprenticeship they received one and a half hours a day teaching from the headmaster and for the rest of their time acted as a teacher in the school. After five years of satisfactory service, those who were successful in a competitive examination were given scholarships for a further period of education in a Training College. A teacher's certificate, which carried the right to an augmented salary and a pension, was granted either on the successful completion of the Training College course or to those passing an external examination for practising teachers. The certificated teachers were, however, the elite of the profession. In 1855, for example, almost all certificated teachers had headship, and even at the end of the century a shortage of Training College places, especially for women, meant that not only were many teachers uncertificated, but that many of the certificated teachers were untrained.

The effect of the pupil-teacher system was to produce several generations of teachers who had been educated within an almost completely closed system. Only the period at Training College was, for those who achieved it, a break from the elementary school, and even this was an enclosed world within the elementary tradition. Moreover the educational background, even for the teacher who had been to Training College, was inevitable limited. For the rest, 'it was impossible to expect a high proportion of "cultured" teachers from pupil-teacherdom with its one and a half hours of instruction a day, after a hard day's work, and with a tired teacher and tired pupil-teachers,' especially when we remember that full-time education for these young people had ended at the age of 13. As benefitted their social origin and limited educational background, teachers were expected to be humble, to show gratitude for the 'charity' to which they owned their education and training, and to reform from any excessive ambition to improve their lot. Indeed, during the middle years of the century in particular teachers were constantly under fire for their conceit and ambition. A particular cause of complaint was the teacher who after training used his education to move into a better-paid job.

At the other extreme from the elementary school teachers were the masters at the major public schools. 'The task of a master in a public school was to teach the classics to the sons of the upper class and to those who were being educated with them. He had to be acceptable both to the parents and to the headmaster on academic and personal grounds, and his background was a matter of some importance.' Not only was an Oxford or Cambridge degree almost essential but there was a tendency on the part of public schools to recruit from amongst their own boys, which reached an extreme form at Eton. According to Bamford, 74 per cent of those appointed to Eton between 1801 and 1862 were old Eton boys. In the main the masters at the major public schools were of middle-class professional origin, and the headmasters often came from eminent families.

The high status of the public school master was maintained not only by means of his educational background but also by his connection with the Church. Until the second half of the nineteenth century it was customary for the masters as well as the head to be clergymen. 'The first significant number of lay appointments for Eton, Harrow and Rugby occurred in the 1850s but not till 1870 for Shrewsbury.'

The position of the headmaster was particularly important. Not only was he in complete control of his school and its staff, but he enjoyed great prestige outside the school. Moreover, even after the introduction of laymen as masters, the headmaster remained a clergyman. Frequently, too, the headship of a major public school was only a 'stepping stone to higher things.' Promotions to deaneries and bishoprics were common, and even an archbishopric was by no means out of the question.

It was customary too for the headship to command a high income even where the assistant masters were poorly paid. Indeed, in spite of their qualifications, assistant masters in all but the top public schools were frequently not only very badly paid but had little hope of promotion. In such schools the turnover of staff was often high. Moreover, below the ranks of the public schools, in the endowed grammar schools and preparatory schools, salaries were so poor that frequently the master looked jealously at the rapid improvements which were being made in the training and education of the masters of schools of a lower grade.' Nevertheless, even if poorly paid, the grammar school teachers shared in the public school rather than the elementary school tradition and enjoyed a higher status than elementary school teachers.

The completely separate elementary tradition did not, however, outlast the nineteenth century. Modifications to the system had started in the 1880s with the development of pupil-teacher centres in the large towns, where pupil-teachers were taught in central classes. At the same time attempts were made to improve the teaching in the Training Colleges and to bring them into closer contact with the universities. Gradually, however, educational opinion was moving away from the view that elementary education needed to be narrow or rudimentary, and with this change in attitude towards the nature of the education to be provided came severe criticism of the systems of teacher-training and the teachers it had trained. Instead of the pupil-teacher centres, *The Report of the Departmental Committee on the Pupil Teacher System* of 1898 'looked forward with confidence to the use of secondary schools as the best means of overcoming that narrowness of intellectual and professional outlook which had long been felt to be one of the weakest points of the profession and which, it can hardly be doubted, was largely due to the inhuman and deadening influences under which generations of pupil-teachers had been educated.' With the reorganization of secondary education that followed the 1902 Act normal entrance to the elementary teaching profession was only through the secondary school.

The immediate effect of this change of policy was tragic for the existing teachers. Branched as 'uncultured and imperfectly educated—creatures of tradition and routine,' they were considered as no longer fit even for those posts in the inspectorate and the training colleges that they had previously held. At the same time the higher-grade work which had been developed in the elementary schools in the 1880s and 90s was transferred to the new secondary system, which tended to be staffed by teachers from secondary or public schools. Even in the long term the ending of the pupil-teacher system did not remove the cleavage within the profession. In practice the elementary school teacher continued to be recruited from the training colleges and the secondary school teacher from the universities. 'Until the 1940s', asserts Tropp, 'only unemployment could drive the graduate into the elementary school.' The abolition of the elementary system in 1944 was a further and indeed a major step in the unification of the profession, but the elementary tradition is still perpetuated, partly by the distinctions operating within secondary education, and partly by the continuation of the college training. These differences, which will be examined in more detail later in this chapter, perpetuate many aspects of the dual system even within the framework of a unified profession.

The development of teacher training in Britain has been described at length because it is paralleled in general terms, if not in detail, in all the European countries and in other parts of the world. The education of the poor, that is to say, has developed separately from the education of the elite. Whereas secondary education has always had close ties with the universities in its outlook and its subject-matter and has had as its function the transmission of 'culture', elementary education in its origin at least was simply intended to 'gentle the masses'. Consequently whereas the teacher in the secondary school needed to be educated in the full sense of the word, the elementary school teacher had only to be trained. Primarily, it was the limited conception of the education of the masses which entailed the narrowness of the education and training of their teachers, and only as the standards expected of elementary education have risen do we find any major changes in the pattern of teacher training. Thus the normal schools of continental Europe were designed as institutions parallel to the academic secondary school, giving some limited general education and some practical training for teaching. For example, in the normral schools set up in France by a decree of 1833, the sons of small farmers and manual labourers were trained as elementary teachers. 'They received a moral and religious education, lessons in reading, grammar and practical geometry. They were given some notions of the everyday applications of science, of French history and geography. They were shown how to draw up certificates of births, deaths and marriages, and how to graft and prune trees. They were initiated into teaching method by attending the primary schools attached to the *Ecoles Normales*.'

Gradually the level of education in the normal schools was improved and entrance standards were raised, but frequently they have remained a separate system, recruiting from elementary rather than secondary schools. In France the *'ecole normale* has remained as a parallel to the academic secondary school although, since the war, the rigid separation between elementary and secondary education has ended. It is, for example, possible now for a student at normal school to prepare for the *baccalaureat* and pass on to a university, or for a pupil from the *lycee* to enter elementary school teaching after a shortened course at the normal school. In Germany the situation prevailing at the present time is much nearer to the English system. The *Pedagogische Hochschule*, which prepares for elementary school teaching, demands as an entry qualification the leaving certificate of the academic secondary school or its equivalent but, like the English training colleges, it is not yet a full part of the university structure.

In the United States the progress towards a unified system of teacher-training has gone much further than anywhere in Europe, even though standards initially were just as low, and improvements during the nineteenth century were no faster than in Britain. Normal schools were founded from the 1830s onwards, but the growth in their numbers was very slow. Moreover, like their European counterparts, entry requirements were so low that one of their main functions was to complete the pupils' secondary education. Many went straight into teaching on leaving school. Improvements in Teacher-training in the United States have occurred chiefly in the present century, and it is in this period too that the system has moved away from the European pattern. In 1910 two-year normal schools were common, following after two years or less at a high school. By 1930 the normal schools were being supplanted by teachers' colleges organized to provide a three- or four-year programme and asking for four years of high-school preparation. Today a bachelor's degree representing four years of preparation beyond high school is almost universally required, and the teachers' colleges are themselves undergoing transformation into multi-purpose institutions. An even more important development is that elementary and secondary teachers are frequently trained in the same institutions, although secondary school teachers are usually expected to have higher qualifications.

In attempting to understand the reasons for the direction taken by teachers' education in the United States, the absence of a distinctive elementary and secondary tradition must take pride of place. The early appearance of the comprehensive high school, and its dominance in the field of secondary education, has meant that all prospective teachers pass together through the high school. At the same time the meaning of secondary education has been altered. It is no longer a selective education, preparing a minority for elite status, but must cater for the needs of all children. Moreover, the frequent absence of streaming and setting in the schools, and the existence of many small schools, means that the specialist subject-teacher is rare in the American context. Consequently, not only has much greater attention been paid to teaching methods in the training of secondary school teachers, but their education is much less subject-centred than is customary in Europe. Bachelors' degrees held by both elementary and secondary teachers are normally degrees in Education. Indeed critics of the American teacher-training system frequently argue that American teachers are inadequately prepared for academic teaching.

The scope and flexibility of American higher education also makes it easier to integrate it with teachers' education than is likely to be possible in most of Europe, where university teachers often show resistance to a closer relationship with teacher-training institutions. This is partly because of the greater willingness in the United States to accept practical and vocational subjects as part of higher education. At the same time, the existence of what Riesman calls the academic procession allows an aspiring teachers' college to turn itself into a multi-purpose college or university. Consequently, even if the education of teachers frequently has less prestige than other kinds of higher education, this is not a distinction which creates a rigid barrier within the profession.

Teachers in universities in Britain are not normally regarded as members of the same professional group as school teachers, although they share with the public school teachers the same origin within the Church. Changes in Oxford and Cambridge and the growth of the newer universities has ended the relationship with the Church, but university teachers are still recruited on the basis of their ability as scholars, even if notions of scholarship have now widened to include science and technology. Recruits to the profession are not trained in teaching methods, nor is ability in teaching a criterion, and achievement in scholarship or research is the most important ingredient in professional success. In this sense the image of the scholar or, increasingly, the scientist, is dominant over that of the teacher.

At the same time there have been quite rigid distinctions between teachers in universities and teachers in other forms of higher education in terms of qualification and pattern of recruitment. The teaching staff in colleges of education, for example, have been recruited principally from the ranks of practising teachers, and have for this reason tended to represent the higher reaches of the teaching profession, rather than to link up with the university teachers either in interests and attitudes or in their sense of identity. The technical college teacher has also been quite sharply differentiated, in part by the tradition of part-time teachers, in part by the emphasis on industrial experience. Technical colleges also seem to attract recruits from school teaching, although not of course to the same extend as the colleges of education. At the same time the range of work carried out in technical colleges means that the qualifications of the staff very accordingly, and nowadays, although many, especially of those doing advanced work, hold degrees or degree equivalents, others hold lower qualifications such as the H.N.C. or craft qualification. In no sense, therefore, can we talk of teachers of higher education as a single group.

In the United States, in contrast, the structure of higher education does not allow for differentiation of quite this kind, although as we have seen, there is a distinct tendency for status distinctions to occur between departments and also between institutions, according to their position in what Riesman has called the academic procession. Nevertheless, teachers of higher education can be and are viewed as a single group in a way that is at present impossible in Britain.

However, the pattern of recruitment to college teaching in the United States still has much in common with the more elitist European tradition from which it sprang, and entry to the profession it still governed entirely by academic qualifications. This emphasis is supported by the pattern of doctorate training which is now the major pathway for entry into the profession, for very few Ph.D. programmes include any provision for teacher training and they can be viewed essentially as apprenticeships in research. At the same time the main promotion opportunities arise as a result of publication and research. Indeed it could be argued that there is even less emphasis on the teaching function in the United States than in Britain. The effect of this is not only to differentiate college teachers from school teachers, but to emphasize loyalty to the discipline rather than to the profession as such, with implications that will be discussed in a later section.

At the same time the very rapid development of college education in the United States since 1900 has meant an enormously rapid expansion in the number of college teachers, so that they now represent a vast and historically unique professional class in American society. The consequences of this enormous expansion are likely to be very far-reaching both for the standards of the profession and for its status in the community. Some of these implications will be taken up later in the chapter.

The Social-class Background of Teachers

The social origin of the teaching profession is closely related to the method of recruitment, and the availability of training. As we have seen already the pupil-teacher system is nineteenth-century England was an important avenue of social mobility for the clever and ambitious working-class child. At the same time the lowly social origins of the elementary school teachers was a factor in the low status given to the teaching profession. Consequently it is of interest to examine the few studies which give us accurate information on the social origin of teachers. Fortunately, the study by Floud and Scott based on a sample survey of teachers in England and Wales in 1955 provides us with a very detailed picture of the social origins of the profession, which confirms the impression received from earlier and smaller studies. Their results show clearly that although teachers are recruited from all levels of the status hierarchy they come predominantly from the lower middle and the skilled working classes. These overall figures however are less interesting than the differences which the study shows to exist within the profession. The following Table 5.1 sets out these differences as they occur not only between various types of school, but between men and women teachers.

Table 5.1

Social Origin of Teachers in Grant-earning Schools, England and Wales, 1955

Father's Occupation when teacher left School	*Type of School* Primary %	Modern %	Maintained grammar %	Direct-grant grammar %
(A) Men				
Professional and administrative	6.0	7.5	12.5	19.8
Intermediate	48.3	45.9	55.1	61.9
Manual, skilled	32.5	36.5	25.3	14.6
Manual, semi- and unskilled	13.2	10.1	7.1	4.0
All	100.0	100.0	100.0	100.0
(N)	1,251	1,178	1,209	544
(B) Women				
Professional and administrative	8.8	11.4	17.8	30.4
Intermediate	52.2	54.8	63.1	57.4
Manual, skilled	29.6	28.1	16.4	10.4
Manual, semi- and unskilled	9.3	5.7	2.7	1.8
All	100.0	100.0	100.0	100.0
(N)	1,449	1,083	1,100	733

It will be noticed that women teachers in all types of school, but particularly in grammar schools, have a higher social origin than men teachers. This undoubtedly reflects the greater alternatives open to men, and particularly to male graduates. Teaching still offers more opportunities to the educated girl than most other careers open to her. The other important distinction is between those schools inheriting the elementary tradition and those still influenced by the secondary tradition. The social origin of the teachers is quite considerably higher in the grammar schools than in either the primary or secondary modern schools. The difference between the maintained grammar and direct grant grammar is an interesting reflection of the relationships generally found between the social class of the pupils and of their teachers. Nevertheless, although teachers of working-class origin are rare in the direct-grant grammar schools, it is true for these schools, as for the rest, that the largest group of teachers are from the lower middle classes.

Floud and Scott have also tried to trace changes in the recruitment of teachers by means of a comparison between cohorts of teachers entering the profession at different periods. Such a comparison shows remarkably little change in the proportion of elementary school teachers from working-class families entering the profession before 1920 and of those entering since 1945. On the other hand, there has been a fairly steady decline in the social-class origin of grammar school teachers. In the case of men teachers this has mainly taken the form of a decline in those entering from the professional and administrative classes, but for women teachers there has been in addition an increase in those entering from manual-worker families.

It is more difficult to get comparable information from the United States. According to Brookover and Gottlieb, 'most studies of the social class background of teachers do not provide us with a foundation for generalizations about teachers across the nation.' The studies available to us, however, suggest that the social background of teachers in the United States does not differ very profoundly from that of Britain, and that, although a sizeable minority are from working-class families, the largest group are those from the lower middle classes. There is also evidence that women teachers have a higher social origin than men teachers. On the other hand, although secondary school teachers are frequently expected to have higher qualifications than elementary school teachers, there is no evidence that they are of a higher social origin. Indeed a study by Carlson suggests that the reverse is true. He found that female elementary school teachers had the highest social origins, and male secondary school teachers the lowest. As many as 48 per cent of male secondary teachers, according to his study, are from the working or lower classes as compared with 23 per cent of female elementary school teachers. While these findings may not be typical of the United States as a whole, and while they may conceal important differences within secondary education, they do lend support to the impression that the United States system has avoided the stigma of the elementary tradition.

This is not to assert, of course, that differentiation is absent from the American teaching profession, any more than it is absent from the American school system. Rather it is less institutionalized than in Europe with its sponsored mobility and selective secondary school. It may well be, for example, that there are differences in social origin within schools between teachers trained in different ways or teaching different subjects. There also seems to be differentiation between schools of the same type according to the social characteristics of the pupils. There is some evidence, for example, of 'a tendency for Negro teachers to be placed in schools where there are strong concentrations of Negro youth,' and it may well be that teachers of working-class origin are to be found predominantly in working-class schools. Becker, for example, in his study of the Chicago public school teacher found that one major career pattern consists in moving from the lower-class school, in which teaching begins, to a school with a higher proportion of middle-class pupils.

Becker's findings are reinforce to some extent by the recent study by Herriott and St. John. They report that teachers in schools where the pupils are in the lowest socio-economic status come from a background 'which can be characterized as more urban, more "blue collar", with less formal education and lower incomes than those of the teachers from schools of highest socio-economic status.' Of these differences, however, only those relating to the type of community and father's occupation were statistically significant. Moreover, nowhere are the differences extreme. In the case of father's occupation, for example, 30 per cent of teachers in schools of high socio-economic status, and 43 per cent of teachers in schools of low socio-economic status had fathers in 'blue collar' occupations. Thus, even in schools where the majority of pupils were from low-status families, the majority of teachers had come from 'white collar' homes.

The social origin of college and university teachers is to

some extent governed by the social background of the college and university student and, as we have seen, this is likely to be predominantly middle class in character even in countries like the United States. There is, however, some evidence that American college teachers are of lower social origin than other comparable professional groupings. This is probably because of the emphasis placed upon academic distinction rather than social and financial considerations in recruitment to the profession. It is likely, however, that as in the case of school teachers there are considerable differences in social origin of college teachers both nationally and between different types of institution. Wilson, for example writing in 1942, compared the American college teacher 'with the new quasi-proletarian intelligentsia of the USSR.' rather than with the 'aristo critically inclined university staff of pre-Nazi Germany.' It is very likely, too, that in Britain university teachers have a higher social origin than those teaching in other forms of higher education. We should also expect to find that the differences in student composition between Oxford and Cambridge and the provincial universities are also reflected in the social origin of their teaching staffs.

The Status of the Teacher

The social origin of any occupational group both reflects and is a reflection of the status of the group; and undoubtedly the social origin of the teachers is a reflection above all of the ambiguity of their status, which needs to contain the two traditions : the teacher of the rich and the teacher of the poor. Undoubtedly the status of the grammar schools teacher, in Britain as in Europe generally is higher than that of the elementary school teacher, yet in judging the profession as a whole it is the influence of the elementary tradition which seems to be the stronger. The Registrar General, for example, places school teachers in Class II, the Intermediate class, and not in the category of higher administrative or professional employees in Class I. Similarly, the London School of Economics, in its study of social mobility, found that the elementary school teacher was ranked by members of the general public alongside the news reporter, the commercial traveller and the jobbing master builder, but below a non-conformist minister, and certainly below the traditional professions.

In the United States, too, the status of the teacher is an intermediate one. In 1947, in a study of the status of various occupations, the National Opinion Research Centre found that the school teacher was ranked in public opinion surveys only slightly above the average. Indeed, Lieberman in a critical survey of the teaching profession in the United States concludes that 'teachers are finding it more difficult than ever before to maintain their present intermediate status, let alone raise it to the level of such occupational groups as doctors and lawyers.' Moreover, even though teacher-training is now carried out more and more frequently in multi-purpose institutions, Conant, amongst others, has pointed to the low esteem in which degrees in education are generally held. It is therefore worth looking closely at some of the factors influencing the present status of teaching as an occupation.

One of the major problems facing the teaching profession is its very rapid rate of expansion. At first this affected only the elementary school teacher, and we have already examined some of the effects of this expansion on recruitment and training. During the twentieth century, however, secondary and, later, higher education have experienced rapid development and, although the United States was affected earlier and more profoundly, since the last war there have been rapid increases in both secondary and further education in most European countries. Both the scale and the rapidity of the expansion have meant that there has been an almost continuous shortage of qualified personnel to staff the schools, and at all times, but particularly during periods of rapid expansion, the profession has included large numbers of unqualified teachers. In the nineteenth century the proportion of unqualified women teachers was as high or higher than those who were qualified, and even in 1900 as many as 40 per cent of teachers in elementary schools were not qualified. During the twentieth century, however, standards in elementary school teaching have risen considerably, and a survey in 1962 by the National Union of Teachers found that only six per cent of teachers in primary schools were unqualified. However, this figure appears to be rising. On the other hand teaching, even secondary school teaching, is a long way from being a graduate profession. Although the majority of teachers in grammar schools are graduates, this is true of only a minority in the secondary modern schools, who are still recruited in large part from the training colleges. The N.U.T. survey found 20.2 per cent of graduates amongst men teachers in secondary modern schools and 13.0 per cent of graduates amongst the women. In maintained grammar schools they were 81.5 per cent and 72.7 per cent, respectively. Primary schools are staffed almost entirely by non-graduates.

In the United States the teacher shortage is more serious and the problem of unqualified staff more acute. We have already noticed the low level of education of elementary school teachers, which lasted into the early years of the present century. Even as late of 1908 a study of 735 high-school graduates in the State of New York showed 117 of them directly entering teaching, as compared with 122 going to the normal schools. The very rapid increase in the number of high-schools at the end of the nineteenth century also produced a similar problem in the secondary schools. Indeed it has been estimated that the development of high schools had outrun the available supply of college-trained teachers as early as the 1870s, and 80s, and the situation was to worsen later. Moreover, there were substantial variations even among neighbouring states.

From the 1920s the level of education of school teachers gradually improved, but so did the standards expected of the profession, so that the number of unqualified teachers continued to be high. Moreover, since the 1940s there has been a serious shortage of teachers, which has accentuated the problem. Consequently although the great majority of teachers in elementary as well as secondary schools by the 1950s had a bachelor's or higher degree, in 1955 'there was not a single state in which every elementary teacher processed at least four years of college training.'

Consequently, as Lieberman points out, although the higher requirements now expected of teachers 'may eventually help to raise the status of education as a profession, the present status of education as a profession is based chiefly upon the much lower requirements in force during the past four decades.'

Another problem for the teachers is that although their educational level is rising, so is that, not only of other professional occupations, but of the population in general.

Consequently the improvements in the last 50 years have enabled teachers to maintain their status but not necessarily to improve it. This is particularly true in the United States, where the meaning of a bachelor's degree has changed radically, due to the rapid expansion in higher education. In Britain, however, as in Europe generally, expansion in higher education has been at a much slower rate, and it seems likely that the improvements in the educational background of the school teachers has done more to improve their status than have the even greater improvements in teacher education in the United States.

A further characteristic of the teaching profession which is closely related to its status is the balance within it of male and female teachers. The proportions of women in elementary school teaching in the United States is so high that it can be reasonably described as a women's occupation. A survey made by the National Education Association in 1956 found only 14 per cent of elementary school teachers to be men. Teachers in secondary education are, however, fairly evenly balanced between men and women. Altogether about 75 per cent of all school teachers in the United States are women. This preponderance of women has characterized the profession since the end of the nineteenth century. Men, however, predominate in educational administration, including the post of school principal.

The proportion of women in education in the United States is probably greater than anywhere else in the world. In Britain, for example, although the proportion of women teachers is higher than in many European countries including France and Germany, it is less than in the United States. About three-quarters of teachers in primary schools are women and roughly half of those in secondary schools. This is another reason to believe that the status of teachers in Britain and in Europe generally, is higher than in the United States.

One of the main reasons why teaching can still attract women into the profession when it is hard to recruit men, lies in the lack of alternatives open to the educated woman, even when there are many such alternatives available for a man with similar qualifications. Not only is the salary scale favourable in comparison with what she could earn elsewhere, but working conditions, hours and holidays are often not only reasonable in themselves but fit in well with the responsibilities of a family.

The profession is, therefore, particularly attractive to the girl who is looking for a job she can return to after she is married.

The fact that many women in the profession see it as a temporary job rather than as a permanent career also has a profound effect on their expectations. The initial salary, the length of training, the possibility of re-joining the profession after a break of several years : all of these considerations are of more importance than ultimate salary or promotion possibilities. Consequently, the aspects of jobs which deter potential male recruits may not appear as disadvantages at all to many of the women entering the profession.

At the same time, the very appeal of the profession to women may diminish its attractiveness to men; for once any occupation becomes accepted as a woman's job, the idea grows that it is unsuitable for a man. According to Brookover and Gottlieb, 'teaching is associated with motherhood, with the training and socialization of the young, and with the protection of the needy. So farmly entrenched is this popular image in our society that is becomes difficult for a man who wants to enter the field to withstand the social pressures against doing so. The authors have talked with numerous college girls who are majoring in elementary education and find that few of them would be willing to consider as a husband a man who makes teaching his life's work'.

The size of the teaching profession is also an important factor in the status it is awarded and, particularly, in the extent to which it can expect high rewards for its services. The cost of maintaining a well-qualified and highly-paid teaching profession in the context of mass secondary education and an expanding system of higher education requires the baking of a community which is not only wealthy, but highly committed to education and willing to spend generously on the public services. The United States, with its tradition of private affluence and public squalor, is not likely to be willing to reward the large number of school teachers on the same level as the doctors. Lieberman has calculated that in the year 1954-55 equalizing teachers' salaries with the incomes of doctors would have required a sum larger than the total amount spent upon public education in that school year.

The rapid expansion in the number of teachers also makes

it difficult to maintain the standards of entrants not only, as we have seen, in the short run but, as the size of the profession goes on increasing, equally in the long term. Indeed Lieberman has suggested that *already* in the United States within the limits of the country's resources of skilled manpower it is doubtful if additional teachers can be secured without lowering the qualifications for teaching. It is true that the present shortage of skilled manpower must be seen within the context of a considerable waste of ability, but in the absence of any immediate expectation of solving this problem it is difficult to see how the current teacher shortage is going to be met. Lieberman's own solution is essentially a more efficient use of teachers, both by the development of a more advanced educational technology, and by changes in the organization of the teaching role. In particular, he advocates the utilization of semi-professional assistants on the model of the medical profession. Pointing out the routine nature of many of the teachers' activities, he suggests that the use of assistants by teachers to carry out routine tasks would permit larger salaries to be paid to the professionals.

On the other hand, the teaching profession also suffers, as Bryan Wilson has pointed out, from the high level of diffuseness of the teaching role. The roles of the doctor or the lawyer, for example, are easier to define; there is a definable expertise involving an objective body of knowledge which is almost completely lacking in the case of teaching. It is true that teachers sometimes attempt to claim such a body of knowledge, and in the United States in particular there has been a widespread development of courses in 'education,' but such courses have not yet met with general acceptance as either desirable or even necessary for the intending teacher. Conant, for example, points out that 'many academic professors believe that the courses given by professors of education are worthless.' In Britain, teachers in grammar schools frequently have had no training for teaching at all. Consequently there is a tendency for teachers to fall back on the subjects they are qualified to teach, and where this is a highly esoteric body of knowledge in its own right, teachers can often command high prestige. Yet such a ranking system, by confusing the difficulty of a subject with the difficulty of teaching it, does less than justice to the role of the primary school teachers and, indeed, to the whole primary stage of the education process as well as to the education of the less able child. The development of teaching skills is therefore vitally necessary for the education process itself as well as for the status of the teacher. Although prejudice is an important factor in the attitude to courses in 'education' as a part of teacher-training, there is no doubt that some of the criticisms of educational courses are valid and that on the whole this aspect of teacher-education has serious weaknesses, many of which spring from the relatively underdeveloped state of the 'education sciences'. Since research in this field is now increasing, it is likely that our knowledge of the educational process will increase in future with results of value to the practising teacher. It is unlikely, however, that teacher skills will ever command the mystique that surrounds the skills of the medical profession.

One of the main characteristics of a profession is the high degree of self-determination allowed to and practised by its members; but as we saw teachers, particularly in the United States, have very little control over many aspects of educational policy which would come within their expert competence if they were truly a profession. Lieberman has argued that if a decision requires expert skill and knowledge is should be reserved to the proper expert authority, and he lists amongst the decisions that should be made by educators, but which are frequently in the hands of laymen, the choice of textbooks and teaching materials and the choice of subjects and courses of study. Control over entry to the profession is also, Lieberman believes, essential to full professional autonomy, and this is denied to teachers both in Britain and the United States.

The status of the college teacher, although it would appear to be invariably higher than that of the school teacher, is also subject to considerable ambiguities, of which the most important is the discrepancy between the economic rewards of the profession and its educational level. This seems to be particularly acute in the United States, where academic salaries, especially at the lower end of the professional hierarchy, are not only strikingly low but have declined in relative terms since the pre-war period. Thus 'by 1957, physicians had gained 93 per cent over their 1939 real incomes—and over 400 per cent in dollar income; dentists had gained 54 per cent; lawyers about 45 per cent. During the same period the real income of the academic man actually *declined* 8.5 per cent—from an income already inadequate in 1939.'

Because their earnings are so much less than others of similar educational background, it has been argued that 'there is a strong tendency for academics to withdraw from the general middle class population and establish a distinctive and relatively isolated subculture'. There is also evidence that some college teachers, at least in the United States, experience a high level of status anxiety. For example, Lazarsfeld and Thielens in a study of social-science professors found that a large proportion of their sample felt themselves held in low esteem by other occupational groups and particularly by businessmen.

We can only speculate on the reasons for the relatively low socio-economic status of college teaching in the United States. It is likely, however, that the rate of expansion has reduced the elite nature of the profession, especially when it has meant the inclusion under the general higher-education umbrella of colleges offering courses and subjects at different academic levels. To this we may add the low prestige of intellectuals in the United States.

In Britain, too, there is a discrepancy between economic reward and educational qualifications, although it seems likely that this is less acute than in the United States. There is also less insecurity in the lower levels of the profession as tenure is customarily obtained at an earlier age. The small size of the profession in comparison with the United States is also an important factor in maintaining its elite status, while distinctions within higher education maintain a fairly clear status differential between university teachers and those in colleges of education and technical colleges. It is likely, too, that the Oxbridge don, with his distinctly upper-middle-class associations, still dominates the popular image of the university teacher.

One way in which college teachers are undoubtedly closer to professional status than are school teachers is in the much higher degree of self-determination which is generally accorded them, and which has its roots in the historical development of the profession. In the medieval university, teacher and student guilds were self-governing, and the tradition of college autonomy remains strongly entrenched in the ideology of the profession. Bureaucratic control, favoured by the increase in the size and complexity of educational institutions, is now a marked feature of college and university control in Britain and in the United States, but it is considerably tempered by what Burton Clark has called professional authority in federated form. He points out that 'as the campus moves from the characteristics of a community to the characteristics of a loosely-joined federation, faculty authority moves from the meeting of the assembled faculty and the informal interaction of a small body to the numerous dispersed units (departments, sub-schools, sub-colleges) that are the foci of the disciplinary interests of the faculty and to a more formal representative government in which there is greater differentiation between those who participate and those who do not'.

Within this general picture there is, of course, considerable variation. In the United States, as we have seen, there are very wide differences in the form of control of higher education, and in some colleges and universities there is very strong lay control, leaving the college teacher with very little autonomy at the level of policy-making. In English universities, faculty control is well established, but this is much less true of other types of higher education, and colleges of education, for example, like schools, are under the control of local education authorities.

It should also be noted that even where professional autonomy is strong, the democratic tradition has often been lost. Some forms of university government, for example, are essentially oligarchic with power tending to fall into the hands of departmental heads, leaving those at lower levels of the hierarchy with little formal autonomy.

The Teacher Organizations

No account of the teaching profession would be complete without some consideration of the part played in its development by the various teachers' organizations, and it is useful for this purpose to make a comparison between the professional teachers' organizations in Britain and their counterparts in the United States, and to attempt to assess their contributions to the professional status of the teachers in the two countries.

The largest organization of educators in the United States is the National Education Association, founded in 1857 when the presidents of 10 State educational associations issued a call to the teachers of the country to form a national organization. This organization, then the National Teachers' Association, joined in 1870 with the National Association of School Superintendents and the American Normal School Association to form the N.E.A. Membership of this Association is open to anyone actively engaged in the profession of teacher or other education work. This means that not only teachers, but principals, superintendents and other professional workers are all members, leading to the charge on the part of many teachers that the N.E.A. is dominated by administrators.

The main achievement of the N.E.A. has been in meeting the needs of its members for specialist information. The Research Division, which was created in 1922, provides members with information and consultative services on a very wide scale. The N.E.A. has also published an impressive list of periodicals, pamphlets, yearbooks and so on. The other main professional activity is the National Commission on Teacher Education and Professional Standards, which was established in 1946 with the declared aim of the advancement of professional standards, including standards for institutions which prepare teachers. The establishment of this Commission, 'marked the first time the N.E.A. specifically charged one of its agencies with responsibilities for spearheading the professional standards movements in education', Lieberman has argued. 'For this reason, the creation of the N.C.T.E.P.S., and of the various state and local T.E.P.S. commissions, must be regarded as one of the most encouraging developments since before World War II insofar as the professionalization of education is concerned.'

On the whole, however, the N.E.A. in spite of its size and importance, has not been a particularly militant organization, largely because of its limited view of its function. Indeed, Lieberman points out that for many years it took the view that as a professional association it was not concerned with things like teachers' salaries. Consequently, its predominance has been seriously challenged by the teachers' unions, the overwhelming majority of which are affiliated with the American Federation of Teachers. This is essentially a trade union of teachers, and superintendents are excluded. The A.F.T. is itself affiliated with the trade-union movement as a whole in the form of the Combined American Federation of Labour and the Congress of Industrial Organizations. Although the first teachers' unions date from the beginning of the century, the spread of the movement was handicapped by the general opposition to trade-union activity in the United States, which led to severe opposition from local school boards including the dismissal of teachers who were union members. Since the 1940s, however, when the general opposition to trade unionism began to decline, membership of the A.F.T. has increased rapidly, although the total membership is well below that of the N.E.A.

The A.F.T. has been concerned in the main with salaries and conditions of service rather than with the wider issues of professionalism. Consequently, although active in the field of teachers' civil and professional rights, including such issues as racial discrimination, it has tended to neglect those professional functions which have been the main concern of the N.E.A.

By contrast the National Union of Teachers, the largest and most important of the English teacher organizations, is, according to Lieberman, 'a far more effective professional organization than any educational organization in the United States'. The N.U.T. was founded in 1870 largely, as Tropp has related, in response to the Education Act of that year. Although originally formed to protect the interests of the elementary school teacher it now includes in its membership teachers from both primary and secondary schools. Like the American Federation of Teachers the N.U.T. does not include administrators who have their own association.

Apart from the N.U.T. there are also four secondary associations, mainly representing teachers in the grammar schools. Headmasters, headmistresses, assistant masters and assistant mistresses each have their own association. There is also a breakaway organization, the National Association of Schoolmasters, the members of which have been brought together mainly by their opposition to equal pay. The N.U.T. is, however, very much the dominant organization, representing as it does about 80 per cent of the whole profession, and this dominance is reflected in its position on the Burnham Committee, the joint committee of local authorities and teachers which negotiates salary scales. The N.U.T. has 16 seats on the Teachers' Panel, in comparison with only six for the Joint Four Secondary Associations.

Although the N.U.T is not, strictly speaking, a trade union, it has from the start concerned itself with issues arising out of the conditions of employment of teachers. Foremost of these is teachers' salaries which, since the end of the First World War, have been settled by negotiations between representatives of the main teachers' associations and the local authorities, subject to government approval. Apart from salaries : superannuation, security of tenure, and the freedom of the teacher from outside interference have all been issues of central importance. In this respect the N.U.T. resembles the A.F.T. rather than the N.E.A. At the same time the N.U.T. has always been deeply concerned with the professional status of teaching, and has worked constantly to raise the level of recruitment to the profession. This was a particularly acute problem in the nineteenth century, when not only were there large numbers of uncertificated teachers, but in times of sudden demand for staff the standard of the certificate would be lowered. This happened for example after 1870 when there was a demand for teachers to meet the provisions of the 1870 Act. In an effort to prevent this serious dilution of standards, the N.U.T. worked for many years to take control of the entrance to the profession into their own hands, in imitation of the older professions like medicine or the law. Although they were completely unsuccessful in this, their efforts to resist dilution have often succeeded. For example they were able to block suggestions made in the mid-1950s for either a general lowering of the standard of entry or some kind of apprenticeship scheme. They have also been successful in resisting the large-scale recruitment of teachers' assistants. Moreover, although they have failed so far in their aim of a graduate profession, their pressure for a three-year rather than a two-year training for the non-graduate has recently been successful. On the other hand, it has proved difficult to persuade graduate entrants of the need for training.

The success of the N.U.T. as a professional organization can be attributed in part to the early development of a sense of professional awareness, clearly defined objectives and a militant and able leadership, but above all it has made itself into a powerful and influential pressure group at both the local and the national level. From the very early days of the N.U.T. every effort was made to influence the local School Boards, the Department of Education, and Parliament itself, and this tradition has continued to the present day. Moreover, as early as 1877 the N.U.T. began to plan the election of a teacher M.P. and in 1893 the first two sponsored candidates were elected. Immediately they 'began pressing the views of the union in the House of Commons. They were both able, modest, unpretentious and gifted speakers who made immediate impressions on the House. While other means of pressure were not neglected, the union was now assured that, with two of its leaders in the House, its views on educational matters would not be overlooked.' By the 1950s there were 23 N.U.T. members in the House of Commons. The N.U.T. has also exercised considerable influence on local education authorities as both elected and co-opted members.

From time to time in its history the N.U.T. has also undertaken more direct action. In 1907 teachers were withdrawn from schools in West Ham, and in 1914 the N.U.T. forced the closure of schools in Herefordshire, as part of its aim of a national salary structure. More recently the N.U.T. has entered another militant phase and in 1956, as part of its fight against the Superannuation Bill, called on its members to cease collecting school savings. Since then, token strikes, the refusal to supervise school meals, and to work with unqualified teachers have been employed as part of the fight for changes in working conditions and salary scales.

Undoubtedly, too, the existence of two rival organizations in the United States limits the efficacy of both the N.E.A. and the A.F.T., whereas the N.U.T. is without a serious rival. So, too, does the higher proportion of women teachers in the United States. As Lieberman points out, 'the woman teacher interested chiefly in marriage and a home is not likely to take a strong interest in raising professional standards and in improving the conditions of teaching. Indeed, such women are frequently opposed to raising professional standards; such action runs contrary to their personal long term interests. On the other hand, women are in the majority in the teaching profession in Britain, too, although not, it is true, to the same extent.

Nor is the higher status of the teaching profession in Britain the responsibility of the N.U.T. alone. A less favourable market situation for the graduate and the smaller relative size of the teaching profession continue to ensure that teaching is better able to maintain the standards of recruits to the profession than in the United States, in spite of the longer training of the American teacher. Nevertheless, even in Britain the teaching profession is at a disadvantage compared with many other professions. It is, therefore, surprising that the teachers' organizations have been unwilling to consider the many suggestions that have been put forward for teachers' aids or assistants, especially since such a solution to the problem could have considerable professional advantages. Yet in recent years the N.U.T. has been firm in its opposition to such proposals. Undoubtedly, however, the opposition is a result of the constant struggles against dilution which have characterized the whole history of the N.U.T. For any such scheme to raise rather than lower the teachers' status it is necessary that it should be controlled by the teachers, both in order to gain their confidence and to ensure that it is not in practice used to flood the schools with untrained teachers. There are also many practical difficulties in its implementation. It would require, for example, not only a drastic reassessment of the teacher's role in the classroom, but in order to be fully effective, serious research into teaching methods, and changes in teacher-training. For this reason, although we are likely to see the increased use of teachers' assistants, it is unlikely that the teaching profession is yet ready for the drastic reorientation that a scheme such as Lieberman's necessarily implies.

Teachers in higher education are also organized into professional associations, but so far these have attracted very little attention from researchers into either the sociology of education or the sociology of the professions. Both the Association of American College Professors in the United States, and the Association of University Teachers in Britain are, however, important bodies which do much to safeguard the interests of individual members as well as to work towards professional standards and improved salaries and working conditions. There is, however, a lack of consensus as to the kind of professional association required by university teachers, as well as the kind of activity is should undertake. Neither the

Association of College Professors nor the Association of University Teachers is a particularly militant body, and it is likely that in this respect they are only reflecting the views of many of their members.

Logan Wilson argued in 1942 that the academic was too individualistic to submit to collective bargaining, and this may well still be true in that financial improvement is sought by means of individual preferment rather than collective action. At the same time the pull of divergent interests and disciplines may also hinder the development of a loyalty to the profession itself, and individual may feel it more important to give their attention to the association which serves their own academic discipline than to the association which represents them as teachers. This division of loyalties is strongly reinforced by the conflict between the teaching and the research function, which has reached an acute stage in the American university. Other professional groups, which do not share in this dilemma, or share it in a less acute form, like doctors and lawyers or, indeed, school teachers, are likely to find it easier to establish a genuine professional identity. For these reasons, if for no others it would seem that the college teacher is a particularly interesting subject for study.

Conclusion

This review of the teaching profession has drawn attention primarily to the ambiguity of the teachers' position in modern society. This arises for several reasons, but mainly because the size, complexity and diversity to be found, not only amongst those who perform the teaching function, but also in the role itself. Some of the ambiguity arises from the attempt to bring unity to a profession which has, in the past, been divided in terms of function, social origin, qualifications and experience, and it is this division which creates many of the problems that arise in attempting to generalize about the teaching profession as a whole. It may be advisable to unify the profession for tactical, political or ideological reasons, but, sociologically speaking, it confuses many of the issues that we are attempting to unravel. It is necessary, therefore, for the sociologist to consider differences within the profession as much as, if not more than, the similarities.

The diversity within teaching is also responsible for some of the controversy which surrounds the issue of professional status. There is no exact definition of profession, but there is fairly general agreement that a professional occupation is one that involves a long period of specialized training, and a defined field of knowledge. It is usual, also to look for a set of ethical principles, or an ethical code, relating the practitioner to the client, and a conception of service rather than simply profitability at the basis of the relationship. Control over entry, and a degree of autonomy in the practice of the profession, are usually, although not inevitably, included in the definition.

If we apply these canons strictly, no group of teachers, except possibly university teachers, can be said to be a profession. Indeed Lieberman, as we have seen, expressly denies that school teachers in America are a professional group. On the other hand, Tropp in his study of English teachers concluded that, in spite of their failure to achieve professional self-government, they had succeeded in attaining professional status. Musgrave, although rather more cautious, also concludes 'that there is an arguable case for saying that there is a teaching profession'. These different conclusions are a result of varying emphasis in the definition of a profession, but they also reflect the differences within the profession itself. Thus, teachers vary in terms of their educational level, their professional qualifications, the degree of control over their conditions of work and the way in which they carry out their tasks and their adherence to a professional code. It is not easy, therefore, to draw any conclusions which will apply to all teachers, even within a single country, and more difficult still if we attempt national comparisons.

So far, the discussion of the teachers' position has concerned almost exclusively the wider society, and we have considered the role of the teacher in the school only indirectly. Yet it is the relationships within the school that are central for an understanding of the teacher's occupational role. It is time, therefore, to consider, as far as the evidence will allow, the teacher in the school itself, and for this purpose the school will be treated both as a formal organization, and as a network of social relationships. This is one of the most neglected aspects of the sociology of education, and there are very few definitive conclusions to be drawn so far.

6

Education and the Economy

The Education Explosion

A consideration of the theoretical scheme outlined makes it clear that in any society the educational system will be linked to the economy, in so far as it must train its young people in the skills they will require as adult members of the society. It by no means follows, however, that these skills will be taught wholly or even mainly within the school system, even where such a system exists. In pre-industrial societies all such skills are taught 'on the job' either within the family itself or at the work place. Even after industrialisation, 'on the job' training has retained its importance, until recently, for many of the lower levels of industrial skill. What characterizes an advanced industrial society is the extent to which skills at all levels of the occupational hierarchy are increasingly acquired within formal educational institutions.

The new tools, new techniques and new materials which transformed nineteenth-century Britain, were only the start of a continuous process of technical development which has, in the twentieth century, accelerated rather than declined. Contemporary innovations, particularly in the field of automation, are so far-reaching that it is customary to talk and write of a second industrial revolution. At the same time innovation itself has become institutionalized, and research in pure science and in technology is harnessed to the needs of higher productivity. It is no wonder, then, that corresponding changes in the scope and the content of education are so often seen in terms of the needs of the economy. The purpose of this chapter will be to describe the relationship between these two aspects of society, and to consider in particular how far changes in modern educational systems can be explained in economic terms. Schelsky has described the way in which science and technology have influenced the amount and kind of skill required of the labour force, and the changes which the future is likely to bring. He shows that the proportion engaged in manual work has declined and the proportion in white-collar and professional and managerial work has risen. Many new professional and semi-professional occupations have grown up, based upon the developing sciences and technologies. Within manual work itself the nature of skill has gone through many changes, as the traditional craft skills of a pre-industrial society gave way to new skills appropriate to new and changing technologies. Moreover, in recent years, especially where automation has been introduced, the traditional distinction between skilled and semi skilled manual workers and clerical and technical staff is practically being obliterated. As a result of these changes the formal educational system of school and college, hitherto required mainly for an elite group of professional occupations, has expanded to provide for the needs, not only of a growing number of professional and semi-professional occupations, but also a skilled labour force which increasingly needs to be literate, adaptable and mobile.

The consequence has been what can only be regarded as an educational explosion. The establishment of universal literacy has been followed by a lengthening of school life, a widening and deepening of the curriculum and the gradual extension of higher education to a wider section of the community. This expansion of education has not followed the same pattern everywhere, and is considerably more advanced in some industrial societies than in others, but the general lines of the educational explosion can be traced in all advanced industrial societies.

At the same time the attitude to education has changed. An abundant and increasing supply of highly educated people has become the absolute prerequisite of social and economic development in our world. It is rapidly becoming 'a condition of national survival', Drucker argues, and increasingly educational expenditure is seen as a vital investment in human beings. A growing interest in the economics of education have produced efforts not only to reach a more precise measurement of the cost of education but also a more accurate estimate of the contribution that education can make to economic growth. So far, however, no general agreement has been reached on this issue and there is still considerable debate on the extent of education's contribution, particularly in the developing societies.

This association between the development of an educational system and the growth of the economy carries, perhaps misleadingly, the implication of a mechanistic relationship. It is indeed quite reasonable to imply that an advanced economy 'needs' literate workers and educated scientists and technicians if it is to maintain its efficiency. It is, however, easy to show that the 'response' to this need by the educational system is far from automatic, and many other factors can be shown to have an influence on educational expansion, some of which may operate to inhibit its growth. At the same time some of the educational expansion that has occurred can be shown to be the consequence of influences which are ideological rather than economic.

One important limiting factor on educational expansion is, however, itself an aspect of the economy, for it is only an advanced economy that can afford a highly developed educational system. In counting the cost of such a system, moreover, it is not enough to estimate only the provision of buildings and the salaries of teachers; it is also necessary to include the cost of training and foregone earnings during the years spent at school and college when the student entry to the work force is delayed. Another hidden cost is the drain on skilled personnel that the provision of teachers represents, and this can be particularly important when there is a general shortage of educated manpower.

The age-structure of the population is another highly relevant factor. When the child population rises, the cost of educational expansion is high, and even the maintenance of existing standards will entail an increase in expenditure. When the child population falls, however, educational standards may rise even if expenditure remains the same. Consequently a fall in the birth-rate may have very considerable advantage for educational provision, just as a 'baby-boom' can lead to over-crowded classes and inadequate school provision.

Another highly important aspect of the cost of education is its quality. The standard of accommodation and equipment, the level of teachers' salaries, the teacher/student ratio are all highly variable items, and their provision on a generous scale can make any considerable educational expansion a costly venture. It would, for example, be exceedingly difficult to maintain the teacher/student ratio customary in British university education if the proportions of the age-group entering it were as high as in the United States.

Apart from considerations of cost, such factors as the supply of teachers may also have an important influence on educational provision, especially in the short run. This is particularly likely to occur if expansion has been rapid or if the salaries paid to teachers are below those available in competing employment. Shortage of teachers combined with a shortage of buildings have seriously delayed the raising of the school-leaving age in Britain since the Second World War.

It is, however, likely that the most important factor influencing educational development lies in the filed of social and educational policy. National differences in ideology can be shown to lie behind many of the variations in educational expansion both within Europe and between Western Europe and the United States. It is necessary therefore to look at ideological differences in some detail and to consider in particular some of the ways in which they may actually impede the response of the educational system to economic needs.

The ideological conflict between elitist and populist theories of education is found in all industrial societies and is the source of much current educational controversy. It can also be shown to have considerable influence on the rate of educational expansion. The elitist ideology, as its name implies, it traditionalist in its orientation, looking back to the time when education was the prerogative of a small elite. The attitude to education to which it gives rise tends therefore to be exclusive and emphasizes the needs of the few rather than the many.

Such an educational philosophy can be seen very clearly in early nineteenth-century England, where the provision of free elementary education was made by charitable and religious bodies whose aim was primarily moral, and whose conception of the amount of education necessary for this purpose was of a very limited kind. The children of the poor needed to be taught Christian principles and to be able to read their Bibles, but writing was suspect and even dangerous. Moreover, although ideas on what was necessary grew gradually more liberal, the anxiety that the poor would be over-educated and made unfit for their station in life, continued at least until the end of the century. Indeed, in spite of the reforms of the early twentieth century which widened the curriculum and postponed the school-leaving age, the elementary system remained in being until 1944, providing a cheaper and more limited schooling for the children of the poor.

At the same time secondary education was conceived as a distinct system, providing for the needs of the middle and upper classes. Even the recognition by the end of the century of an educational ladder from the elementary school to the university did not really after the conception of secondary education as a distinct system, linked to the elementary system by scholarships and free places, but separate from it administratively and socially. Moreover, attempts from within the elementary system to extend into secondary education were severely curbed.

The 1944 Education Act, as is well known, abolished the elementary school and introduced free secondary education for all, and the secondary school became a stage in the educational process for every child. On the other hand, in spite of the attempts to achieve parity of esteem between the different types of secondary education, the secondary modern school has retained at least some of the traditions of the old elementary system, and it is at the secondary modern school that the great majority of working-class children complete their formal education. It is for this reason that the tripartite system of secondary education since 1944 has frequently been linked with the three grades of secondary education described by the Newcastle and Bryce Commissions of the nineteenth century. Moreover, 'If the ladder between elementary and secondary education as a whole has been abandoned,' Glass has argued, 'it has been replaced by a ladder from the primary school to the grammar school.' At the same time selection by ability has replaced, within the maintained grammar school, the right to entry on the payment of fees. An aristocracy of brains is not, however, any less of an elite than an aristocracy of birth, and in so far as the grammar school selects an able minority of children and prepares them for middle-class occupations it is still fulfilling an elite function and representing an elite philosophy of secondary education.

Evidence that the elite conception of education is out of line with the needs of the labour market is provided very graphically by Taylor's study of the secondary modern school. He shows how full employment and the creation of new jobs which require both a high level of skill and a good educational background have deeply influenced the direction of development of the schools. Not only has there been a widespread provision of extended courses of both an academic and a vocational nature, but the modern schools have been able 'to break the examination monopoly of other types of secondary school, and to participate in, rather than contract out of the process of vocational competition and the promotion of social mobility through education'. Developments within the secondary modern school since 1944 are therefore a particularly interesting example of the sensitive interplay between economic and ideological factors in educational change.

It is true, of course, that the elite concept of secondary education has to a very considerable extend remained the dominant ideology in Britain, but it has by no means gone unchallenged. The emergence of a genuine populist ideology can be seen very clearly as far back as the controversy over the high-grade schools in the 1890s. At the same time the need for skilled manpower, particularly for clerks and school teachers, made possible not only the expansion of secondary education, but he development of higher forms of elementary education. In the years between the two world wars, for example, many local authorities experimented with selective central schools, providing what amounted to a secondary education within the elementary system. The effect has been a compromise in which the elite ideology, populist pressures towards equality, and the needs of the economy have together produced an expansion of secondary education to include all children, but within the framework of an elite system.

The elite ideology in secondary education is at present severely challenged both in Britain and in other parts of Western Europe by the idea of the comprehensive school, and it may be that the selective system of secondary education will eventually give way to some form of unselected school. If, however, we wish to see the effect on secondary education of an educational philosophy in which the populist ideology has long been the major influence we must look to the United States. The controversy between what has come to be called the Jeffersonian and Jacksonian principles of educational provision resulted in an early and almost complete victory for Jacksonian principles, which has expressed itself in the belief that education for all was essential in a democratic society, irrespective of social origins or even learning ability. This has been combined with strong popular support for the value of education.

Unlike the situation in Britain where the education of the masses has been imposed or withheld by powerful elite groups in Church or State, the common school in the United States was founded by 'relatively untutored farmers who established one-room district schools in rural neighbourhoods as they moved across the continent'. In consequence, except in certain regions and neighbourhoods, there is a great deal of public enthusiasm for education and parents on the whole are eager to take advantage of what the schools have to offer. As a result of this, not only is the common high school the normal type of secondary school in the United States, but graduation from high school at the age of 17 or 18 has now become the generally accepted level of educational achievement.

It is, however, in the field of higher education that we find the biggest consequences of differing ideological approaches to educational opportunity. The universities, as Halsey has pointed out, are 'intrinsically inequalitarian', but this tendencies is considerably enhanced when they are restricted to a very small section of the community. The symbolic value of the higher learning has always conferred high status on those who are admitted to it, and in addition it has had functional value, in so far as it has been a limited but possible avenue to positions of wealth and power in Church or State.

The effect of industrial development is to link the university to the economy through the market for professional and scientific manpower, and the benefits of higher education are inevitably extended to cover a higher proportion of the community. At the same time there are wide differences between countries in the actual amount of expansion, and the form the expansion takes—differences, moreover, which cannot be explained solely in terms of economic development. Anderson, for example, using data from a large number of countries in Eastern and Western Europe and the United States showed that, for males only, there is some relationship between a nation's type of economy and the rate of university attendance, but that this relationship is a limited one. 'The underlying factors explaining national contrasts must', he argues, 'be sought in values, customs and public educational policies.' Moreover, for women, none of the differences can be explained in economic terms. Ben-David has also reached similar conclusions using, this time, a world-wide range of data. Even though there is some correlation between the production of graduates and the level of economic development, 'there still remain obvious and glaring exceptions'.

Ben-David distinguished 'three influential academic systems, the European, the American and the Soviet, each of which produces different ratios and kinds of graduates. The positions of the other countries seem to be, at least superficially, the function of respective spheres of influence. The developing countries of the Middle East and Latin America whose academic traditions were imported from Europe, are situated close to and below the European countries, while the Philippines, which used to be an American dependency, are trailing the Unites States. The position of Canada and that of Japan reflect the replacement of European influence by American. Among the communist countries of Eastern and Central Europe there is a tendency to approach the U.S.S.R.'

The European pattern of higher education is strongly influenced by the dominant elite ideology. Only a very small proportion of the age-group enter any form of higher education, and the universities, at the apex of the hierarchically organized system, are particularly narrow in their recruitment. Table 6.1 gives particulars from several countries in Western Europe, and shows that in spite of some variations, the general picture is fairly similar.

Table 6.1
Percentage of Age-Group Entering Higher Education in Selected Countries, 1958-59

	Full-time courses only		*All methods of study*	
	Courses of British degree level %	*All levels of higher education* %	*Courses of British degree level* %	*All levels of higher education* %
Great Britain	4.6	7.7	6.6	12.4
France	8	9	8	9
Germany (F.R.)	4	6	4	8
Netherlands	3	7	3	8
Sweden	7	10	8	11
Switzerland	5	10	5	11

In the United States in contrast higher education is open to a wide range of ability and to a very wide sector of the age-group. There is no attempt to restrict it to a minority of the population. Already, in 1958-59, 35 per cent of the relevant age-group entered college, and by 1970 it is expected to be almost half. At the same time the distinctions within higher education are much less clear-cut than they are in Europe. In Britain, for example, there are clear differences between universities and other institutions providing higher education, and this is true of Europe generally. In the United States, however, there are no formal barriers between institutions and the system is 'in a state of constant flux. The Junior Colleges tend to develop into liberal arts colleges. Professional schools tend to develop general arts and science faculties. The liberal arts colleges themselves, if publicly controlled, seek to become State universities, and the latter soon begin to award Doctorates.' The whole system indeed is one of open competition, an academic procession, as Riesman, has called it, in which it is not always easy to decide on a single scale to rank or prestige.

In the U.S.S.R., too, a populist ideology has led to a rapid expansion of both secondary and higher education. Moreover, in order to appreciate the Russian achievement it is necessary to recall how much needed to be done both educationally and technologically to bring standards even up to those in Western Europe. 'In a country where in 1917 the large majority of people were illiterate there had come by 1958 (when the last major reorganization of education occurred) a system under which a third of the younger people completed a full secondary education.' The development of higher education has also been very rapid and although it has not reached the same level as in the United States it compares very well with many countries in Western Europe, including Great Britain.

The Content of Education

So far the discussion has been concerned with educational expansion, but any consideration of educational development must take into account changes in content as well as in scale. As the demands of the economy have required higher levels of skill, so the nature of that skill has changed, and with it the perception of the educated man. This is not the place to trace these changes in detail, but rather to indicate something of their general scope and direction.

It is sometimes argued that the changes in curriculum which have characterized the development of educational systems as consequence of industrialization have been mainly a trend towards vacationalism. In fact this is true only in a very special sense. The process of education, whatever the agency that has charge of it, is always in part vocational, in so far as it must be concerned with the transmission of skills and values. This was no less true of the schools and universities of the past than of the schools and universities of today. Hofstadter and Metzger make this point very clearly when they write, of the universities of the middle ages, that their work 'was as relevant to the ecclesiastical and political life of the thirteenth and fourteenth centuries as the modern university is to the scientific and industrial life of our time. They provided vocational training for the clerical functionaries of church and state—for notaries, secretaries, legates and lawyers.' This link between the formal educational system and the two great professions, the Law and the Church, has been of vital importance, determining as it has the content of schools and universities for many centuries.

If we are to understand the process by which the classical and literary curriculum—the traditional vocational training of the professions—became the very essence of non-vocational or general education, it is necessary to consider the extent to which the schools and universities have stood apart from the needs of the economy, focused as they were upon the needs of the Church and the State. Training in practical skills, at all levels, has traditionally taken place at home and in the work-place. Moreover, this tradition remained all but unbroken up to and indeed into the nineteenth century.

It is true that science had a place, if only a small one, in some schools and universities, but this had almost always been divorced from the practical processes of industry. So extreme indeed was the separation of the formal educational process from the development of the economy that Ashby could write that 'in the rise of British industry the English Universities played no part whatever.'

The extent to which a modern industrial economy makes demands upon the educational system is not in question. An advanced technology can no longer depend upon the traditional 'on the job' training. New and more complex skills require not only a literate work force but, in the higher echelons, a formal training in science and technology. At the same time the concomitant expansion in trade and commerce gave rise to a demand for commercial skills both at the practical and the more theoretical level. Finally the education explosion itself, with its need for more and more teachers, had a profound effect on the secondary and higher stages of the educational process.

On the other hand the extent to which these pressure are accepted or resisted varies very greatly from country to country. In particular, America and Russia have moved further and faster in this direction than Western Europe. Moreover the reasons for these differences are very complex, including not only the acceptance or otherwise of an elite ideology but the nature of the elite itself. In addition, as Ben-David points out, the rate of expansion of educational provision is itself related in several important ways to changes in educational curricula. For this reason it is necessary to look in some detail at the social proceses involved in harnessing the educational system to the needs of the economy, and in particular to the means by which these processes have ben delayed.

A number of studies have shown how the development of scientific and technical education in Britain has been handicapped by the association of the universities with the training of an elite. 'University education was a matter of luxury, part of the way of life of the upper classes. Originally the clergy was the only profession for which people were trained at universities. Higher civil service and secondary school teaching were added to this during the second part of the last century. All these professions, or important parts of them, were closely connected to the upper class, or were upper-class, callings.' As a result, a university education was in itself a powerful status symbol, indicating membership of the community of the educated, and giving the rank of gentleman.

Moreover, the Industrial Revolution, as Ashby has pointed out, was not accomplished by the educated classes. 'Men like Bramah and Maudslay, Arkwright and Crompton, the Darbys of Coalbrookdale and Neilson of Glasgow, had no systematic education in science or technology. Britain's industrial strength lay in the amateurs and self-made men : the craftsman-inventor, the mill-owner, the iron-master. It was no accident that the Crystal place, that sparkling symbol of the supremacy of British technology, was designed by an amateur.' In consequence for a long time technical education in Britain was seen as appropriate to the artisan and foreman level, rather than at the level of higher education, and there was little appreciation of the practical application of science to industry.

Cotgrove in his study of the development of technical education in England and Wales, has attempted to explain the late start in the nineteenth century and the slow progress in the inter-war years largely in terms of 'the 50 years or more of industrial pre-eminence which had established industrial traditions in which science and research were absent.' This long period of pre-eminence induced a mood of complacency among British industrialists and businessmen which has lasted, to some extent, until recent years.

A second factor which Cotgrove also believes to be of considerable importance, is the lack of scientific and technical qualifications on the part of the proprietors and managers in industry. Either they had risen from the ranks with only a modicum of elementary education or they had been educated in the mainly classical and literary tradition of the middle-class secondary school. Consequently they were not themselves in a position to appreciate the potential value of a scientific or technical education to industry and might even be prejudiced against it. As a result there has not been, until recent years, a demand for men with scientific or technical qualifications, and in much of top industrial management the arts graduate has been preferred.

The same points have been made by Musgrave in a recent study of the British and German iron and steel industries, and their relationship to the labour force. He, too, lays stress on the cleavage between industry and higher education which arose partly out of the tradition of the self-made man, partly because of a belief in the practical rather than the theoretical approach. The general belief was that 'every workshop or factory in the kingdom' was a technical school in which trades could be 'learned with far more efficiency than under the most learned professors.' At the same time the dislike of science and industry on the part of the upper classes and the universities meant that 'many able men were diverted from industry to politics, the professions and the Civil Services.'

Musgrave contrasts the situation in Britain with that of Germany, where science was given a very high place, both in secondary and higher education, and in industry itself. Consequently, by 1900 German boards of management in large firms consisted of highly paid specialists, who were constantly watching for scientific discoveries helpful to their business; under them was a large staff of men trained to university level to develop such discoveries. In the iron and steel industry, mainly large integrated firms, the salaries of such experts ran into thousands of pounds. As a consequence, Germany's technical and scientific development was rapid and, in spite of her late start, was able not only to catch up with Britain but even in some instances to surpass her.

This is not to suggest that there has been no change in higher education in Britain. The new university colleges founded at the end of the nineteenth century were much more utilitarian in their outlook than were the ancient foundations at Oxford and Cambridge with their elitist traditions. Indeed, representing middle-class rather than aristocratic attitudes, the provincial universities and university colleges were willing enough to accept the task of training for the newer technological professions as well as for the growing needs of the secondary-school teaching profession. Nevertheless, although technology has gradually taken its place in British universities, its expansion has been only gradual. Even into the twentieth century, industry has continued to be apathetic and State support has been 'reluctant and inadequate.' Only since 1945 has there been any real willingness to provide money for expansion, and a demand from industry for the large-scale employment of science and technology graduates. Government plans have included the expansion of science and technology faculties at the universities, the setting up of new technological institutions, including technological universities and the provision of more advanced work in technical colleges below university level.

In the secondary grammar schools, too, there has been a major swing over to science teaching since the end of the war. According to the Crowther Report, 'among the maintained boys' schools the proportion of science specialists among boys in the sixth form has risen between 1952 and 1959 from 52 to 65 per cent, leaving out of account for both years boys in a general sixth. In 1956, in those independent and direct grant schools which are members of the Headmasters' Conference, the proportion of science specialists was 47 per cent in independent schools and 54 per cent in direct grant schools, while the proportions which had gone on to full-time courses of university standing in the previous year showed an even stronger bias towards science.'

Nevertheless, in spite of a period of rapid development in the facilities for higher scientific and technological education, the rate of expansion is still much less than in the United States and in Russia. Nor has the rate of change been sufficient to meet the increasing demands of industry. Even more serious is an apparent unwillingness on the part of potential university entrants to take up the places that are offered in science and technology. In the last few years some university faculties in these subjects have not been able to fill all the places offered because of a dearth of suitable candidates. Moreover, this has happened even though many such faculties have been prepared to consider applicants with lower qualifications than those asked for in arts faculties, and in social science faculties and departments. At the same time there has been something of a swing away from science subjects in the schools. According to the Universities Central Council on Admissions, 'Entries at advanced level in the G.C.E. for Mathematics, Physics, Chemistry and the Biological Sciences have shown a tendency to shrink when considered as proportions of the rising total number of advanced level candidates each year.'

It is, of course, possible that these recent trends reflects the shortage of good science and mathematics teachers in the schools. Nevertheless they do indicate something of the complexity of the relationships between economic pressure and educational response, especially in a society where occupational choice is a matter for individual decision. Moreover, there are clear signs that technology as a career does not enjoy the prestige of pure science—a reflection, almost certainly, of its very recent admission as a full academic discipline, and its still uncertain social status as a profession.

At the lower levels of industry there was also for a long time a failure to develop specific technical education. The traditional 'on the job' training for craft and allied manual skills was still, throughout the nineteenth and into the twentieth century, the preferred method, and formal technical education was seen as subsidiary to training on the job. It was, in Cotgrove's words, a 'theoretical supplement of the practical experience of the artisan,' desirable perhaps but not essential. In consequence it had of necessity to be provided in the evenings. Moreover, since it was regarded as a venture in self-improvement on the part of the ambitious artisan, attendance was voluntary, although success might be rewarded by higher pay or perhaps promotion.

This preference for a mixture of learning and earning has influenced not only craft training but also and even more significantly the whole new range of technical and professional employment opened up by changes in industry in the twentieth century. To meet the needs of these students a profusion of courses have developed, leading to a variety of qualifications ranging from a predominantly craft level, like the City and Guilds courses, to the National Certificate Courses catering for largely non-manual occupations such as draughtsmen, quantity surveyors and similar occupations. The whole recruitment and training policy in many industries has also been geared to these part-time qualifications. Such firms have preferred an early entry, at or about the statutory school-leaving age, followed by on-the-job training, and part-time study. These courses have consequently been the route not only to technician level but even, for the determined and lucky student, to full professional status. This part-time route to professional employment has been an important one in Britain in the history of the professions and has indeed in some cases provided a good proportion of its recruits in the past. 'Even now many engineers have learned their skill by some form of apprenticeship with part-time further education, and only about half are graduates.' There is some evidence, however, that those who achieve professional status by this route are at some disadvantage, at least in financial terms. Moreover, even the successful achievement of a Higher National Certificate does not necessarily lead to commensurate promotion. Cotgrove, for example, cites a government enquiry which found that 48 per cent of those obtaining Higher National Certificate in 1952 were in posts in 1958 which did not require H.N.C. as a necessary qualification.

Since students attend evening classes in the hope of occupational reward it is not surprising to find that the popularity of certain types of course is closely related to the expectation of rewards for such studies. In the inter-war period the lack of interest shown by employers in technical education is reflected in the predominance in technical colleges of classes in professional and commercial subjects. Enrolment in professional and commercial classes in 1931 comprised 21 per cent of total enrolment, compared with 13 per cent in classes related to industry. Since the war, however, the growing prestige and security of the technically and scientifically qualified worker in industry is reflected in a relative increase in the number of students enrolling in classes preparing for such occupations. By

1955 enrolments in industrial classes had increased 66 per cent over 1931 whole enrolments in professional and commercial classes had not increased at all.

This change in emphasis in technical college enrolments has a close parallel in the field of secondary education. The greater willingness of clerical and professional employment to recognize the General and Higher School Leaving Certificates and Matriculation exemption, was a powerful incentive to turn the grammar school leaver away from industrial employment, especially when so many firms actively discouraged grammar school recruits by their apprenticeship requirements. Since the Second world War, conditions have changed considerably. Firms are now more flexible in their entrance requirements and the larger firms in particular have frequently make provision for several grades of apprenticeship to meet the needs of the 16– or even the 18-year-old leaver from grammar school. There is also more opportunity in industry for the graduate with a scientific or technological degree. Although, as we have seen, the grammar school boy appears still to have some resistance to technical employment there is evidence, not least in the overall shift to science subjects since the war, of a genuine response to changed industrial conditions.

In recent years there has been considerable dissatisfaction with the present structure of technical education. Cotgrove, for example, points out that 'the application of science to industry requires the widespread dissemination of scientific knowledge, rather than the production of an aristocracy of learning.' He alleges that the present system not only results in a restricted output of men trained at the highest levels, but prevents necessary improvements in the education of the technician. In particular criticism has focused on the part-time route because of the lack of time it allows for study, even when evening classes are supplemented by periods of day release. Wastage is high and is not necessarily related to ability, the attitude of the firm and the motivation of the individual student being perhaps the most important factors. Present government policy favours a rationalization of the courses available, more care in selecting students for courses, and in particular more time for study during the day, including periods of block release, and, particularly at the level of professional training, more full-time courses. Such schemes are, however, still largely dependent on the good will of the firms concerned, and there are many who doubt whether they go far enough to meet national needs.

The United States, on the other hand, has been characterized not only by the rate of expansion but by the breadth of the curriculum in both secondary and higher education. 'In Europe students pursued more or less the same kinds of study in the thirties as they did in the early years of this century, and the variety is still limited. In the United States, on the other hand, growth of higher education took place through a process of constant differentiation. Fields of intellectual and occupational interest which elsewhere remained outside the academic framework became academic subjects in the United States.' It must also be borne in mind that in the United States there is not the sharp distinction customary in Europe between universities and other institutes of higher education. 'In American universities, besides the liberal arts and sciences and the traditional professional schools of law, medicine and theology found in Europe since medieval times, there appeared schools of journalism, librarianship, business methods, nursing and later, practical arts, home economics, physiotherapy. In Europe few, if any of these schools are to be found in universities, but usually in separate institutions of sub-university standard.'

Undoubtedly this variety in higher education has been of vital significance in making possible the high rate of expansion in the Untied States. If, as in Europe, the scope of higher education tends to be restricted to the traditional subjects, expansion on any scale is impossible without overcrowding in the traditional professions. This overcrowding did of course actually occur in may European countries in the inter-war period and is a feature of twentieth-century India and China. The outstanding feature of the system in the United States is the way in which this overcrowding has been averted. Under the influence of pragmatic and equalitarian ideologies the original elitist conception of higher education has been transformed. Universities and colleges in the United States are essentially middle-class rather than aristocratic in their outlook, serving the needs of the new professional middle classes created by the economy.

The situation in the U.S.S.R. is sociologically even more interesting. The traditional elites have been destroyed and the new power group, the Party, has deliberately attempted to fashion the educational system as an instrument of social and economic change. 'The role of Soviet education is to assist in the building of a communist society, in shaping the materialist world outlook of the students, equipping them with a good grounding in the different fields of knowledge and preparing them for socially useful work.' This aim is pursued by the central authority, the Party, consciously and deliberately. Educational policy is shaped with the 'building of a communist society' constantly in mind, and policies which do not appear to be in keeping with this achievement are ruthlessly scrapped. The degree to which the system is consciously guided is heightened by the very high degree of centralization and the degree of uniformity which is enforced throughout the whole of the U.S.S.R. 'From ministerial level command is passed on to provincial or city departments of education, then to district departments, and finally to school directors and teachers. The farther down the chain one goes, the greater the amount of detail laid down for the conduct of the schools. By the time it comes to the teacher, the area of personal discretion is very small. Not only basic policy, but the content of the curriculum, schemes of work, teaching methods, and the like are prescribed for the teacher in considerable detail.'

As part of the drive for economic development the educational system is geared very deliberately to the needs of the economy. The first of the aims of higher education as set out in the Statute of 21 March 1961 is 'the training of highly qualified specialists brought up in the spirit of Marxism-Leninism to be well skilled in the developments of recent science and technology, both in the U.S.S.R. and abroad and in practical matters of production, who should be able to make use of modern technical knowledge to the utmost and be capable of themselves creating the technology of the future.' Accordingly a greater emphasis is placed on science and technology in higher education, even than in the United States, and this bias towards scientific and practical subjects extends back into the secondary schools. In addition there is an attempt to direct labour for the first three years after graduation, in order to ensure that trained personnel go where they are most needed. This attempt is not always successful and there are plenty of cases of evasion and wire-pulling, but it demonstrates the extent to which individual preferences are subordinated to economic needs.

It is no part of the argument in this chapter to deny that the development of the economy is a crucial factor in the expansion of secondary and higher education. On the other hand, it is clear from a comparison of these three very different educational systems that the economic factors do not explain all the variation that we have found. Where there has been a hierarchic conception of society, as in Britain and in Europe generally, there will be strong pressures to retain the elitist elements in secondary and particularly higher education. Moreover, such pressures may operate not only against the expansion of higher education, but against its extension to include non-traditional and non-academic elements. Only where an equalitarian ideology is dominant are there likely to be drastic changes in the scope and content of secondary and higher education. Clearly, therefore, any attempt to assess the relationship between the educational system and the economy must take into account many aspects of a society. Educational changes may reflect its political ideology and its system of social stratification as well as the level of economic and technical development, which may be hindered by adherence to traditional values. It would seem, indeed, that the technical and economic level of a society sets limits on the variations in educational provision but does not operate as a strictly determinist factor.

7

Education and Social Mobility

Education and Occupation

One of the main features of a modern industrial society is the extent to which the educational system is the means by which individuals are not merely trained for but allocated to their occupational roles. This allocative or selective function is a direct consequence of the demands made by an advanced industrial economy for highly trained manpower; demands, moreover, not for traditional, family-based skills, but for new and continually evolving expertise based in large part on a formal educational training. In consequence, entry to these new occupations is increasingly dependent on the acquisition of the necessary educational qualifications. It is not surprising, then, to find that status is increasingly achieved, rather than simply acquired; and achieved, moreover, by means of educational success. It is true that there are many limitations on this development, some of which we shall be discussing in detail in a later chapter. Nevertheless the movement from status ascribed by birth, to status achieved through education, remains accurate as a very general description of the tendencies within modern industrial economies.

The use of the educational system as a means of social and economic ascent is not of course new. The system of scholarships for poor and able boys has a long history and is by no means confined to Western Europe. Nevertheless opportunities for such ascent were rare, and could not be other than rare when the occupations open to the educated man, whatever his social origin, were limited to the learned professions and their ancillaries. Only with the unprecedented expansion in the professions and quasi-professions and in technical and commercial employment does the opportunity arise on any but the smallest scale for social and economic ascent through educational achievement.

One of the effects of the increased demand for scientific and professional skills has been the rise in the importance of formal educational qualifications and the decline in opportunity for the 'self-made' man. As a result there is, in any advanced industrial economy, a close link between educational qualifications and occupational level. Consequently it can be shown that those at or near the top of the occupational structure have more education than those at the bottom. For example, Brunner and Wayland show, for the United States, that professional and similar workers have more than twice as many years of schooling as farm labourers, and nearly twice as many as factory operatives. Using data from the 1950 census they show that, ranking in terms of the median years of school completed by the employed labour force for each major occupational grouping, professional and kindred workers lead, followed by sales workers and managers, and clerical workers. Table 7.1 indicates the relative position of the major groups.

Table 7.1
Median Years of School Completed by Males by Major Occupational Grouping, USA, 1950

Occupational grouping	*U.S. total*
Professional, technical and kindred workers	16 plus
Sales workers	12.3
Managers, officials and proprietors, except farm	12.2
Clerical and kindred workers	12.2
Craftsmen, foremen and kindred workers	9.3
Operatives and kindred workers	8.7
Farmers and farm managers	8.3
Labourers, except farm and mine	8.0
Farm labourers except unpaid and farm foremen	7.1

Although not presented in the same form, and using slightly different occupational categories, Table 7.2 shows that the same pattern, although with some important variations, also applies in Great Britain.

It will be seen that not only is there a general relationship between education and occupation in both countries, but that the pattern of the occupational hierarchy, with the exception of farmers and agricultural workers, is also very similar. The main difference lies in the greater range in the United States. The column in Table 7.2 giving the median years of schooling shows that the differences between the socio-economic groups are smaller in Great Britain.

Table 7.2

Age of Leaving School of Male Population by Socio-Economic Grouping, Great Britain, 1961

Socio-economic Group	*Percentage Leaving School*			*Median years of schooling*
	15 and under	*16,17, 18*	*20 and over*	
Professional	22.1	40.6	37.2	12
Employers and managers	60.2	32.2	7.2	10
Intermediate and junior non-manual	60.3	32.8	6.9	10
Farmers	76.7	19.8	3.5	9
Agricultural workers	92.0	7.4	0.6	9
Foremen and supervisors	92.1	7.3	0.5	9
Skilled manual	92.1	7.7	0.5	9
Semi-skilled manual	94.2	5.3	0.5	9
Unskilled manual	96.4	3.2	0.3	9

A closes relationship between formal education and occupation is bound to have important consequences for occupation and hence social mobility. Under such conditions, educational achievement might well become the most important way to reach a high-status occupation, whether this involves social mobility upwards or the prevention of social mobility downwards. It is customary to use a model of this kind in describing modern industrial societies, and to suggest not only that there has been a movement in this direction in the past, but that it will continue in an accelerated form in the future. Havighurst, for example, suggests that in this type of society 'there is likely to be increased opportunity for people with talent and ambition to get the education they need for "better" positions and to achieve these portions, while those with less talent and ambition will tend to be downwardly mobile. The industrial and democratic society of the year 2000 will be even more open and fluid than the most highly industrialised societies today, so that education will be the main instrument for upwards mobility, and lack of education or failure to do well in one's education will be the principal cause of downward mobility.'

Studies of social mobility have also demonstrated the important part played by education. For example, Glass's study in Britain showed quite clearly the advantages of a grammar school education for those of working-class or lower-middle-class origin. They were much more likely to be socially mobile than those who had received no more than an elementary education. Similar findings have been reported for the United States. In both these studies, although the detail varies, the pattern is substantially the same; within lower status groups a child is more likely to be socially mobile if he has a superior education, and at the same time a superior education lessens the possibility of downward mobility for those in the higher status group.

To demonstrate the education is a factor in social mobility is not, however, to say that it is the only or the most important factor. Anderson for example argues that 'while education certainly influences a man's chances to move upward or downward, only a relatively modest part of all mobility is linked to education'. Using data from Glass's social mobility study as well as other similar studies, he shows that there is far more mobility than can be explained in terms of education, both in terms of mobility upwards on the part of those with a low level of education, and in a downward movement of those with a high educational level. In none of the three countries for which data exist does lack of education necessarily prevent mobility any more than a good education necessarily prevents a fall in status. He does suggest, however, that education is more closely linked to social mobility in the United States than in Sweden or Great Britain.

The strength of association between education and social mobility will depend upon the extent to which formal educational qualifications are a necessary requirement for positions of high status. In so far as status can be achieved in other ways, whether by training 'on the job' or by the possession of special talents, as in the world of sport or entertainment, the importance of education as a factor in mobility is reduced. An advanced industrial economy increases the importance of formal educational qualifications but it has by no means succeeded in imposing them universally.

Another vitally important factor is to be found in the distribution of schooling in relation to the occupational structure. One of the consequences of industrialization is, as we have seen, an increase in the proportion of middle- and upper-level jobs. Where this is combined, as it frequently has been, with a low fertility rate in the middle and upper classes so that they fail to reproduce themselves, there is plenty of room at the top and conditions are favourable for considerable social mobility. If at the same time the educational system, as in pre-war Britain, provides few opportunities for the children of working-class families to receive more than a basic elementary education, then we are faced with the kind of situation Anderson describes, in which a great deal of upward mobility occurs irrespective of education.

Industrial management in Britain today provides us with an extremely clear example of precisely this type of situation. Unlike professional occupations it has not been closely tied to formal educational qualifications, except for certain specific technical functions. Promotion from the shop floor has in the past been an important avenue of recruitment. At the same time is has been a rapidly expanding field of employment, providing frequent opportunities for social mobility. Studies of the educational background of managers reflect this general situation quite clearly. The Action Society Trust, for example, showed that even in the large firms which they examined, 53 per cent of managers had been to an elementary or an ordinary, i.e., non-grammar, secondary school. This is not to suggest that education at a grammar or public school is not an asset in reaching management status. Forty-seven per cent of the managers had been to public or grammar schools, and the authors of the report estimated that, computing these figures with the general population, grammar school boys have had twice the average chance of becoming a manager, and public schools boys about 10 times the average. Nevertheless we are still left with a very large proportion of managers who have almost certainly been upwardly mobile and for other reasons than formal educational achievement.

It is almost certain however that the picture of management qualifications given us by this and other studies is fast becoming out of date. There is a growing tendency to recruit managers with professional and scientific qualifications, rather than to promote from the lower ranks in the firm. Recent years have seen an expansion in the requirement of graduates, and a proliferation of student apprenticeships and other training schemes designed to attract the more highly educated entrant. At the same time changes within the educational system itself are providing a considerable increase in the number available to industry with higher qualifications. Such changes include an expansion in higher education generally and in technical education at all levels. Some of these changes are new, others have been operating for some time and have already produced differences of some magnitude between older and younger managers. For example, younger managers in the Action Society Trust study are more likely to have a degree or some kind of professional qualification. They are also more likely to have had a grammar or public school education.

At the same time it is also very clear that not all occupations of high status have been equally open to those without educational advantages. Even within industrial management it has been much easier for them to get into junior or middle management than into the levels of top management. Moreover, it we look at occupational groups in which formal educational qualifications have been important the picture is a very different one. There are many professional and semi-professional occupations which require a minimum professional or educational qualification and which may involve a high level of educational achievement. Alternatively, special entrance examinations as in the Civil Service may operate in much the same way. Kelsall's study of the higher Civil Service shows that, even including those who have been promoted from below, only a very small minority have not been educated at either a grammar or, in the majority of cases, a public school. In such types of occupation, social mobility is still possible but it will be largely dependent upon educational achievement, and it is this pattern of social mobility which seems to be increasing in importance.

On the other hand, although it has just been argued that an increase in the provision of higher education in Britain is likely to increase the relationship between education and occupation, it is also possible for higher education to become so general in the population that it no longer differentiates sufficiently to act as a criterion for occupational selection. Indeed, it has been suggested that the relationship is already declining in the United States as the proportion with a college education goes on increasing. Under such circumstances it is likely that more subtle distinctions will operate, including the prestige level of the individual college or university, and personality or social status differences.

Yet a further factor of vital importance determining the part education plays in social mobility is the nature of the selective mechanism within the school system. The more efficient this is in predicting school and vocational success, the more closely, that is to say, that educational achievement is related to 'ability', the less likely will it be that ability will operate as a factor independent of schooling, and so serve as a separate factor in social mobility. The study of social mobility is in consequence bound up with the analysis of selective mechanisms and their operation. But before we can begin to consider the question of how efficiently the schools select, we must examine the different mechanisms of selection used in different educational systems.

Strategies of Selection

Turner's well-known ideal-type analysis of modes of social ascent, with their accompanying strategies of educational selection, would seem to be the most useful framework of analysis for studying education as a selective function. Turner distinguishes two modes of ascent: sponsored mobility and contest mobility, both of which are founded upon quite different ideological positions and also different elite structures. For the time being, however, we shall concentrate upon the strategies of selection that accompany them, although it must be borne in mind that the characteristics of these selective mechanisms derive from the differences in ideology.

Sponsored mobility, compared by Turner with sponsorship into a private club, is characterized above all by early selection, followed by a clear differentiation of those singled out from the rest, usually in quite separate institutions. The process that follows has the nature of a special preparation for elite status, and covers not only special skills, but an indoctrination in the standards of behaviour and the value systems of the elite group.

The English educational system of the late nineteenth and early twentieth century was a very close approximation to the ideal type of sponsored mobility. The system of elementary education for the children of the poor was quite distinct from the system of education for the middle classes. Transfer between the two systems was possible, but it was not likely, and was reserved for the working-class child of exceptional ability who showed promise of successful assimilation to the middle classes. The Education Act of 1902 and the Free Place Regulations of 1907 between them destroyed the exclusive hold of the middle classes over the secondary system. Increasingly, after the First World War, working-class children entered the secondary schools until, in certain areas at least, all places were free, and in some schools the majority of children were from working-class families. Nevertheless certain essential characteristics of sponsored mobility remained, notably the stress on early selection and a considerable degree of segregation. It was customary to select children for free places at the age of 10, and to transfer them to the secondary school at 11, leaving the great majority of children in the elementary system. Those who were transferred went to schools with a higher rate of grant, better-paid and better-qualified teachers, and the chance to a acquire the formal educational qualifications which were, as we have seen, a great advantage in the transition to or maintenance of middle-class status.

With the 1944 Education Act the elementary system came to an end, and for the first time secondary education became a stage in the education process, rather than a special type of education appropriate to the middle classes. Even so, however, Turner was still able to characterize the English system of education as one of predominantly sponsored mobility because, within the new system of secondary education, there has been a distinction between types of school, with the new secondary grammar schools carrying on almost unchanged the secondary school tradition. The old scholarship examination has been replaced by the 11-plus, which is undoubtedly more efficient but performs precisely the same function. The new secondary modern schools are, certainly, an improvement on the old senior elementary schools, but the fact of selection and segregation remains. It is true, also, that all secondary education is free, and that success in the 11-plus is the only way to get into the grammar schools, but this is to emphasize the significance of the selection process rather than to diminish its importance. Moreover, even if it is no longer possible to buy a place in the secondary grammar school, there are still opportunities, for those who can afford it, to enter the flourishing independent sector, which still remains as a segregated middle- and upper-class system. Indeed, in so far as the Direct Grant grammar schools and some of the so-called public schools offer scholarships to a small minority of children from the maintained schools, they repeat precisely the pattern of sponsored mobility as it existed in the late nineteenth century.

The alternative system of selection is based on the ideology of contest mobility, likened by Turner to a race or other sporting event, in which all compete on equal terms for a limited number of prizes. The chief characteristic of contest mobility is a fear of premature judgment and not only is early selection avoided, but any open selection is, as far as possible, avoided altogether. The competitors may drop out of the game of their own accord, but they will not be barred from the competition, as occurs under sponsored mobility. Moreover, in order to allow everyone an equal chance, segregation is avoided or postponed or in some way minimized to avoid giving anyone or any group an unfair advantage.

Turner used the United States system of education as an example of contest mobility, although he is careful to point out that existing systems are only an approximation to the ideal type. There are few overt mechanisms of selection in the United States and certainly nothing corresponding to the 11-plus. Although there are specialized high schools, corresponding to the English grammar schools, the common or comprehensive school is the normal pattern in the United States. Moreover, although there is increasing opportunity for students of different ability to take different courses, there is no sharp separation between students of different ability levels.

Entry to higher education in the United States also runs true to the principles of contest mobility. Although private colleges can be, and often are, highly selective in their choice of students, those colleges which are supported by public funds often encourage relatively unlimited entry, at least by British standards, and it has been estimated that 'high school graduates of all levels of ability can gain admission to some institution without going very far from home.' Inevitably, large numbers of students of low academic ability fail to meet the standards of performance expected of them, and those American colleges which practice 'open door' admission policies protect their standards by means of a heavy failure rate which may be as high as one in eight in the first term and continues at a high level throughout the course. It has been estimated indeed that in State universities above 40 per cent withdraw in the first two years. Some of these drop-outs will, however, return later, or will transfer to another college, so that failure need never be seen as absolutely final.

Another approach is that of the two-year junior or community college. Unselective, and tuition free, the junior college takes those students wanting to go to college who are not judged to have sufficient academic ability to manage the four-year senior college course. Such students are channelled into the junior college, which provides not only a one- or two-year programme of vocational or semi-professional training for those students who do not aspire any higher, but the possibility of transfer to the senior college for those who can reach the required standard. By this means the 'open door' policy is maintained and college standards are protected without the wastage of a high failure rate.

Higher education in England follows the general pattern of sponsored mobility. All forms of full-time higher education have high admission standards, and this is particularly true of the universities. This is coupled with an extremely low average wastage rate of only 14 per cent for the universities and seven per cent for Training Colleges or Colleges of Education. Only in the field of further education, with its tradition of part-time study, do we find wastage comparable to the American pattern, and here too we find 'open-door' admission policies which allow entrance to all students who meet the minimum entrance requirements. The Crowther Report survey of wastage in part-time technical courses makes plain that the forces operating here are those of contest rather than sponsored ability. The full National Certificate Course, for example, comprises five stages leading to a Higher National Certificate but of those who start on the course only 10 per cent reach this level unless they are already exempted from the earlier stages. Indeed, as in the American context, the drop-out starts very early on, and the Crowther Report showed that only 68 per cent successfully completed stage one. However, the difficulties inherent in this alternative route to the top only serve to point up the importance of sponsorship in full-time higher education.

In general the European tradition is in line with sponsored rather than contest mobility. The U.S.S.R. is, however, a major exception in that it approaches the pattern of contest mobility to a much greater extent than has been customary in Europe. Soviet schools are, with few exceptions, completely comprehensive. Indeed, not only do the Russians refuse the early selection of an elite, but they reject the whole theory of innate abilities upon which so much elite thinking is based, and argue that, within certain limitations, abilities are learned rather than inborn. Mental testing is 'not merely characterized as theoretically unsound but also, and as a consequence practically misleading,' and it is generally held that if children are slow to learn it is the teaching which is at fault. Accordingly educational psychologists in the U.S.S.R. are concerned not with devising tests for the measurement of ability but rather with the 'study of human learning, and, particularly, learning under the conditions of organized teaching in schools, under planned educational influences.'

Within the schools, comprehensive principles are carried to much greater extents than are commonly found even in the United States. Not only is there a complete avoidance of streaming and setting, but there is an emphasis on all children covering the same course at the same level. This contrasts with the American system, which allows for considerable individual variation within the comprehensive framework. A great deal of emphasis is laid on bringing up the weaker members of the class, and the brighter members of the class are encouraged to help those who are slower with their work, rather than to push ahead with their own studies. Those children who fail to meet the required standards have to repeat the grade. There is some evidence that a fairly high proportion each year do in fact have to repeat the work although the proportion will vary from place to place. Nigel Grant reports that 'according to the Assistant Director of Education in Leningrad, 16,000 out of a total of 450,000 school children in the city were repeating the year's work during the school year 1962-63.' Since Leningrad is better off than most places for teachers and school buildings, the national proportion is probably a good deal higher. In addition, some of the obviously mentally backward children will be placed in special schools and there are various unofficial ways of getting rid of very unresponsive children, including sending them to the school with lower standards or allowing them to leave school before they reach the statutory leaving age. On the other hand, and in spite of a very formal approach and a highly academic content, Nigel Grant concludes that 'more children make the grade than would be thought possible by those conditioned to the values of a selective system.'

The comprehensive principle does not, however, extend right through secondary education. At the age of 15 there is differentiation into three quite distinct types of school, which correspond quite closely to the three sides of the English tripartite system, except of course that the selection takes place at a much later age. The Russian version of the grammar school is the three-year 'general education secondary school' leading to the school-leaving diploma, which entitles its owner to apply for admission to higher education. Some 20 to 25 per cent of the age-group are in schools of this kind. Secondly there is the technicum, which also takes up to 25 per cent of the age-group. Although it is possible to stay on at the technical, and obtain a school-leaving diploma, most of its students do not go on to higher education, at least for the time being. The remaining 50 per cent do not continue in full-time education at all. They are, however, required to attend at afternoon or evening classes of approximately 15 to 18 hours a week, for one, two, or usually three years. The ablest of these pupils are encouraged to go on to the technicum, so that the door is never completely closed, but this part-time route does not by itself lead to the school-leaving diploma. It can be argued, therefore, that there is considerably more selection in the Russian system than in the United States.

Although in theory all who complete the school-leaving diploma are eligible for higher education, in practice the competition is so keen that all kinds of higher education can be highly selective. The institutions themselves have their own entrance examinations, and there are variations in standards, in spite of the theoretical equality of status. Thus it is harder to get into a university than into a pedagogic institute for teacher training. The proportion of applicants accepted also varies according to the popularity of the universities concerned, but nowhere is there room for more than a fraction of those who apply. On the other hand, it is fair to say that this selective entry is a matter of expendiency, and results only from an inability to provide sufficient places to keep pace with the demand. At the same time great pains are taken to try to ensure that the most highly educated do not become an exclusive elite. For example, the principle of polytechnic training, which attempts to ensure that the majority of students in higher education have had some first-hand practical experience of the basic processes of production, is designed to prevent the emergence of a narrow academic elite, Moreover, preference is given in higher education to those who have done some practical work in industry or agriculture. Indeed, 'so much attention is now paid to this qualification, that increasing numbers of school leavers go into industry straight away without bothering to apply for a year or two. At the present time, only about 20 per cent of each intake has come into the institutions straight from school with no other hurdle than the entrance examination to pass; these are mostly mathematicians or physicists.

Although, with the exception of Russia and other communist countries, it has been argued that the European tradition is one of sponsored mobility and that a modified form of sponsored mobility occurs generally at the present time, it is probably true to say that even in Europe the modern trend is away from a differentiated secondary system and towards the comprehensive school. In Sweden, for example, a large-scale reorganization of the school system has been in process since the early 1950s, and by the early 1970s it is hoped that all those in the public sector of education will be in comprehensive schools. In Britain experiments in comprehensive schools have existed since the 1940s and, after a slow start, have increasingly come to challenge the dominant tripartite system. Although at first only a very small part of the secondary system, their numbers are growing year by year. Moreover the government, in 1966, pledged itself to a policy of complete, if gradual, change-over to a fully comprehensive system of secondary education.

This is not to suggest that the process has been a smooth one. Indeed it has been marked by a political and ideological battle of some considerable bitterness, in which the arguments of the two sides have reflected with surprising exactness the ideals of contest and sponsored mobility. It does not follow, however, that by the adoption of comprehensive schools the English system will necessarily reflect the principles of contest mobility to the same extent as in the United States. There is some evidence already that many of the English comprehensive schools show much more differentiation between types of pupils than do the American schools. Pedley, for example, has stated that 'it is the almost universal practice to group incoming pupils on the basis of general ability so that the cleverest children learn together, and so on down the scale'. This emphasis on streaming and the general avoidance of mixed-ability groupings, is an attempt to retain the chief characteristic of sponsorship, notably early selection, within the framework of a common school. Moreover it is at least possible that the private and so-called 'public schools' will increase the part they play in sponsored mobility, especially if the small number of scholarships they now offer were to be augmented. When this is taken in conjunction with the restricted entry into higher education which is likely to continue to a large extent, it seems probable that strong elements of sponsored mobility will remain characteristic of English education for some time to come.

On the other hand, it should not be assumed that under a system of contest mobility selection is less important. What distinguishes such systems is not the fact of selection but the manner in which it is carried out. Contest mobility is characterized by a selection strategy which relies on the 'drop-out' rather than an overt mechanism of early selection, but in the last analysis the prize of elite status, whether in the United States, Britain or anywhere else, can only be for the few. It is legitimate to ask, however, whether these different types or modes of selection differ at all in their consequences. Do they, for example, select for different characteristics, or do the same kinds of people reach the top whatever the system of selection? In general, when sociologists have asked this kind of question they have phrased it more specifically in the context of equality of educational opportunity. Above all they have wanted to know how efficient selection strategies have been in matching opportunities to ability. A great deal of work has been done in this area in recent years, and since it is easily accessible only a brief review will be attempted here.

Equality of Educational Opportunity: Myth or Reality

The usual approach to this problem is to attempt to measure specific inequalities in educational opportunity as they apply to different sections of society, and the most fruitful area so far has been the study of social-class and educational differences. Social class is not a particularly straightforward concept, and there are in fact may differences in the precise definition or classification employed in different studies. This makes comparison difficult especially when international differences are involved. On the other hand, there are sufficient common factors to allow rough comparisons to be made, provided it is remembered that the basis of classification is often not identical. It is usual, for example, to take father's occupation as the main basis of classification and to group the manual occupations as 'working class' and the non-manual occupations as 'middle class.' Most classifications are sufficiently close to this pattern to make it workable, provided all the limitations are kept in mind.

On this basis a few general patterns emerge clearly from a number of national studies and international comparisons. It can be shown, for example, that children of manual workers are less likely to enter and to graduate from higher education, not only in Europe but also in the United States, even with its ideology of contest mobility, and its mass provision of higher education. Thus, it has been shown that children of professional and semi-professional parents have five- and -a-half time as great a chance of graduating from college as children of manual workers, and the chances of children of managerial parents, although smaller, are still two- and -a-half times as great as those of manual workers. Such inequalities, however, are much greater in Britain, where children from professional and managerial parents have 17 times as great a chance of entering university as children of even skilled workers, and 30 times as great a chance as children of semi- and unskilled workers. Moreover, the chances of working-class children relative to middle-class children appear to be even lower in France and Germany than in Britain. In the U.S.S.R. in 1958, between 30 and 40 per cent of university students came from worker and peasant backgrounds. This is about the same proportion as in the United States. On the other hand, workers and peasants account for a much higher proportion of the population in the U.S.S.R. and the chances of a working-class child obtaining a higher education there appear to be closer to chances in Britain than in the United States.

Table 7.3

Proportions Obtaining Education of a Grammar-school Type Among Children of Different Classes Born in the Late 1930s

Father's Occupation	*At ages 11-13*	*At age 17*
Professional and managerial	62	41½
Other non-manual	34	16
Skilled manual	17	5
Semi-skilled manual	12	3
Unskilled	7	1½
All children	23	10½

When secondary education is of different types, working-class children can be shown to be less likely to enter the more academic schools and, once there, to be more likely to leave early. Table 7.3 which is adapted from an article by Little and Westergaard, shows clearly the class differential at entry to the school, and the increase in the differential as a result of early leaving, as they occur in England and Wales.

Class differences are however much less important within the sixth form itself. As Little and Westergaard point out, among sixth-formers leaving school at 17 years or over in 1960-61 the proportion of boys who left with at least two 'A ' level passes varies very slightly in terms of social class. Only the sons of semi-skilled and unskilled workers fall below the average level of achievement. For girls the social class differences are larger but they to not begin to approach the earlier differential. There is also evidence that at university level social-class differences are eliminated altogether. This suggests that those who are seriously handicapped by their working-class background have already dropped out.

Table 7.4

Proportions of Recruits in Relation to Parental Occupation Who Took a Vocational Part-time Course at any Time During the First Three Years After Leaving School

Parental Occupation	*Took course*	*Did not take course*
	%	%
Professional and managerial	65	35
Clerical and other non-manual	55	45
Skilled manual	52	48
Semi-skilled manual	41	59
Unskilled manual	27	73
Other groups	33	67
All occupational groups	46	54

If we consider the so-called 'alternative route' of part-time education we find the same social-class differences repeated as for the more orthodox full-time route. The Crowther Committee, for example, in their Survey of National Service Recruits found that not only are middle-class boys more likely than working-class boys to go on to full-time further education, but they are also more likely to go on to vocational part-time courses. This is illustrated in Table 7.4.

At the same time there is a relationship between social-class origin and the level of course. The Crowther Report draws attention to the small number of higher-grade trainees deriving from the semi-skilled and the unskilled manual homes and how many come from homes of non-manual workers. Even the skilled manual group provides for fewer at the higher levels of training than its numerical predominance would warrant.

Table 7.5

School Background of Men in Different Types of Training

	Type of School					
Training before National Service	*Inde-pendent (efficient)*	*Grammar*	*Technical*	*Modern and all-age*	*Other types*	*Total*
	%	%	%	%	%	
Craft apprenticeship	trace	12	11	76	1	2,770
Learnership	2	22	7	66	3	1,241
Graduate and student apprenticeship	6	60	15	17	4	217
Articled clerk, etc.	16	63	10	7	4	195
Other training	14	50	7	26	3	122
Abandoned training	1	10	8	79	2	299
No training	5	19	3	70	3	3,147
Percentage total	4	19	7	68	2	7,991

Indeed, although part-time vocational education can serve as an alternative route of the working-class child who has attended the secondary modern school, it is more likely to operate in this way for the grammar school boy who is unable or unwilling to follow the normal full-time route, and the evidence in the Crowther Report indicates that the secondary modern school leaver is at a serious disadvantage in part-time education. Table 7.5 illustrates this point clearly, showing as it does that not only do modern school boys preponderate in the lower-level craft crses but that they are more likely than boys from grammar or technical schools to drop a course without completing it. They are also less likely to have started a course at all.

It is clear that the part-time route does not operate in such a way as materially to lessen the class differentials in educational opportunity. Nevertheless Cotgrove has argued that it has in fact been important in the past in providing access to the middle ranges of the occupational hierarchy, for those in the two lowest status groups. Using data from David Glass's social mobility study he has shown that, taking only those of semi-skilled and unskilled social origin, 74 per cent of those with same part-time education achieved social mobility compared with 45 per cent of those who had no further education at all. On the other hand, recent trends away from part-time courses, coupled with increases since 1944 in grammar and technical schools, may well diminish even further the effect of the part-time route in the future.

In other Western European countries the general pattern would appear to be of a very similar kind. Working-class children are less likely than middle-class children to enter the more academic types of secondary education and even if they do so they are less likely to complete the course. Indeed the evidence that we have indicates that on the whole differences between social classes are even greater than in England and Wales. Ben-David, for example, quotes evidence from Germany which suggests that working-class entry to academic secondary education has been considerably more restricted than in England and Wales. Recent studies in Switzerland and Belgium also illustrate the same order of class differences.

In the United States, too, the pattern of class differences is much the same as in Europe. It 'has been demonstrated many times that the socio-economic background of the child is related to school retardation, academic grades, age of leaving school, and percentage of youngsters who remain in school to any designated level.' Nevertheless, although class is an important factor in completing high school its main influence is felt at the point of entrance to college. This is because the biggest drop-out in the whole of the United States educational system occurs at this stage and not, as in the European system, at the statutory leaving age. Accordingly there are in the United States large class differences amongst high-school graduates who go on to college. However, once in college, as in Britain, class differences are much less important. This point is well illustrated in Table 7.6, adapted from Wolfle.

Table 7.6

The Relation Between Father's Occupation and Probability that a High-school Graduate will Enter College and that a College Entrant will Graduate

Father's occupation	*High-school graduates who enter college* %	*College entrants who graduate from college* %
Professional and semi-professional	67	60
Managerial	50	55
White-collar	48	57
Farmer	24	44
Factory, craftsmen, unskilled, etc.	26	58

This brief review of the main findings on class differentials in educational opportunity has indicated that in spite of national differences the children of the working class are always at a considerable disadvantage, compared with middle-class children. It remains to consider how far this is because working-class children are of lower potential ability than middle-class children, or how far it is genuine waste of talent. In attempting to assess the efficiency of education systems as selection processes, it is usual to define ability in terms of intelligence as measured by tests. This is a useful approach to the problem, in so far as it provides us with an efficient and standardized measuring instrument that can be used for a wide variety of comparative studies. Ability so defined is not, however, the same as potentiality, although it may well be the nearest we can get to it at present. A child's score on an intelligence test is to some extent influenced by environmental factors, including his or her own educational experience. To this extent inequalities are built into the measure of ability. Nevertheless intelligence tests can be a most useful way of answering the extent to which wastage can be said to occur, always provided it is remembered that this method will always tend to underestimate the amount of wastage that exists.

A number of methods have been used to assess the 'wastage' of ability in this sense but probably the most useful is the method adopted by the Crowther Committee in their Survey of National Service Recruits. By comparing the educational experience of the main social classes at various ability levels, they were able to show wide class differences even at the highest level of ability. Table 7.7 indicates the extent of such differences as they apply to the age of leaving school.

Table 7.7

School-leaving are for (a) All Men in Ability Groups 1 and 2 and (b) Sons of Manual Workers (Except in Agriculture)

	Number		*School-leaving age*		
	= *100%*	*15 or earlier* %	*16* %	*17* %	*18 or earlier* %
All men in ability group 1	681	9	33	17	41
Manual workers' sons in ability group 1	295	19	44	13	24
All men in ability group 2	1,824	65	22	6	7
Manual workers' sons in ability group 2	1,286	75	20	3	2

It is clear from Table 7.7 that even in the highest ability group, representing the top 11 per cent of the population, there is considerable wastage of working-class ability. Similar findings reported by the Robbins Committee show clearly that 'wastage' can occur at even higher levels of the ability range, and is considerable at slightly lower levels.

Table 7.8

Higher Education of 'Able' Children of Different Classes, Born 1940-41

		% obtaining higher education of the following kinds			
I.Q. at 11	*Father's occupation*	*Full-time degree level*	*Other full-time*	*Part-time only*	*Total*
130+	Non-manual	37	4	10	51
	Manual	18	12	10	40
115-129	Non-manual	17	17	4	38
	Manual	8	7	9	24

It will be noted that although the social-class discrepancy is fairly small for those with an I.Q. at the age of 11 of 130-plus, those in the manual group are more likely than the non-manual group to receive their higher education outside the universities.

There is no reason to suppose that this wastage of ability is confined to the British system of education. The pattern of selection in Western Europe leads us to suppose that at least the same order of wastage is repeated there, and that in some cases it will be higher. Moreover it is easy to show that this general pattern is by no means confined to systems of sponsored mobility. Wolfle has made it clear that a similar pattern occurs in the United States.

Even at the top ability level only 69 per cent of high-school graduates graduate from college, and this figure drops steeply as the ability level falls, until of the top 20 per cent, only 34 per cent graduate from college. It can also be shown that much of this wasted ability follows social-class lines. Using scholastic performance as her criterion Natalie Rogoff shows that, of the top quartile of scholastic ability, measured in each school, 83 per cent of the top socio-economic status quintile plan to attend college, and only 43 per cent of the bottom socio-economic quintile.

On the other hand, it would be wrong to assume that all wastage of ability in the United States or elsewhere is to be explained in terms of social-class inequalities. Some attention has also been paid to regional inequalities, and in particular to the problem of the educational backwardness of many rural areas. Children in such areas have been shown to be at a disadvantage in Europe, including the U.S.S.R., and in the United States. One of the main problems in rural areas would seem to be the difficulty of making adequate educational provision in sparsely populated districts, but this basic limitation common to all such areas can be strongly influenced by administrative arrangement, and cultural and educational traditions. Nor are these the only kind of regional differences. In the United States, for example, it has been found 'that the college-going propensities of youngsters attending high school in the very largest cities is almost as low as that of youngsters residing in the smallest towns and villages.' A similar distinction between the suburbs and the inner areas of big cities is also found in Great Britain. In addition, wherever there is an element of decentralization in educational policy-making, differences in ideology will be reflected on the regional as well as on the national level. In England, for example, local education authorities have pursued widely different policies with respect to the provision of selective secondary education, so that it is much easier to enter a grammar school in some areas than in others. In the United States, because of the relative autonomy granted not only at the State level, but even down to the local school board, regional differences are also very great, both in terms of the proportion of the age-group entering college, and the financial support given to the schools.

Yet another source of educational inequality is found wherever there are distinctive minority groups. The most striking example of such a minority is the American Negro, who is disadvantaged not only by actual discrimination on the grounds of colour but in many cases by the presence of all the other disadvantages which affect white lower-class communities. Moreover not only Negroes, but also 'the French Canadian of parts of New England, Orientals, and the Spanish-speaking immigrants of the southwest all illustrate the better utilization of high intellectual potential of minority group members.' On the other hand, there are times when membership of a minority group has the reverse effect. Wolfle, for example, points out that 'the great esteem which Jewish culture gives to higher education has overcome quota barriers and other forms of discrimination with the result that a Jewish boy is more likely to graduate from college than is a Gentile of equal ability.' In the same way the Welsh and the Scottish working classes have traditionally been more interested in education than their English counterparts.

The final area of inequality to be discussed is that between the sexes. The Robbins Committee on Higher Education was very much aware of the wastage of girls' ability that occurs at the level of higher education and in the senior forms of the secondary schools. Girls were less likely to get 'O' levels than boys and less likely to go on to higher education. Only 7.3 per cent of the age group entered full-time higher education in 1962 as compared with 9.8 per cent of the men. Moreover with higher education girls were less likely to enter the universities. Indeed only 28 per cent of all university students in Britain in 1962-63 were women. If we include all forms of full-time higher education, however, the figure is 40 per cent. On the other hand women take only a very small share in all part-time forms of higher education.

In the United States girls are more likely than boys to graduate from high school but less likely to go on to college. The proportion of women to men in higher education is 40 per cent, which is the same as in Britain, if we include those in Colleges of Education. America would seem therefore to waste as much female ability as Britain, in spite of its different educational system.

In the USSR there is strong belief in equality between the sexes, and women play a very active role in the occupational system. There also seems to be less discrimination against them in employment than in either Western Europe or the United States. The proportion of women to men in all forms of higher education is 45 per cent and, in full-time higher education only, 42 per cent. The situation is, therefore, one of near rather than complete equality and does not differ radically from the United States or Britain.

We are now in a better position to discuss the extent to which contest mobility as a mode of selection succeeds in achieving its goal of equality of opportunity. Clearly even the United States has not eliminated class and other differences from its educational system, and the data from Wolfle indicates that at the point of entry to college there is considerable wastage of ability. In the U.S.S.R., too, in spite of its opposition to streaming and to early selection, there are considerable class and regional differences at the entry to higher education. On the other hand, it would appear that the United States has succeeded in providing opportunities for secondary and higher education for a higher proportion or working-class children than has Europe, both in absolute and relative terms. What features of the American system can be said to have contributed to this measure of success ? The ideology of contest mobility lays great stress on the postponement of selection, and this is, undoubtedly, an important feature in the situation. Husen, for example, has drawn attention to the loss of ability which can follow from mistakes in selection.

At the same time the postponement of selection does not necessarily led to greater opportunity, as we can see from the example of the U.S.S.R. It has been argued that what is chiefly distinctive about the United States system is not its postponement of selection alone, but its combination with a highly flexible system of both secondary and higher education. Ben-David, for example, points out that the 'much wonder scope of studies creates a more flexible standard of achievement and, as a result, a greater variety of attitudes and motivations can be satisfied within the educational system. This is why secondary and higher education in the United States can cater to a wider range of class differences and to people with a somewhat wider range of motivations and intelligence test scores than elsewhere. Educational mobility and the rapid expansion of higher education were made possible by this flexibility.

In Europe, on the other hand, secondary education in particular has been relatively inflexible. The curriculum, especially in continental Europe, places considerable emphasis on the acquisition of items of the traditional culture of the upper middle classes. It seems likely that this characteristically narrow and essentially academic curriculum is an important factor in the loss by early leaving of many able working-class children in the academic type of secondary school. Universities in Europe have also been more narrowly based than in the United States and so have been less attractive to working-class children.

The flexibility of the American system is closely related to the ideology of mass rather than elite education. With the prolongation of school life, and the unprecedented expansion of higher education, 'educationalists are compelled to face the fact of different educational needs and have to adopt measures in order to cope with them.' These measures, as we have seen, include flexibility and variety not only within institutions but between them, so that the umbrella concept of higher education covers an enormous range of institutions, catering for a wide range of abilities and interests. A colleges education in itself is no longer conceived of as limited to an elite either of class or of intellectual ability. On the other hand, within the whole range of higher education there are important status distinctions, which operate as hidden selectors, so that the American system is in fact less open than it appears.

In spite, therefore, of its success in opening higher education to the working classes it still remains true that there are important differences in educational achievement in the United States, and in recent years a great deal of research has been undertaken to explain why they occur. In Britain, too, research has focused on this same problem as it was realized that the changes in the organization of secondary education that followed the Education Act of 1944 did not in fact do a great deal to remove educational inequalities. Most of these enquiries have been concerned with class differences in what has come to be called educability and, so far at least, most attention has been paid to their source in the family and the neighbourhood. It is to this aspect of educational sociology that we must now turn.

8

The School: Its Relation to Culture

The origin of the school. Cultural concepts which have influenced American education. The growth of American education. Unresolved issues.

Culture accumulates. From the most primitive society, which is almost, but never wholly, free of social controls, to the modern world with its complex social structure and cultural heritage, so rich and so varied that no one person can now comprehend it, each generation has passed on to each succeeding generation all, or some portion, of the values it has nurtured. Ways of behaving under prescribed circumstances—the folkways and mores; basic social patterns regarding property, sex, and religion, which have crystallised into law and become formalized by institutions; and the we-feeling—with its corresponding they-feeling—based upon myths or facts of origin and the sense of rightness of its own social organization, all these social values must be preserved if the group or society is to survive. The preservation of the cultural heritage is the primary function of education carried on through the informal agencies of primitive society; it still is and must remain a major function of the modern school. These two facts—the accumulation of culture and the necessity for its transmission as an agency of social control—form the framework in which the educational sociologist must view the educative process in general and the school in particular. But within this framework, he must also point out the ways through which the school may direct the social processes and provided for a creative role in personality development.

The Origin of the School

Education takes place in all human societies; the school, of comparatively recent origin, arose only because other agencies failed adequately to pass on to the succeeding generation the cultural heritage of the group—clan, tribe, race, or nation.

That education has existed universally is attested to by anthropologists in their descriptions of primitive societies. Sumner and Keller aptly describe the status of primitive man: "No myth was ever farther from scientific truth than that which represents mankind as starting in a state of nature in which there were peace, love, truth, justice, gratuitous abundance, liberty, and equality." Scarcity, rather than abundance, characterized his environment and struggle, rather than sloth, his manner of existence. Under such conditions, social organization was inevitable, although varying in both degree and character. It required mutual adjustments, limitation of individual freedom, and the imposition of responsibility for the welfare of the group.

Informal Transmission of Cultural Pattern

In primitive society, restrictions and taboos are passed on informally through the usual associations of the primary group. Cultural heritage is simple, consisting primarily of methods for procuring the basic necessities of food, shelter, and protection. The close relationship between behaviour and security makes nature and effective teacher. The family and the clan provide the necessary instruction, and the child learns through trial and error, observation, and imitation. Although the extent to which such enforcement of taboos and assumption of responsibilities is deliberately directed varies with the group, as shown in Mead's interesting contrast of the children of Manus and those of New Guinea, children early accept the stern realities of life.

Self-preservation is often itself a struggle against great odds and even small children must contribute their part in eking out an exisence in a resistant environment. Herskovitz describes the responsibilities of boys and girls at various ages in one primitive group. By six years of age, boys have begun o assist in pegging out goats, to scare birds from newly sown fields and from crops, and to accompany the family on sowing and harvesting parties; form six to nine, to the above listed activities are added helping in house building, assisting in sowing and harvesting, and toward the end of the period, going out with the herd boys, and assisting in caring for the poultry; from nine to twelve, full responsibility for cattle herding and caring for poultry, assisting parents in care of crops or, if the father is a craftsman, helping him and "learning by looking", from twelve to fifteen, real farming of their own plots, leading the younger herd boys, or assisting the father in his craft. Comparable responsibilities, differentiated by sex, are assumed by girls and at fifteen, girls have "a responsible part in all domestic duties of everyday life and of those associated with ceremonial occasions."

In primitive groups, the boy models toys after the tools and weapons of his father, and as soon as a lad is strong enough, he begins to accompany the father in quest of food or in pursuit of enemies. The girl likewise learns the household tasks of her mother. One other fact should be noted in Herskovitz's description—the specialization of the craftsman. Division of labour and responsibility could have been described in greater detail, since they include the specific functions of the tribal leader, and the role of the medicine man and others in the ceremonials. Even these knowledge and skills are acquired by observation and imitation.

The descriptions previously given of the Acomas and Navahos illustrate groups that have advanced beyond the stage of merely providing economic necessities, but include the rudiments of intellectual aspects of cultural heritage: art, mythology, songs and sagas of heroes, and involve taboos and ceremonials. The Acomas, like all the Pueblo Indians, have advanced still further in tribal organization and allocation of function to members of the tribe, but the need for the school is not felt. The day-to-day association within the primary group, the repetition of the songs and the ceremonials, and the swift punishment for the violation of taboos transmit the cultural heritage without change or modification. In the ceremonial dance and other tribal rituals, tiny feet begin to pattern their steps after the longer ones of their elders; in the propitiation of the gods, the children learn from the grown-ups.

The Initiation Ceremony

One of the earliest kinds of formal education is the initiation ceremony. In groups in which the cultural heritage has accumulated to the point that it can no longer be left wholly to trial and error, a special period for instruction is set aside, individuals are assigned specific roles and instruction is to a varying degree formalized. Through this short, but tense and highly realistic, period of "schooling," the elders transmit to the adolescent the cultural heritage of the tribe, thus bridging the gap which would otherwise have been left by the inadequacies of wholly informal educational agencies.

Transition to Formal Instruction

Only with the development of language characters, as in China, and of the alphabet and the number system in other early culture groups, did cultural heritage accumulate beyond the point at which it could no longer be entrusted even to the initiatory ceremony. Then it was that the school was established in China, Egypt, Babylonia, India, Greece, and Rome. Even after the development of paper and the invention of the printing press, formal schooling was confined chiefly to those areas of highest culture accumulation—written language, religion, philosophy, and mathematics—and given only to the children of priestly and noble families. The great mass of humanity still continued to acquire the lore of the past and the mores of their current culture through the informal channels of their primary groups. Extension of the school to include "all the children of all the people" is a recent development, actually of the last hundred years. There are still more than a million native-born adults in the United States who have never attended a school.

The Navahos and Acomas illustrate the transition from informal to formal schooling within our own time. Without written language, the natives had no school; their mores and ceremonials were passed on by action and word of mouth in close association within the family, and, among the latter, within the tribe. When these Indians came into contact with Western civilization and took on, more or less unwillingly, the white man's culture, then schools were established—not, however, by their own initiative. Etymologists have attempted, with indifferent success, to develop a written language for several of the tribes, but that which does not evolve from within the group is not readily accepted as a part of its culture.

This concept of the origin of the school as developing to meet the need for the transmission of the cultural heritage—a need created because of culture accumulation and the consequent inadequacy of existing agencies—is fundamental in the appraisal of the function and activities of the modern school. As stated by Woody: "Preliterate peoples knew nothing of the education of mental discipline and effort, the conning of lessons and tasks unassociated directly with life. Till men had languages, literatures, philosophy, and sciences, there was no occasion for disciplinary, mental effort on the part of new generations. Men lived and learned; they did not immune themselves from life. When, however, society had acquired these instruments, systematic training was instituted so that the new generation might learn quickly and well what society itself had learned slowly and with difficulty."

This basic premise raises one of the most controversial issues of modern education. It appears to exclude the entire concept of the school's responsibility for the development of the personality of the individual, especially in its extreme form of the "child-centered school." But even the extremists recognized that the full development of the child involved an appreciation of the cultural heritage and the mastery of such skills as are essential to participate effectively within the total social pattern.

From the point of view of the educational sociologist, the development of personality and the inculcation of the cultural heritage are but two aspects of the same process—the establishment of skills, knowledges, appreciations, and values in a dynamic world as the basis for enriching experience for the development of new social patterns and for providing situations to stimulate creative abilities.

A parallel issue is the degree to which the school at all levels only reflects the culture of the dominant group or has a primary responsibility to seek to develop new cultural patterns. The implications of these issues will be discussed later.

Cultural Concepts which have Influenced American Education

Thus far, the basic premise that the school reflects the patterns and values of the culture in which it develops has been illustrated from its origins. But is might likewise have been illustrated from education in any culture during the long span of recorded history. It is equally true in our own country.

Every aspect of culture has had its influence upon the development of education throughout our history. The multiplicity of old-word backgrounds that were brought to our shores, the rugged individualism essential to carve a home and a nation out of an often resistant environment, the rich heritage of natural resources which made possible both westward expansion and industrialization, the growth to a position of world leadership—these are but a few of the cultural influences which have affected every aspect of our development. It would be interesting to trace each as it has affected education. But only four basic concepts of our democratic way of life are selected . equality of opportunity for all; university of civic responsibility; right of free choice; and shared responsibilities for individual and public welfare.

Equality of Opportunity for All

"All men are created equal . . . they are endowed by their Creator with certain inalienable Rights . . . among these are Life, Liberty and the pursuit of Happiness." These words, inherent in our Judeo-Christian tradition, have been more than just idle phrases, they have been a basic aspiration in terms of providing the opportunity for each individual to achieve all of which he is capable. They are the core of what the editors of *Fortune* have aptly termed USA.: *The Permanent Revolution:*

> These natural Rights have not been mere theories in America. They have lived in the hearts of the people. They actuated the Revolutionary War, the Civil War, and much thereafter. Indeed, the thesis can be sustained that in the last analysis American history has been a struggle to define and implement these Rights, and that this struggle is still going on. The great social issues of our time, for example, can be construed as attempts to redefine the Right to Life in terms of an industrialized society. From the Right to Liberty, on the other hand, there spring all the *political* safeguards that Americans have erected to protect the individual. And the Right to the Pursuit of Happiness, if as yet less well defined, opens up for the individual the opportunity to develop himself according to his own cultural and spiritual lights.

Of course these goals have not been achieved in full nor, perhaps, can they ever be in human society. Class and caste lines still divide a local community; freedom and equality of opportunity are still restricted by many factors other than the innate ability of the individual. But it is the struggle to achieve that has characterized our short but intense history and in this struggle, education has been and remains a vital force.

Universality of Civic Responsibility

"Religion, morality and education, being necessary for good government and the happiness of mankind, schools and the means of education shall forever be encouraged." These words from the Ordinance of 1787 which set aside one section for education and one for religion in each township in the states of the then Northwest Territory—Ohio, Indiana, Illinois, Michigan, and Wisconsin—express another basic concept.

If representative government were to succeed, it was essential that each individual should be educated sufficiently to assume his obligations of citizenship. As first conceived, these responsibilities, and especially the right to vote, were limited to free white males, and individual states added other qualifications; however, these limitations have, across the years, been swept aside as suffrage has been made available almost without restrictions.

But the assumption of civic responsibility is very much more than the intermittent casting of a ballot. It increasingly involves intelligent participation in community life, including local government. It involves understanding issues that far transcend the locality and involves the state, the region, and the entire nation. Today, as never before, it requires also an appreciation of world issues and the extent to which events that occur anywhere around the globe may be influenced by America's foreign policy and, in turn, influence our day-to-day living.

No aspect of society, and least of all the school, can fail to assume this ever broadening responsibility. It has been a major factor in the increasing emphasis upon social values, in the expanding of the curriculum, and in relating the school more closely to the community—local national, and world-wide.

Freedom of Choice

A third basic factor, closely allied to the first, is the right of the individual to freedom of choice, limited only by transgression upon the equal freedom of others. No one of the many cultures transplanted in America was permitted to dominate nor given the sanction of law. This resistance of legal sanctions and conformity has been the basis of individual freedom, whether of religious affiliation or occupation or loyalty to political parties. Standards of value and the things one likes or dislikes are matters which the individual may decide for himself within the bounds of law. Censorship in any form is abhorrent to many, though concern for the public morals and public welfare must entail specific restrictions. Complete freedom is anarchy; for freedom must be limited by responsibility!

As has been emphasized earlier, the cultural heritage is a further factor restricting total freedom for the individual. But the basic premise holds for all but relatively limited areas of our behaviours. The school has evolved within this basic concept and rightly retains its freedom to learn and to teach.

Shared Responsibility for Individual and Public Welfare

A fourth and final characteristic in this brief analysis is the sharing of responsibility for individual and public welfare. This sharing is twofold : among the various levels of government and between governmental agencies and voluntary organizations.

As isolated settlements joined in commonwealths and territories and as these in turn formed the union of states through the establishment of the Federal government, each level of government reserved certain responsibilities, for itself. Others were recognized as bring more effectively carried on by the next larger unit. These functions of local, country, state, and Federal government have not remained static but have reflected the changing aspects of an expanding economy and a mobile population. The establishment of the United Nations carried certain governmental responsibilities to the international level.

Paralleling the changes in governmental functions has been the development of an endless number and variety of voluntary organizations. There is hardly a specialized interest—religious, social, cultural, vocational, industrial, or professional—that does not have its own voluntary association. At a recent conference of representatives of 140 national organizations, it was estimated that, as a result of individuals belonging to several organizations simultaneously, their combined membership exceeded the total population of the United States!

The functions of voluntary organizations—local, state, national, and international—vary with the interest of the group but, almost without exception, each accepts some responsibility for service to its members, and frequently to non-members beyond that of an egocentric interest. Thus voluntary organizations and governmental agencies share many responsibilities which neither could meet adequately without the help of the other.

Illustrations could be drawn from almost any aspect of our economic or social life. One of the most interesting is that of responsibility for the public welfare. The term was at first narrowly conceived and related primarily to the care of the sick and the poor. Families sought to care for their own but, when unable to do so, the local government assumed a share of the responsibility. Records of early Town Meetings are mute testimony to the concern of the community for its "indigent poor."

Even when welfare is thus narrowly defined, cities, countries, states, and the Federal government now share in providing essential care. City departments of social welfare, county homes for the aged, state mental hospitals, and Federal maternal and child care and widows' pensions are but illustrations of the interrelated functions of levels of government. Illustrations of the activities of voluntary organizations in this field are too numerous to cite.

When the concept of individual and public welfare is expanded to include sanitation, water supply, food protection, health in all its preventive and curative aspects, counselling, control of deliquences and crime, social work, and education, the sharing of responsibility becomes all the more obvious. In each of these and other related fields, the continual shifting of functions among the levels of government and between government and voluntary organizations is inevitable in adapting to the needs of a dynamic society.

It is within the general framework of these basic concepts that our schools and colleges have evolved. They have not only reflected these aspects of our culture but have sought continually to enrich them. They have expanded to provide greater equality of opportunity for education; they have sought to provide the understanding essential to assume civic responsibility; they have aimed to provide the knowledge, skills, and sense of values for wiser choices; and the responsibility for education has been shared by the various levels of government and between government and voluntary organizations. Perhaps more than all else, the school, like the culture of which it is an integral part, has been dynamic, continually seeking both to retain the "hard core of universal values" and to adapt to the changing needs of the times.

The Growth of American Education

The history of American education clearly shows its relationship not only to the concepts described above but also to our whole cultural pattern. This could be illustrated from many aspect of our educational system : the retention of control in lay boards of education, the active participation of teachers at all levels in planning the programme and curricula, the development of new fields of study to meet expanding needs, the increasing relationships between the school and its community, the increasing professional preparation, both pre-service and in-service, of teachers and administrators, and many more.

Some of these will be touched upon later, but the phases of the development of education which most specifically show the inter-relationship of education and culture are these : the religious influence in our schools and colleges, the rise of publicly controlled education, the education of women, trends in control and support of education, the role of the Federal government, and the development of voluntary professional organizations.

Religious Influence

Colonial education in America differed little from that of the country from which the settlers came—Puritan in New England, Catholic in Maryland, Quaker, Lutheran, and others in Pennsylvania. The Church provided the schools and determined the curricula. The earliest colleges, such as Harvard and William and Mary, were "to train up learned man for the clergy." The dominance of the Church is shown in the contents of the *New England Primer*, the most used of all elementary textbooks for more than a hundred years and reprinted as late as 1830. It begins with the alphabet:

In Adam's fall we sinned, all
Thy ways to mend, God's Book attend

and so on through the alphabet, ending with :

Youth forward slips, death soonest nips;
Zaccheus he did climb the tree his Lord to see.

The following quotation from the *New England Primer* indictates the contents, which are illustrated by vivid woodcuts:

I in the burying ground may see
Graves shorter there than I;
From death's arrest no age is free,
Young children, too, may die.

My God, may such an awful sight
Awakening be to me
So that by early grace I might
For death prepare'd be !

The earliest legislation regarding school were the so-called Satan Acts (to keep children busy and so out of the clutches of the Devil) passed by the Colonial Legislature of Massachusetts in 1642 and 1647. Based on the English Poor Law of 1601, the law of 1642 required only that all children be taught "to read and understand the principles of religion and the capital laws of the country." There were no provisions for the establishment of schools, this being left, as in England, to the family and the Church. Only five years later the second act remedied this defect and made schools mandatory : "Every town having 50 householders should at once appoint a teacher of reading and writing, and provide for his wages in such manner as the town might determine;" and "Every town having 100 householders must provide a grammar school to fit youths for the university." Penalties for failure to provide such schools were designated.

The individual colonies differed widely in the extent to which they sought to require education and, reflecting the influence of the dominant religious group, varied also in the degree to which elementary education was left primarily to the Church. Many private schools also developed and wealthier families employed tutors for their children.

Secondary education, likewise, was developed by religious denominations although private "academies" shared in providing secondary schools for the very limited number who continued beyond the grade school. As previously stated the religious motivation was strong in the establishment of colleges and universities although the greatest number of denominational colleges was established in the early part of the nineteenth century. In the field of higher education, including professional schools, many were founded by individuals and were neither denominational nor publicly controlled.

The close relationship of Church and State during the entire colonial period is indicated by the passing of the Ordinance of 1787, previously described. The first sentence of the First Amendment to the Constitution is, even today, highly controversial as to its intent and meaning: "Congress shall make no law respecting an establishment of religion, or prohibiting the free exercise thereof." But whatever the intent, especially of the first part of the sentence, religious denominations have played an important role in the development of our educational system and, as will be emphasized later in this chapter, we have retained a dual system of education. The discussion of the role of the Church as an educational institution and the relation of religion and education will be discussed later.

Rise of Public Education

As indicated by the early Massachusetts laws through which the colonial government required the establishment of schools, local and state governments began almost immediately to express an interest in the education of children, especially at the elementary school level. But the establishment of free public schools and institutions of higher education was not achieved without a long and continuous struggle. In fact, some of the issues have not yet been resolved.

The recency of free public education in the United States is startlingly brought home by the struggle to eliminate "pauper schools" and the "rate bill." The former is illustrated by Pennsylvania. After more than two decades of controversy, the Free School Law passed in 1834. Even by this act, local school districts were to decide whether or not they would tax themselves to establish free schools, and it was not until 1873 that the last district in the state accepted the system. The so-called "rate bills" required each student to pay a fee varying with the school and the grade in which he has enrolled. In New York State, the matter was twice voted on by referendum; it was not, however, until 1867 that New York abolished rates. New Jersey, the last state to throw off the practice of rates, did so in 1871.

The expansion of education is shown by the fact that in 1800 the average person had only 82 days of schooling during his life-time; in 1850, 321 days; and by 1900, it had reached 998 days—the approximate equivalent of five school years. The average soldier of World War I had completed only the sixth grade; in World War II he had just entered his junior year of high school. In 1953, the average person of 25 years of age had completed high school, and there is strong pressure to make minimum education include two years of college.

The greatest numerical growth in relation to population has taken place in the public secondary school. The Latin Grammar School on the British pattern was gradually supplanted by the tuition-charging "Free Academy." By 1840 some 6,000 such schools were in operation. The free public high school was first established in Boston in 1820. The movement rapidly grew, especially after the Kalamazoo Case of 1872 when the courts upheld the right of a district to levy taxes to provide education at all levels. Today the high school has virtually replaced the academy, although a few communities still cling to the name. In 1952, there were approximately 28,000 secondary schools in the United States, of which more than 90 per cent were publicly administered. In 1890, only 3.5 per cent of 17-years-olds were high-school graduates; in 1952, 55 per cent had graduated; then only 7 per cent of those 14 to 17 years of age were in secondary school; in 1952-53, 83.1 per cent—almost twelve times as high a percentage.

In higher education, only 38 colleges had been established by 1820; 92 were begun in the decade 1850-59, and a total of 300 within the 40 years 1850-89. The period of rapid increase in church-controlled colleges has been followed since 1900 by a tendency to loosen or in many cases sever the relationship with the denomination. Publicly administered colleges and universities developed in the first quarter of the last century, but had their greatest growth after the passage of the Morrell Acts of 1862 and 1867 that gave lands to the states for the establishment of colleges, especially to give instruction in agriculture and home economics.

Publicly administered universities developed in response to the growing demand to liberate education both from its selective factor based on economic status and from denominational control. For the most part, these universities are supported by the state, although a score of cities have established municipal universities, and more than 300 have organized junior colleges. Although the number of privately administered colleges and universities exceeds that of those

Table 8.1

Number of Institutions of Higher Education by Type and Type of Control, 1952-53*

Type of programme	*Total*	*State control*	*District or city control*	*Private control*	*Denominational control: Protestant*	*Denominational control: Roman catholic*	*Denominational control: Jewish*
1	2	3	4	5	6	7	8
(a) Terminal-occupational (below bachelor's degree)	41	12	4	21	3	1	—
(b) Liberal arts and general	142	6	5	54	39	37	1
(c) Liberal arts and general and terminal-occupational	317	[1]20	168	59	53	17	—
(d) Primarily teacher preparatory	133	80	26	19	3	5	—
(e) Both liberal arts and general and teacher preparatory	428	74	9	83	154	108	—
(f) Liberal arts and general, terminal-occupational, and teacher preparatory	171	36	46	21	45	23	—
(g) Professional or technical only (not including teacher preparatory)	216	[2]22	2	111	69	9	3
(h) Professional or teachnical, and teacher preparatory	64	7	—	46	9	2	—
(i) Professional or technical, and terminal-occupational	14	1	1	10	1	1	—
(j) Liberal arts and general with one or more professional schools	260	79	9	71	58	42	1

Institutions attended predominantly by Negroes							
(a) Terminal-occupational (below bachelor's degree)	1	—	—	—	1	—	—
(b) Liberal arts and general	1	—	—	—	1	—	—
(c) Liberal arts and general and terminal-occupational	5	1	1	1	2	—	—
(d) Primarily teacher preparatory	11	8	2	—	1	—	—
(e) Both liberal arts and general and teacher preparatory	38	8	—	6	24	—	—
(f) Liberal arts and general, terminal-occupational, and teacher preparatory	26	8	1	6	11	—	—
(g) Professional or technical only (not including teacher preparatory)	3	1	—	1	1	—	—
(h) Professional or teachnical, and teacher preparatory	2	—	—	1	1	—	—
(j) Liberal arts and general with one or more professional schools	16	6	—	3	6	1	—
Total:							
White institutions	1,786	[3] 337	270	495	434	245	5
Negro institutions	103	32	4	18	48	1	—
Grand total	1,889	[3] 369	274	513	482	246	5

**Educational Directory*, Part III, page 11. Washington, D.C.: Office of Education, Department of Health, Education and Welfare, 1952.

1. Includes 2 under Federal control.
2. Includes 5 under Federal control.
3. Includes 7 under Federal control.

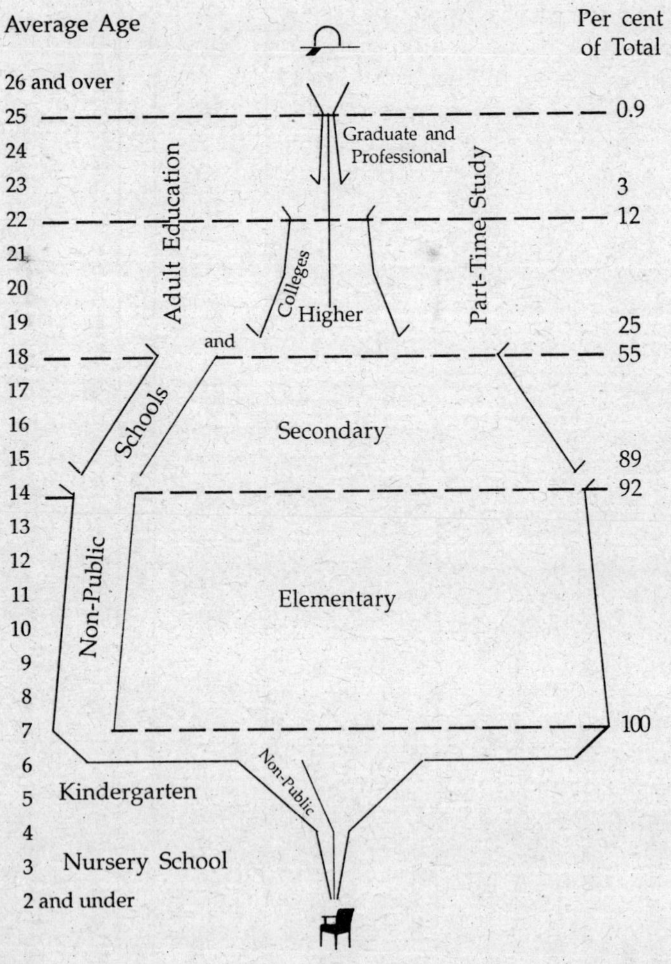

Figure 8.1 : Per cent of Persons by Age in Attendance in All Schools and Colleges and in Non-Public Educational Institutions, 1951-1952.

publicly administered, as shown in Table 8.1 the latter enrol approximately 51 per cent of the students. There appears a very gradual but persistent tendency for publicly controlled institutions to absorb a larger proportion of the increasing enrolment in higher education.

The emphasis upon the retention of the right of the individual to choose the type of school he wishes to attend is clearly indicated in the above account. From early colonial times, when education was provided primarily through the initiative of church bodies and of individuals, to the present, we have retained a dual system of education, part publicly controlled and part privately controlled. In fact, it might better be described as a triple system for the privately controlled schools and colleges are of two types : those that are related to a religious denomination and those that are independent institutions of education including both those operating on a non-profit basis and those that are operated for profit.

Each type of institution has made and is continuing to make a significant contribution to our national life. The proportion of elementary school pupils in private schools has increased from 7.2 per cent in 1900 to 12.2 per cent in 1950. At the secondary level the proportion has declined during the same period from 17.6 per cent to 10.6 per cent. However, this trend was reversed during the decade 1939-40 to 1940-50. The relative importance of private schools in the total educational system is shown in Figure 8.1.

But even more important than numbers is the fundamental principle that every parent has the right to choose the type of institution he desires for the education of his child and that the maturing individual has the same freedom for himself in the selection of his college.

The Education of Women

The education of girls and women even more concretely illustrates the development of schools to meet changing needs. Throughout the Colonial period and until the middle of the last century, girls attended the elementary schools, but only a very small proportion went beyond the eighth grade. Daughters of well-to-do parents were sent to finishing schools, under either private or church control. These Female Seminaries gave instruction in literature, art, music, and conduct, but not in subjects of practical value in homemaking, and curricula did not have an employment objective. As the public high school developed on a co-educational basis, the number of girls who went on into secondary schools rapidly increased, and for the past 50 years has equaled or exceeded their brothers in number.

By 1825, agitation to provide higher education for young women had begun, but of the 61 colleges established by 1834, not one, as Daniel Chandler stated, "was dedicated to the cause of female education." During the quarter century from 1850 to 1875, much of the battle for higher education of women had been won. Auburn Female Seminary was moved in 1855 and became the Elmira Female College and granted its first baccalaureate degrees in 1859. Other female seminaries became colleges, and new institutions were established : Vassar, 1861; Wells, 1870; Smith and Wellesley, 1875. State universities had almost from the first been co-educational, thus accounting for the development of women's colleges in the East but few in other sections of the country. The following statement, made as late as 1871, however, suggests the attitude still held by many people : "If females persist in attempting to endure the rigour of hard study, hospitals and asylums must need be erected alongside of colleges for women. The training provided for girls in our common schools even largely incapacitates them for the duties and the joys of their natural future and without raising either their character or their intelligence. .. It is a mistake full of unreason and fruitful of sorrow."

How surprised the author of this statement would be if he could return to any one of the 279 colleges for women, the 1,186 co-educational institutions, or to the high schools and vocational schools and find women competing on an equal basis with men in courses varying from welding to Oriental literature. Or if he could have watched the procession of 558,050 girls (505,394 boys) receiving their high school diplomas in 1949-50 and the 103,217 young women (328,841 men) being given their first college degrees, 16,963 (41,220 men) their master's degree and 643 (5,990 men) their doctorates.

With some exceptions, professional schools tended to resist the admission of women students longer than other schools within the university. In the field of medicine the Womans Medical College of Pennsylvania was established in 1850, because of the inability of women to gain admission to medical schools. Today, however, there is little if any discrimination.

Although there are many factors which influence school

and college attendance, it is significant that though there is a considerably larger number of girls than boys who graduate from high school, the proportion is reversed in the numbers attending college. In 1889 the ratio was two men to one women; by : 1939-40 women's enrolment had risen only to approximately 40 per cent of the total. During World War II the numbers were approximately equal, but as a result of the large number of veterans enrolled women comprised but 30.8 per cent of college enrolment in 1949-50; in 1952-53 it was 35.5 per cent. Perhaps even more significant is the fact that of the total bachelor's degree awarded in June, 1950, women received approximately 25 per cent; of master's, 29 per cent; and of doctor's only 9.7 per cent.

During 1952 the American Council on Education convened a national conference to appraise the education of women in the light of the changing needs of modern society. Following the conference a comprehensive study was initiated by the Council.

Trends in Control and Support of Education

The principle of shared responsibility among the levels of government and between government and voluntary organizations is clearly evidenced in the control of education. Basically education is controlled by the citizens of the community through its lay school board. In 1949-50 there were 85,000 separate administrative units, each responsible for the major aspects of education within its jurisdiction, from a one-room rural school to a great metropolis like Chicago or New York City. In a few states, the country is the ultimate administrative unit.

The local board of education shares certain of the responsibilities with the State Government, primarily in the interest of maintaining uniform minimum standards throughout the state. The minimum and maximum age of required school attendance is established by state law. Minimum requirements for teaching certificates and the minimum number of days schools must be in session are set by the state. In many states, the State Department of Education prepares the list of approved textbooks from which schools may select and, in a few states, there is state-wide adoption of textbooks. Likewise a few states provide state-wide examinations of educational achievement. Beyond these few specific areas, there is wide variation in the extent of state control of education. The role of the Federal government will be discussed later in this chapter.

The same basic principle of shard responsibility applies also to the support of education. The increased cost of education is due not only to the expanding enrolment previously described but also to three other factors. One is the decrease in the purchasing power of the dollar. Increased cost is caused in part by higher prices, but, even more, by the need for higher salaries to provide adequate financial incentive for an increasing number of young people to enter teaching. Another is the continually expanding function of education. The modern school require plant, equipment, and personnel to provide for the health care of its children, their recreational and leisure-time interests, guidance and counselling, and concern for moral and spiritual values. The third factor is the news type of instructional material—audio-visual aids and laboratory equipment—continually to improve the teaching process.

The Board also develops programmes based on Memoranda of Agreement rather than contracts. Participating institutions jointly plan graduate and professional work in order to have complementary specialities within a total regional programme and to avoid unnecessary duplication. Memoranda of Agreement have been executed in forestry, pulp and paper, city planning, marine sciences, and petroleum sciences. In addition, the Board appoints committees and commissions to conduct research on educational needs and resources of the region and sponsors various short-term projects, such as its recent Southern Regional Conference on Educational Television.

Groups of states in the West and in New England are initiating similar regional planning and co-operation. The Western group intends to establish administrative offices in Salt Lake City, Utah, in the summer of 1953. By careful planning, unnecessary duplication of facilities in professional and graduate education can be prevented and the quality of existing facilities can be strengthened.

As previously indicated, public schools and colleges were established to provide free access to education for all able to profit from it. States established teachers colleges, universities and landgrant institutions. Many cities and some counties extended their educational system through junior college and municipal universities.

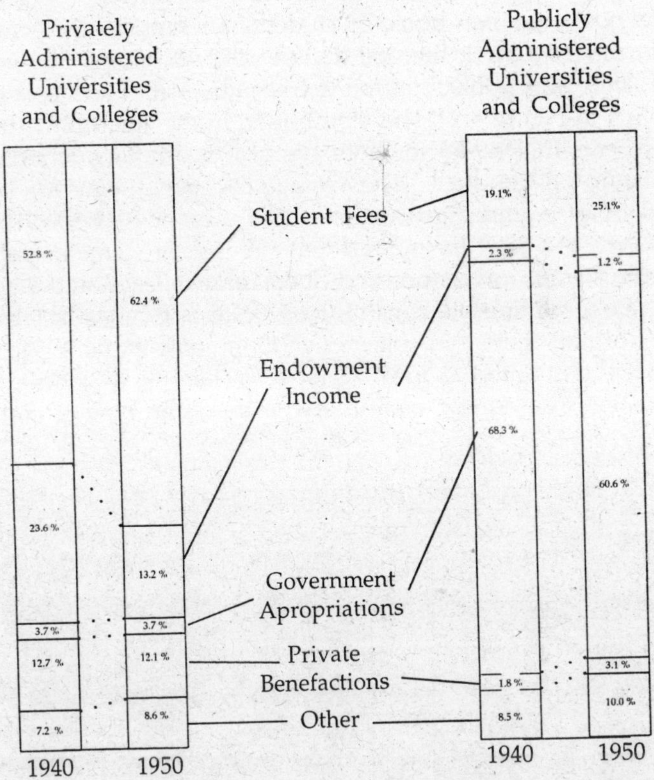

Figure 8.2 : Sources of Income for Higher Educational Institutions, 1939-1940 and 1949-1950. (Data for 1939-1940 from *Report from the Committee on Educaiton, U.S. House of Representatives,* "Effect of Certain War Activities upon Colleges and Universities." Washington, D.C.: U.S. Government Printing Office, 1945. Data for 1949-1950 from Richard H. Ostheimer, *Student Charges and Financing Higher Education*, page 12. Published for the Commission on Financing Higher Education, New York: Columbia University Press. 1953.

Within the past three decades and especially since 1945, a reverse trend has been evident that may have serious effect upon college and university enrolment. This trend is the decreasing degree to which public education, and especially public higher education, continues to be free. The proportion of total operating costs borne by students has consistently increased. The change during the one decade 1939-40 to 1949-50 for both privately and publicly administered universities and colleges is shown in Figure 8.2. The distribution in the amount of student payments in 1949-50 for both types of institutions is indicated in Figures 8.3 and 8.4. The average cost per student for tuition and other required instructional fees was, in 1949-50, $123 for resident and $279 for nonresident full-time students in publicly administered universities and liberal arts colleges; and $392 for privately administered institutions. The last varies in terms of type of university and college : $540 in nonsectarian institution; $362, Protestant; and $337, Catholic. There is, of course, wide variation also among institutions of the same type of control.

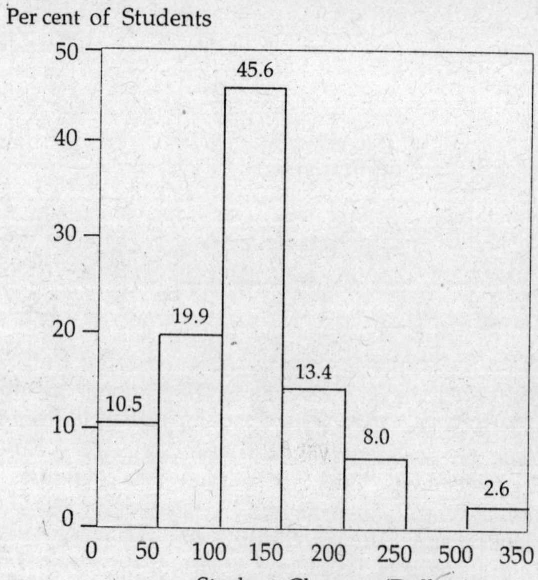

Figure 8.3 : Resident Student Charges (tuition and other required instructional fees) Paid by Full-Time Students in 101 Public Universities and Liberal Arts Colleges, 1950.

A study made during the academic year 1952-53 even more significantly points up the increasing costs of higher education to the student. A total of 358 accredited four-year colleges and universities were included in the survey; the results are shown graphically in Figure 8.5. Of the 160 publicly controlled institutions 123 had increased the student fees during the decade 1942-43 to 1952-53. The range of increase was from 1.3 per cent to 487 per cent with an average of approximately 65 per cent; 129 made a still further increase for 1953-54 averaging 19 per cent. Non-resident fees were increased even

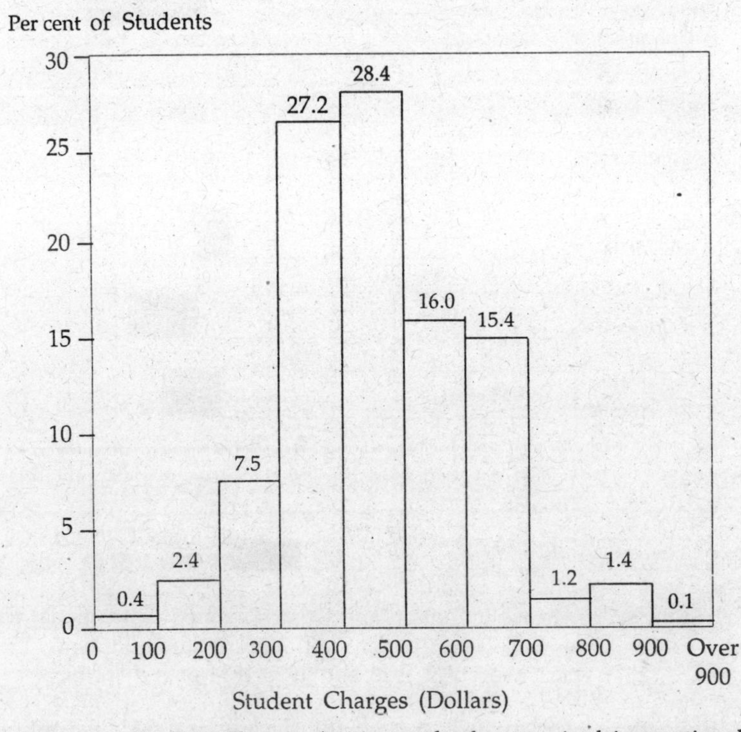

Figure 8.4 : Student Charges (tuition and other required instructional fees Paid by Full-Time Students in 473 Private Universities and Liberal Arts Colleges, 1950. (Reproduced by permission from Richard H. Ostheimer, *Students Charges and Financing Higher Education*, pp. 30-31, published for the Commission on Financing Higher Education. New York : Columbia University Press, 1953).

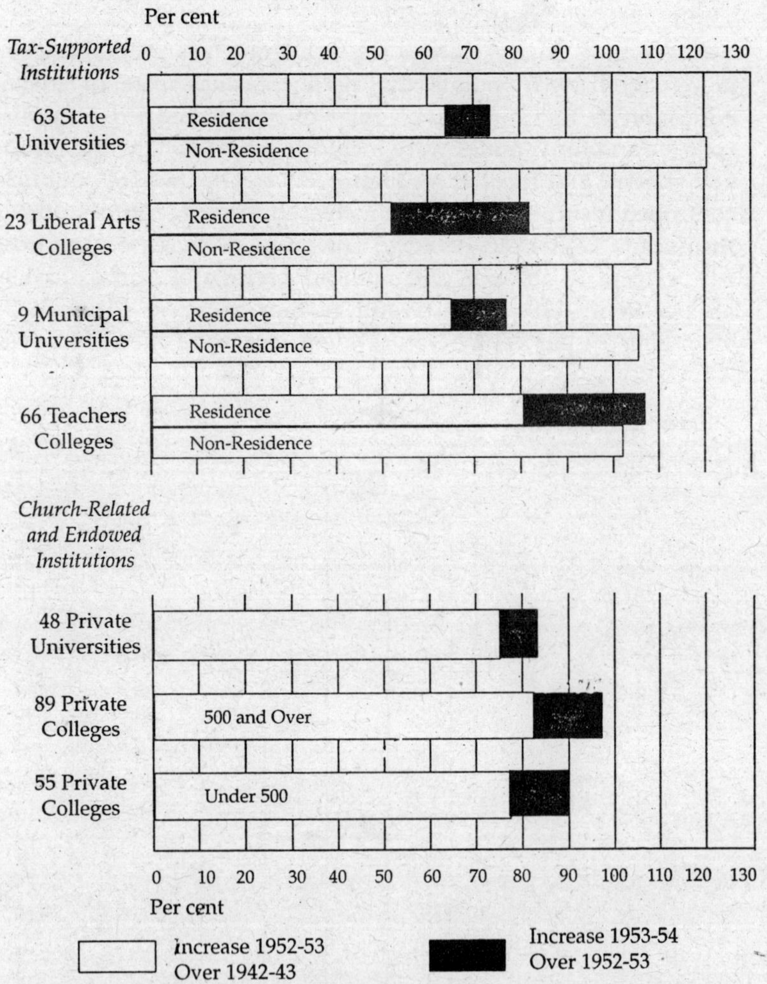

Figure 8.5 : Increase in Tuition and Other Required Instructional Fees for Full-Time Resident and Non-Resident Students, 1952-1953 over 1942-1943 and 1953-1954 over 1952-1953.

more than resident fees during the decade and 131 institutions increased their fees again in 1953-54 for non-resident students though the amount of the increase was not included in the survey.

Of the 198 private institutions, all but four had increased tuition and other instructional charged during the decade; the range was from 6.9 per cent to 300 per cent, the average 78 per cent; nearly half, 85, added a further increase in 1953-54 averaging approximately 12 per cent.

The increase is forcefully demonstrated in the changes in tuition and required instructional fees of one large state university, which is typical. In 1918-19 a student who was a resident of the state paid a total of $20 an academic year for tuition and by signing a statement that his parents were unable to pay, even this was waived; students from outside of the state paid a non-residence fee of $50 per academic year. In the 1953-54 catalogue the tuition and required instructional fees of a resident of the state is $130 a year and of a nonresident, $300. Thus, it may well be that the equalization of opportunity, at least at the higher education level, has reached its peak unless some means can be found to reverse the present rising cost to the student. Work opportunities, institutional and state scholarships, and the GI Bill are ameliorating factors, but may prove inadequate. The President's Commission on Higher Education in 1947 proposed a national system of scholarships based on ability and financial need but this proposal has not been enacted into law. Municipal institutions and teachers colleges have resisted the rise in student fees more successfully than state and land-grant colleges and universities. The rapid expansion in both number and size of municipal community colleges, also recommended by the President's Commission, is a significant effort to retain the concept of free higher education easily accessible to able students.

Much of what has been said above about public education is applicable also to private education. Although privately controlled schools and colleges have the right to restrict enrolment to children and young people who accept the specific purposes of the institution, all have shared in the expansion of educational opportunity. Likewise, there has been a tendency for greater co-operation both among private institutions and between public and private schools and colleges. They have sought, especially at the higher education level, to broaden the base of their support by joint appeals to industry. More than half of the states now have a state organization of higher education, often, however, not including all private colleges.

Both in per cent and in dollars private institutions at all levels, and again especially of higher education, have increased their tuition and required instructional fees. This increase raises very serious problems as to the point at which such institutions may price themselves out of the market for students, especially if the currently expanding economy goes into reverse.

There is also the issue as to the extent to which private education at all levels should be entirely autonomous or subject to minimum requirements established by the state in which it is located. Shyster trade schools and diploma mills do exits in states in which the only control is the initial granting of the charter. On the other hand, too rigid control will defeat the basic purpose in retaining our dual system. The general practice and perhaps the safe middle ground, is to be assured that private institutions meet at least minimum standards established by the state. This is not a problem in established denominational and non-church-related schools and colleges; it is a problem in relation to some other types of institutions.

The Role of the Federal Government

The interest of the Federal government in the education of its children and young people did not await the establishment of the Office of Education in 1867, then the Bureau of Education. Reference has already been made to the Ordinance of 1787; as new states were admitted, public lands were set aside for education and in some instances direct grants were made. Specific grants were made by the Congress very early in out history to several private colleges. The Morrell Act of 1862 and subsequent legislation established the principal of Federal aid for specialized types of education, a principle that has been extended to vocational education, of the physically handicapped, and many more.

Contrary to popular opinion, there is no fixed policy of granting Federal financial assistance to public schools and colleges only. School lunches are available to children without regard to the type of school they attend. During the expansion of higher education to provide for veterans, the Federal government spent approximately $360,000,000 to put temporary building on the campuses of both privately and publicly controlled institutions. Federal scholarships and fellowships are available to students regardless of the type of control of the school in which they enroll. Conversely, aid for vocational education and financial assistance in construction and operation of schools in federally impacted areas, such as those in which military establishments or Federal research plants are constructed, are illustrations of grants-in-aid restricted to public educational institutions.

The vast extent of Federal support of education is indicated by the fact that during the school year 1950-51, a total of $2,550,642,812.95 of Federal funds was allotted to the states for education. An additional $350,000,000 was obligated by the Department of Defense for Federal educational programmes.

One of the most significant and the most extensive scholarship programmes ever made available by any governments is that for veterans of World War II and those of the Korean conflict. Under Public Laws 16 for disable veterans and 346 for those not disabled, a total of more than 8,000,000 of the 14,000,000 eligible veterans took advantage of the education and training provided under the Acts. Of this number 41 per cent were enrolled in institutions of higher education, 29 per cent in institutions below college grade, 19 per cent in on-the-job training courses and 11 per cent in on-farm training. Through June 30, 1953, the Federal government had invested more than $15,000,000 in this scholarship programme which will continue in decreasing amount to 1956.

Public Law 16 has now been indefinitely extended and in 1952 the Congress enacted P.L. 550 providing similar educational opportunities, but with lesser payments, to veterans who had served attractive duty in the armed forces since June, 1950. It is estimated that when this programmes rashes its maximum, there will be approximately 750,000 veterans in education and training each year until the Congress or the President declares the termination of the present emergency. Of this number, some 300,000 will be in college.

Further activities of the Federal government in education are illustrated by the educational programmes of the Department of Defense, exclusive of the military training programmes. In March, 1953, approximately 365,000 students in college were in the Reserve Offices' Training Corps of the Army, Navy, and Air

Force. In 1951-52, more than $7,000,000 was spent for the education of military personnel in other than R.O.T.C. programmes in civilian educational institutions. In addition, the United States Armed Forces Institute has provided correspondence courses in which the 2,000,000th student enrolled in June, 1952, and through contracts with civilian organizations, provided funds for the accreditation of military experience and the evaluation of educational attainment while in service through the General Educational Development Tests. It is estimated that more than 1,250,000 veterans have thus earned a secondary school diploma without returning to high school and at least half as many have gained advanced standing in college as a result of these programmes. It is impossible to estimate the saving in man-years to the veteran and in funds to the taxpayers by permitting students to continue their education in terms of what they have achieved rather than from the point where their formal education was interrupted by military service.

One other illustration of the Federal government's interest in education is the provision of student deferment. The National Defense Act of 1950 specifically provides that a student in high school cannot be inducted through Selective Service until he has completed high school or reached the age of twenty, whichever is earlier. Likewise, a college student may not be inducted during the school year in which he receives his first order for induction. The Act also permits the deferment of selected students enrolled in college and university until they have completed their education, in order that they may be of greater usefulness when they enter military service and upon their later return to civilian life. In March, 1954, 185,000 students in college were postponing military service as a result of the Federal government's policy of student deferment, in addition to those in R.O.T.C.

Although legislation to provide general Federal aid to education has been introduced into every session of Congress for more than three decades, it has not been enacted into low. It is a logical extension of the principle of equalizing educational opportunity through the expansion of the tax unit to include the entire United States. Although the gap between the expenditure by states per school child is narrowing, in 1949-50 New York spent $295.02 per child in average daily attendance in public elementary and secondary schools and Mississippi spent $79.69—approximately one fourth as much. Yet Mississippi invested a higher proportion of its state income in education than did New York. The accident of birth or residence still determines the effectiveness of a child's education.

Two basic issues, both a reflection of our culture, have thus far prevented the enactment of this legislation. One is the extent to which the general support of education is a responsibility of the Federal government as related to the principle of states' rights. The other is whether such general financial aid should be available to both public and private schools or restricted to public schools, an issue sharpened by the principle of separation of Church and State.

In spite of the vast Federal funds invested in education and the concern of the Federal government for educating the youth and in spite of the trend toward state-wide financing of public elementary and secondary education, American education has remained essentially a local school system. The old adage "He who pays the fiddler calls the tunes" has not characterized education. The Office of Education serves in an advisory capacity only; it cannot dictated to education; there is no Ministry of Education. Private and church-related schools have received special types of aid but have remained free and autonomous. America has retained the principle that the control of education must remain in the hands of state and local communities and that the individual has the right to select the type of education which he desires for himself and his children. This is a democratic concept which developed out of our culture, resisted adopting the nationalism of European countries and is almost unparalleled among the nations of the world. No nation has taken so literally its own ideal of education. Never has a nation sought so earnestly to provide free education from the kindergarten through the graduated and professional school. Never has any country left education as free from state and Federal control or translated into a system of schools and colleges its faith in education as the means through which the state can achieve its objective of a free people in a free nation.

Voluntary Organizations

Equally unique and equally indigenous to our culture is

the rise and increasing significance of voluntary organizations in almost every field of human interest. They arise from at least two basic factors: the resistance to government control, however benevolent; and the individualism which inspires local initiative.

In education, there is hardly a field of specialized interest that does not have one or more national organizations: classroom teachers, supervisors, principals of each of the different types and levels of schools, curriculum specialists, teachers of each subject, parents, university professors, college and university presidents, members of boards of trustees, and many more. There are also a hundred or more organizations, not of persons, but of institutions: independent schools, church-related institutions of many of the denominations, liberal arts colleges, land-grant colleges and universities, and others. Many of these national organizations have state and local branches. In addition, there is scarcely a city or village that does not also have one or many local organizations interested in education at the community level.

Sometimes these organizations work at cross-purposes. A few which appear to champion education and whose names would indicate this as their purpose, actually work against the interests of education and use the organization to advance their own interests or to promote their own conception of education. But on balance, the voluntary educational organizations exert a powerful and instructive force in the further advancement of education.

Three voluntary organizations which illustrate differing types of service to education are : the voluntary accrediting associations, the American Council on Education, and the National Education Association.

Voluntary Accrediting Organizations : Accrediting associations arose to develop and maintain educational standards within the particular geographic area or type of institution each serves. They are independent of government, though in an number of the professional fields which require licenses and approval of schools for veteran education, state governments and Federal agencies may accept the lists of institutions drawn up by the accrediting agencies. But the significant fact is that through their own organizations the institutions themselves, rather than the government, establish the standards for evaluation. They do not, however, include public elementary education nor all of public secondary education which are controlled, as previously stated, by the local school board supplemented by the state departments of education. Private elementary and, to some degree, secondary education lies outside the present surveillance of the regional accrediting groups.

Accrediting Organizations are of Two Major Types: Those which accredit the institution as a whole, such as the North Central Association of Colleges and Secondary Schools, and the five other regional organizations; and those which accredit only the professional schools in its field such as medicine, nursing, law, and business administration. In an effort to develop closer co-operation between the two types of accrediting agencies, the National Commission on Accreditation was established in 1950. The present trend is toward strengthening the regional associations though the professional organizations will continue to have an important role, through co-operation with the regional associations, in establishing standards and in evaluations the effectiveness of the education in its field of specialization.

American Council on Education: The second type of educational organization, those whose members are institutions or other organizations, is illustrated by the American Council on Education. Its membership on March 1, 1954, was 144 national or regional organizations and 945 educational institutions, of which 838 were accredited colleges and universities.

Its Purpose is Stated in its Constitution: "The general object of the Council, and the purpose of membership therein, shall be to advance American education in any or all of its phases through comprehensive, voluntary, co-operative action on the part of educational associations, organizations, and institutions and in the fulfilment of that purpose to initiate, promote, and carry out such, systematic studies, co-operative experiments, conferences, and other similar enterprises as may be required for the public welfare and approved by the Council or the Executive Committee. The Council was organized to meet national needs in time of war and will always seek to render patriotic service. It will also encourage international co-operation in educational matters."

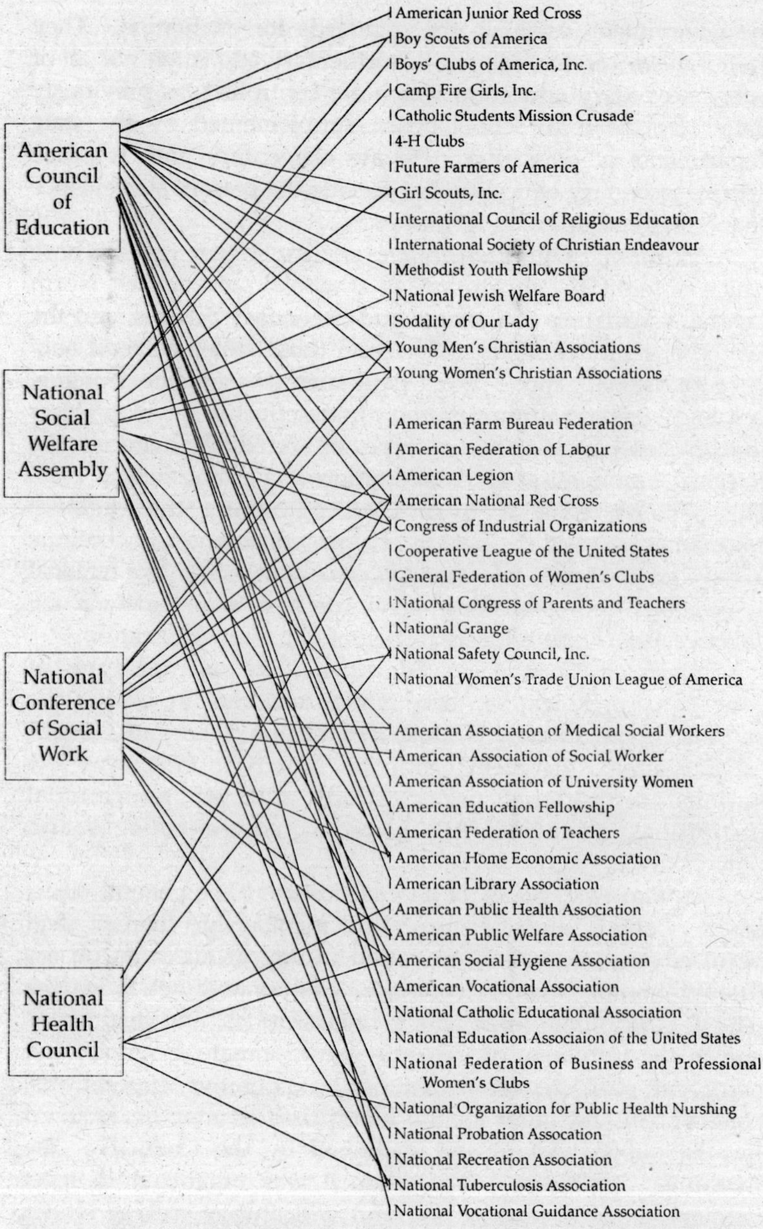

Figure 8.6 : Forty-Five National Youth-Serving Organizations and Their Affiliations with Four National Co-ordinating Bodies. (From Chambers, M.M., *Youth Serving Organizations*, page 8, Washington D.C.: American Council on Education, 1948).

Its activities include liaison, in matters of education, between government agencies and the institutions and organizations; research; national conferences; and publication. They are carried on through a central staff of approximately forty persons and some thirty committees and commissions. Some of the major recent projects include educational television, religion and education, international cultural relations, equalizing opportunities in higher education, institutional finance, intergroup education, and improvement of college teaching.

National Education Association: The third type of voluntary organization is that whose members are individuals. The National Education Association illustrates this kind of educational organization. By June 30, 1953, its membership had just passed the half-million mark, the great majority of whom were teachers and administrators in public schools. Its primary purpose is to improve the profession of teaching at all levels through its national, state, and local organizations. The various levels and fields of interest with the total structure are represented in separate departments. In a few instances autonomous but affiliated organizations represent their own special interests; such are the National Association of Secondary School Principals, the American Association of School Administrators, and the Association for Higher Education.

The headquarters in Washington, D.C., has a staff of more than 500 persons. There are also state and some local NEA offices. Its activities include national, regional and state conferences; research; publication; and direct contacts with public interest groups and with state and Federal governmental agencies.

It would appear from the above analysis that the total pattern of voluntary organizations is relatively simple. This is by no means true. A school system or a college may belong to more than twenty separate organization and, in addition, the individual members of its staff may be members of as many and more organizations with personal membership. The intergroup relationships are even more complicated by the fact that the interests of organizations, institutions, and individuals often extend into filed other than education. Something of the complexity of organizational structure is shown Figure 8.6. In commenting on this chart, M.M. Chambers states:

> Let no one be unaware of the fact that the picture at this level is literally chopped from the context on either hand. Developments in international organization are of extreme interest and import and are now in a particularly fertile stage. ... At the other side, the reason for being and the lifeblood of national voluntary associations is in what they can accomplish for good "at the grass roots" in local communities where their activities tough and influence the lives of the youth of the land. It is there that the problems of young people are met at first hand, and there that the need exists for a constant inflow of information which will keep the community and its young people aware of the changing scene at the national level and will stimulate them to assess and utilize their own local and individual resources to best advantage.

It should not be implied that voluntary organizations operate without regard to governmental agencies. While independent of government, they frequently work in close co-operation with government at the Federal, state, and local levels. The Mid-century Whitehouse Conference of Children and Youth was convened and partly supported by the Federal government and participated in by 33 work groups and more than a thousand delegates representing hundreds of national and state voluntary organizations. State Commissions on Children and Youth such as those in Ohio and New York work very closely with the schools, churches, and other institutions. Minneapolis, Chicago, and many more cities and other local governments have appointed Commissions and Mayor's Committees which co-operate with the schools on a community-wide basis.

Unresolved Issues

Education faces many issues in its relation to culture. Some have been previously mentioned. It needs increasingly to determine cultural goals and the best means of achieving them. It should recognize that science, technology, and materialism are amoral; they may be used for the improvement of human welfare or for man's own self-annihilating. It is the human element that will determine the choice; education must discover and utilize the ways through which a sense of values is developed. The following statement, though overcritical in its generalizations, is worthy of serious consideration:

> The schools flag far behind the march of events. Although the service they render in their present form is indispensable to the functioning of our society, they fall well below the requirements of the age. In their programmes they reveal little grasp of the character of industrial civilization, except in its more superficial aspects. They teach the findings of science, but fail to instill the spirit of science or to convey an understanding of what science is doing to the world and human institutions. They transmit the words of the tradition of human freedom, but fail to arouse concern or to apply old meanings to new conditions. They encourage the development of egoistic and competitive impulses suited perhaps to the society of yesterday, but fail to foster effectively the social and co-operative tendencies, the devotion to the general welfare necessary for successful living in the society of today. They do a magnificent job in preparing for war when the occasion demand it, but they have yet to formulate a bold and imaginative programme to build a peaceful world. They have vast potentialities that remain undeveloped. They lack a generous and realistic conception of their task. They are without vision.

Nor has education fully achieved its own goal of equality of opportunity. In many rural areas, children cannot procure an education equivalent to that provided for the majority of urban children. Race still is a discriminatory factor. The differential between opportunities for white and Negro children is narrowing and education is to be commanded on the progress made. In 1854 George Fitzhugh in his Sociology for the South made his impassioned plea of the education of poor whites on the following basis:

> Educate all Southern whites, employ them, not as cooks, lacqueys, ploughmen and menials, but as independent freemen should be employed and let Negroes be strictly tied down to such callings as are unbecoming white men, and peace would be established between blacks and whites. The whites would find themselves elevated by the existence

> of Negroes amongst us. Like the Roman citizen, the Southern white man would become a noble and privileged character, and he would then like Negroes and slavery, because his high position would be due to them.

What a long way we have come in a century and at a positively accelerated rate! Within states which have maintained separate school systems many publicly controlled institutions and a number of privately controlled colleges and universities are now admitting Negroes, especially to their graduate schools. But there is still a long way to go. There was a time when the educational opportunity provided for majority groups was our own affair; today it has international significance in the world-wide struggle of democracy and communism.

In the field of higher education there is the basic issue as to the degree to which colleges and universities should select only students of high ability or should accept responsibility for all for whom further education may be in the national interest.

Equality of opportunity requires also physical facilities, staff, and instructional material. Additional floor space equal to a one-story building, 52 feet wide, extending from New York City to San Francisco, is needed to house adequately the nation's elementary and secondary school population. More than 160,000 new teachers will be required each year to meet the demands of a school enrolment now increasing at the rate of over 1,600,000 annually. Yet the American people are investing only approximately three fourths as high a proportion of the national income for education as in 1940!

Many needs can be postponed but those of education cannot safely be delayed. Failing to meet them even for a few years will leave an irreparable gap in the education of those who will shortly face future issues that may well be more portentous than those of the present.

Summary

Even so brief a resume of the development of the school as that presented above clearly indicates the close interrelationship of education and culture. Whether among primitive groups or in modern America, the school, on the one hand, reflects the cultural values of those who maintain it; and, on the other, seeks to instill those qualities of personality which make for the progressive adaptability of culture to new situations.

The relative emphasis of these two seemingly conflicting relationships between culture and education varies with the group. In a group characterized by relative homogeneity and cultural isolation, as among primitives or the Indian groups previously described, culture is predominant and remains virtually unchanged through the centuries. In modern society, with its heterogeneity and its culture contacts, education assumes increasing importance.

The rapid and unparalleled increase in enrolment in American schools is itself a reflection of culture. Inherent in democracy is the right and responsibility of each individual to express judgment on local and national issues, both directly and through elected representatives. Such a concept entails a need for the greatest possible education for the largest possible number. As the spheres in which such judgment have multiplied and become more varied, education has increased both in the numbers it has served and in the breadth of its programme.

But the interrelationship of culture and education is shown not only in the over-all picture : it is equally evident in the state or community. To a considerable degree, the development of education reflects the degree of cultural isolation. A rural community that even yet is fairly autonomous in its social structure is content to continue the type of traditional education which the adults themselves were given; it is lax in its enforcement of compulsory attendance laws; and teachers are poorly paid. In contrast, a rural community rich in its social contacts insists that its school provide the kind and quality of education which will assist its youth to face the complex problems of the modern world.

Cultural isolation is not the only factor, other than economic, which influences the development of education. Basic attitudes play an important role, as is illustrated by the failure of many communities, especially in the deep South, to provide equal educational opportunities to Negro children. One northern community, however, shifted the zoning of its school districts with sufficient frequency to keep the Negroes registered in the older, poorly equipped schools. In contrast are the communities, even those in which a dual educational system is maintained, in which education opportunities are the same for all children.

World War II changed many of our cultural patterns; it broke down the last vestige of isolation in many American communities and weakened isolation sentiment in others. Even if the Federal government had not passed legislation providing education for all veterans, there would have been an expansion of education similar to, if not greater than, that which followed World War I. This expansion is not only in numbers, but in scope and content of the subject matter and activities of the school. In an age of atomic energy, with speed of travel faster than sound, and with the spoken word communicated to all the world almost instantaneously, the demands upon the school are many times those which prevailed even a decade ago.

The school reflects the culture of the community or the nation, but it is also a major force in changing the cultural pattern. In its choice of content and relative emphasis upon selected values, the school is both limiting and directing the learning of children and youth; in its policies and procedures it is shaping the attitudes in both the less fundamental and the basic concepts of human relations. By providing the fundamental background of knowledge and by developing resourcefulness and initiative in the individual, the school provides the basis for further advancing the boundaries of understating of both the physical and the cultural world.

9

The School: The Development of In-Group Relationships

Holding-power of the school. Reappraisal of goals. Development of the in-group. The role of the teacher.

Approximately one in four of the total population of the United States is engaged full time in some phase of education; 29,000,000 in elementary schools; 7,500,000 in secondary schools, 2,250,000 in colleges and universities; and 1,250,000 in teaching and administrative positions. Perhaps an equal number is engaged in some form of part time education. This fact places the school in a strategic position as an agency for social control; it is the only agency established by society devoted exclusively to this end. The school occupies more working time of a larger proportion of children and youth than any other institution, including the average family; its teachers are more specifically trained to perform their tasks than are the great majority of parents. School administrators and teachers have a great degree of freedom to direct the operation of the processes of social interaction within the school to achieve almost limitless social goals.

Holding-power of the School

Yet this fact and the more detailed analysis of the expansion of our educational system must be paralleled by data that should be a serious concern to all interested in the education of children and youth. Figure 9.1 presents these data graphically. Out of every 1,000 children in the fifth grade in 1943, 847 finished the eighth grade, 807 entered high school and only 505 graduated. Of these, only 202 entered college and a little more than half of those who entered, 111, will graduate in June, 1954.

These drop-outs are not statistics, but children.

There are many reasons for school mortality. The differences in abilities of individuals to profit from the higher levels of education is important not only to the individual but to society's further investment in his education. But all too frequently such differences are used a rationalization for selectivity rather than as a challenge to adaptation to meet such abilities.

The economic factor is important among the many reasons why the school has failed to hold a higher proportion of children and young people for more years. More than half of the men queried while in the armed forces during World War II listed "had to go to work" or "had to held at home" as their reason for quitting school. The third reason for not going onto College was "no school near home." An interview study conducted in Louisville, Kentucky, of 440 young people who had dropped out of school before graduation from high school showed that 19.4 per cent had left because of economic need but 47.7 per cent gave dissatisfaction with school as the major factor. Another 11.7 per cent gave "lure of a job" as the reason, but this might well be included with school dissatisfaction as the job appeared more attractive than further education.

These same replies would indicate, if worded differently, that the basic factors involved were low family income, the failure on the part of the school to challenge the interest of the children or their parents, and inadequate school facilities. Certainly if America is to achieve its goal of equality of educational opportunity, and, for all, a minimum education which some would place at the level of completion of the first two years of college, schools and colleges must continually reappraise their goals, internal organization, teacher training, the curriculum, and the relation of the school to the community which it serves.

Figure 9.1 : Undeveloped Human Resources. (Reproduced with permission from *The Growing Challenge*, p. 9. Washington, D.C.: Education Department, U.S. Chamber of Commerce, 1952).

Reappraisal of Goals

Education is not static. It could not be in a dynamic society. Although in each generation there are those who look back to the "good-old days" and decry the passing of the "little red schoolhouse" and the failure to teach the "Three R's" as they presumably learned them, education has continually sought to meet better the needs of the changing world. In its effort to shake off the dead hand of the past education has sometimes gone to extremes, but there is always the striving to find the way that will be in the best interest both of the individual and of society. Neither can be considered independently of the other.

Education as Learning

A basic characteristic of institutional procedures is that those which are introduced to meet an imperative need in one generation become formalized in the next. The school has not escaped the operation of this process. The newer methods of teaching developed in the seventeenth century were soon crystallized and developed into a formal system of memorization and repetition. This emphasis reached its extreme in the

Lancastrian system, developed first in England, and brought to the United States in the early 1800's.

The Lancastrian system was based on the use of monitors. The pupils were divided into groups, usually of 10, with a selected student in charge of each group. The ideal seating arrangement was in vertical rows, each row constituting a group. The teacher taught a lesson to the monitors, then each, in turn, took his group to a "station" around the wall or in their row and taught the lesson to the others. The teacher called the group together, and the monitor checked the results of the instruction. In this member, one teacher was able to instruct several hundred pupils.

Many schools adopted the system, and North Carolina almost enacted it into the educational law of the state. By 1840, the system had virtually disappeared, but it left two heritages; the emphasis upon rote learning and the organization of the school into classes.

For another half century the emphasis upon rote learning dominated education. Recitations were but little more than reciting the lesson in the textbook, with major emphasis upon isolated facts. Periodic examinations measured the extent of the child's retention, and the pupils who had memorized the minimum required for promotion were moved up to the next higher grade, where the process was repeated over again.

In spite of powerful influences in the development of educational theory under such leaders of Pestalozzi, Herbert, and Froebel, abroad; and Horace Mann, Suzzallo, Parker, Dewey, and many more in the United States, too many children still repeat formal lessons and master skills unrelated either to the experience of the child or to the society in which he lives. The following excerpts from the stenographic report of a lesson in eighth grade citizenship are much too typical. It is all the more significant since the report was taken while post-war developments were creating new instruments of government and shifting the relationships among its major divisions.

> "Yesterday we learned that there were three major divisions of government. What are they, John? . . . That's right—the executive, the legislative, and the judicial. Can you tell me again the function of each, Mary? . . . You could if you

had paid attention yesterday. Sarah? . . . That's right. Our lesson yesterday was on the executive branch; today it is on the legislative.

"Harry, what is the legislative body called? . . . Good. Now, what are its two divisions? . . .

"What are the qualifications of a senator, George? . . . Is that all? You didn't study your lesson. Who can tell me? All right, Sarah. . . . Are the requirements for a representative the same as those for a senator, Jack? . . .

"Susan, are their terms of office that same? . . . Well, if they're different, what is each? . . . Then how do you know they aren't the same! Ralph? . . . Are there any kinds of legislation that must be initiated in either the House or Senate, Joe? . . . Does anybody know? Well, look it up and I'll ask that question again tomorrow.

"Clara, what the salary of a Congressman? . . . You say it is the same for both? Does the class agree? Are there any special privileges which a Congressman has, Florence? . . . It tells you on page 243 in you'd read your lesson.

"What is meant by a quorum? I didn't call on you, Ruby. Sarah, what is it? . . . If a bill passes in the House, for example, but does not pass in the Senate, does it become law? George? . . . Right. If it passes both House and Senate, is it law? . . . That's good, George. . . .

"That's all for today. For tomorrow study the section on the judiciary."

In the entire 40 minutes, there were no references to any of the far-reaching legislative proposals then before the Congress and which were being discussed in every newspaper. There was no discussion of the function of standing or special committee in which the real responsibility for preparing legislation rests nor mention of the role of pressure groups. No reference was made to the role of investigating committees of the Congress nor to the shifts that occur with changes in the majority of political parties. The entire time was given to question and answer on facts as though they had no bearing at all upon the lives of those who memorized them.

Learning is an essential aspect of education, but to be of value, such learning must be in terms of the inter-relatedness of human knowledge and in terms, too, of the lives of those who learn and the society in which they live. This does not mean that learning must be of immediate value, for it may lead also to appreciations and long-range values.

Education as Self-expression

Beginning as a revolt against the formal character of traditional education and growing out of the increasing number of studies of childhood, the pendulum of educational theory swung to the other extreme. By the 1920's, educational literature for parents and teachers contained constant reference to such terms is "self-development" and "child-centered."

Although seldom recognizing the source of the theory in the individualism of the French Revolution and, more specifically, in Rousseau's *Emile,* the exponents of progressivism ignored his Social Contract and accepted only his dictum that "everything is good as it comes from the hand of the Creator and deteriorates in the hands of man." "The very words 'obey' and 'command' will be excluded from his vocabulary, still more those of 'duty' and 'obligation'." Thus, the best education is that which gives the child the most complete opportunity for self-expression. Supported by a current school of psychology that raised the fearful sector of inhibitions, frustrations, and complexes, parents were admonished that they should never say "no" to a child, that they must provide only natural consequences of the child's acts, and that alternative choices must be provided, rather than direct commands.

Taking its touchstone from John Dewey's oft-quoted phrase, "I would have a child say not 'I know,' but, 'I have experienced,'' the so-called "new education" far outran the social emphasis so definitely included in his *Democracy and Education* and in his little masterpiece *School and Society,* first published in 1899. By lifting such sentences as the above out of their context, Dewey was made the revolutionary apostle of freedom for the child. The phrases and thoughts seized upon by his disciples were "spontaneous interests and intentions," "lift activities," "doing, not listening," "child development," "activity leading to further activity," and "Education is all one with growing; it has no end beyond itself."

The words were translated into educational practice. The intervening step was the "project method" developed by such leaders in education as Fred and Frank McMurray, Kilpatrick, and others. Projects might be planned and carried out by the group, such as building an Indian village on the sand table, making and operating a store, or an excursion to the park. The project might be, and in the upper grades frequently was, an individual undertaking solely directed by the child's own interest. In one school, for example, each class engaged in one major project each semester. The first term the children were little Indians; the second, medieval knights and ladies; later they became postmen and printers; in the eighth grade the school sought in one year to teach necessary knowledge and skills lest their students show too great gaps upon entering high school.

Perhaps the most extreme contrast between the "traditionalists" and the "progressivists" was that drawn by Rugg and Shumaker:

> Picture, then, children who cannot get to school early enough, and who linger about the shops, laboratories, yards, and libraries until dusk or urgent parents drag them homeward. Observe these busy and hard-working youngsters who seem to play all day, who do not seem to have lessons and recitations, yet who do not wait for teachers to make assignments.
>
> Here is a group of six and seven-year-olds. They dance; they sing; they play house and build villages; they keep store and take care of pets; they model in clay and sand; they draw and paint; read and write; make up stories and dramatize them; they work in the garden; they churn, and weave, and cook. . . . A breakless group is stocking a new aquarium to be sent to the third grade; while over in the corner white rabbits, mice, and guinea pigs—even a turtle—loll in well-attended ease.
>
> What a contrast between this picture of happy, purposeful living and that of the old school! . . . In that pattern, children are pigeonholed in long rows of desks, filed in stereotyped classrooms as alike as the cabinets in which the methodical principals preserve their records. Children must sit quietly, study their lessons silently, obey

> the teacher promptly and unquestioningly. Speech is only on permission, in well-mannered, subdued tones; and movement means marching in orderly rows, two abreast, at the signal for dismissal. . . .
>
> Small wonder that the indignant protagonist of the new school rebels against this regime which , says he, "reeks of restraint and suppression and the inarticulate child."

Both of the above descriptions are accurate of a few schools representing the worst of traditional education and the best of progressive education. But just as the latter was a revolt from the former, so there has been a revolt against the extreme of progressivism. Why should the child go through the slow and painful task of rediscovering through experience that which man has acquired through the centuries? In biological inheritance, each individual begins anew where his parents also began; in social inheritance, the person begins at the level of the culture into which he is born. No individual can exist in a social vacuum, and the self-expression of each is limited by the necessity of granting the same right to each other. Education is more than living and experiencing in childhood; it is also preparation for richer living and deeper experiencing in the complex world of the adult.

Across the years, the difference between progressive and traditional education has gradually broken down as progressive schools have recognized that fundamental social values must be instilled and traditional schools have reappraised their procedures and curricula in terms of the needs of the changing modern world. World War II influenced both types of schools—training for military effectiveness in the technology of modern war was both functional and disciplinary and recent developments have indicated a primary need for an understanding of human relations and the factors which influence inter-group behaviour.

These changes are well summarized by Ashburn: "Few adults now out of school for twenty years can grasp the revolution that has taken place in school teaching. Methods, texts subjects are different, and the end is not yet. Progressivism is embedded in America today. On the other hand, progressivism is itself quite different and chastened since its scudding days when theory was untrammelled by experience. The fine progressive schools have been tempered by practice and conflict, and the starry-eyed parent who still dreams of fitting a child for society by unlimited self-expression, who holds that sweetness and light are entirely adequate substitutions for hard work and thoroughness may have a difficult time finding a school dedicated to such pleasant and irresponsible theories. . . . The fact is that the good progressive schools today are remarkably conservative and the good conservative schools are remarkably progressive. They are still different, and that is a social good, but their points of difference are more marginal than central."

Development of the In-Group

One of the most significant developments since the close of World War II has been the increasing emphasis upon human relations and group dynamics. Many factors have stimulated the development but perhaps the most important has been the realization that man has discovered the means for his own annihilation and only a better understanding of interpersonal and inter-group relations, extending to the international level, can save man from himself.

In the development of this understanding, the school and the classroom provide a unique and as yet not fully realized opportunity. If the school is to make democracy a way of living rather than only a verbal concept, it must provide experiences which develop a sense of the mutual responsibility of the individual for the group and the group for the individual. This is the essence of in-group relationships.

The means through which awareness of group relations may be developed are many. Jennings states them as the warmth of the teacher, activities which permit a high degree of interaction, and the use of democratic methods. Giles presents a "blue-print" "of the practice of human relations through joint purpose, jointly arrived at through joint planning, joint work and joint evaluation." From the point of view of educational sociology, it is necessary to take a prior step, namely that of appraising the cultural differences of the members of the group.

Recognition of Individual Differences

Teachers have always recognized that students differ in ability and, for more than a quarter of a century, such differences have been subject to measurement through objective tests. Such measuares of ability, wisely and conservatively used, have been invaluable in assisting teachers in adapting instruction to the ability level of the child. Tests have been detrimental when used in discriminately and as a sole basis for the classifying and sectioning of children throughout a school. They have given, also, an attitude of determinism expressed by the child who said to a schoolmate, "You're a dumb bunny or you wouldn't be in 4B5. I'm in 4B1," or the teacher who said, "I can't do much with my class this term. I've got the 4B5's."

Participation in Shared Responsibilities

The second step in creating a we-group of the class and the school is to provide for the participation of each child in a shared responsibility. It is not necessary to revolutionize school procedure or curricula to accomplish this end. No "new school" is necessary, nor need the "shared responsibility" be a physical activity. A stimulating group discussion or maintaining standard of group achievement may be as much a group responsibility as putting on a play or going on a field trip.

The most obvious illustration of participation is that of taking part in class discussion, yet, on the whole, teachers are not alert to this elemental necessity. A simple device to check on pupil participation is a seating chart of the classroom and a code, such as that shown in Figure 9.2. In this average classroom, 9 of the 32 children did not respond at all; 7 only once; and 8, twice. Three others took part three times each, but the majority of the class period was taken up with the teacher and 5 children. The most unfortunate fact was that pupils asked few questions and offered few independent statements. If a similar check has been made in another class, it is probable that, with some shift of the role of the teacher, each child would have shown approximately the same extent of participation.

The substitution of movable furniture for the rows of desks in many classrooms has facilitated group participation but it is

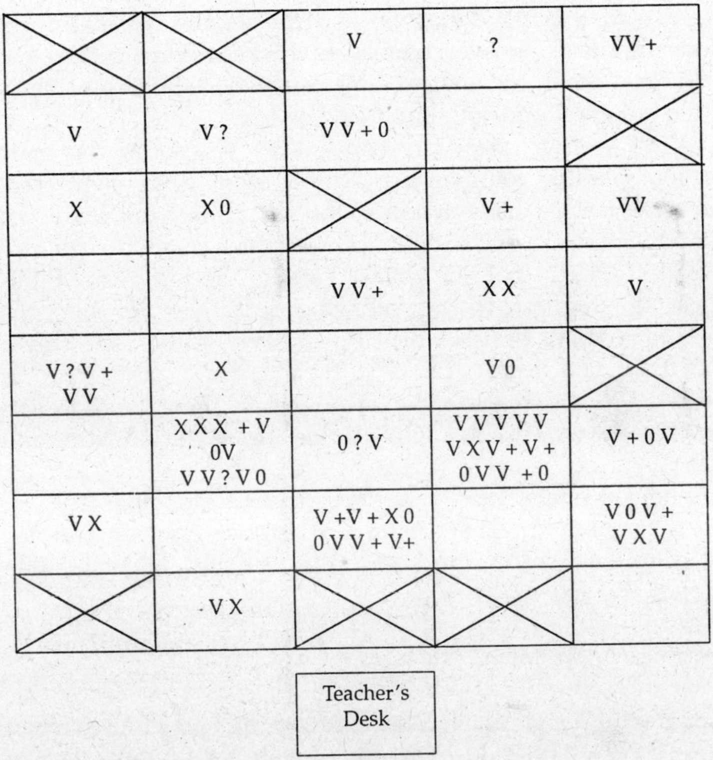

X = "Yes" or "No"
V = Short Statement
V + = More Complete Statement
0 = Independent Comment
? = Question
[vacant seat symbol] = Vacant Seat

Figure 9.2 : Student Participation

no guarantee of it. It is assured only by an atmosphere in which the teacher and each student have a sense of responsibility for the group.

To some degree, variation in classroom response is the reflection of the child's personality, but to a large extent it is the result of the failure of teachers to provide for wider participation. Gradually, the child accepts a role, whether passive or aggressive, and senses his oneness—or lack of it—with the group. The sensitive child may tend increasingly to withdraw from the group, and the foundation be laid for serious maladjustment problems later. The over aggressive child should be curbed and the more reticent, encouraged; both can be done by an awareness of the situation and an abundance of tact.

The words "shared responsibility" instead of the more frequent phrase "common experience" were deliberately used. Too often teacher have assumed that an activity need have no end beyond itself; that experience is of value in and for its own sake, but this is not the case. Dewey has emphasized this phase of education in the following quotation: "To have the same idea about things which others have, to be like-minded with them, and them to be really members of a social group, is therefore to attach the same meanings to things and to acts which others attach. Otherwise there is no common understanding, and no community life. But in a shared activity, each person refers what he is doing to what the other is doing and *view versa*. . . . There is an understanding set up between the different contributors; and this common understanding controls the actions of each."

Operation of the Social Processes

The third step in developing the we-group feeling involves many types of procedures which provide for the operation of the social processes, especially opposition and co-operation. The classroom provides abundant opportunity to direct the functioning of all three types of social interaction described earlier: one with one; one with group and group with one; and group with group.

Chief in the interaction process is the teacher-pupil relationship. All too often this is one of opposition in its undesirable aspects, rather than of a wholesome character or of co-operation. Frequently, a minor conflict is developed into one of major consequence. Rare is the teacher that knows when to be "blind" and "deaf" yet be able to keep children from taking advantage of situation. With skillful handling the trivial but often irritating conflicts can be utilized in creating an atmosphere of group responsibility. Group unity is based upon the little things well as the big, whether the group is a family, a play group, a class, or adult society.

The school likewise provides many opportunities for desirable opposition both among persons and between groups, yet with recognition of the varying ability of each individual member of the group. Among such opportunities are : extracurricular activities, sports and games, neatness of work, quality of prepared assignments, orderliness of rooms and desks, promptness or tardiness, and many more.

Group solidarity and the child's identification with the group may be broken down by undesirable opposition. The wide differences between members of the group may be exaggerated in the classroom by cliques, often based on place of residence, economic status, or religion. The teacher may inadvertently or deliberately be excessive in praise of certain students and in criticism of others. Such statements as "Why can't you get your work done as well as John? He always has his lesson," may seem inconsequential, even complimentary, yet is may lead to John's loss of status with the group.

This brief discussion of the social processes may be further elaborated. Their importance in the classroom is preparing children for participation in the larger society is forcefully stated by Ruth Cunningham and her associates at the Horace Mann-Lincoln Institute of School Experimentation:

> Democracy demands skills as well as attitudes and understandings—skills of leadership and group membership, skills in delegating responsibility, skills in evaluating individual and group contribution to democratic life. As with other skills, these skills are learned. As with other learning, learning of these skills takes place when three is meaningful experience. Boys and girls, as well as teachers, see new meanings and importance in democratic action as they learn to put into practice the skills necessary to its attainment. And, as they see through experience how skills contribute to such action, they learn to respect the skills. Circular thinking? No—spiral experience, in which democratic skills and democratic action each reinforce the other toward a growing democracy.
>
> Practice of democratic skills and development of democratic concepts within the classroom are of paramount importance. They provide the bases of understanding of

the wider group dynamics of the community, of democratic society, of world co-operation. It is with the equipment of such skills and concepts that individuals and groups are able to operate as forces in community betterment, whether the term "community" means "my school friends," "my neighbours and I," "Centerville," "my country," or "one world."

Importance of Social Status

The emphasis upon group behaviours may seem to imply a failure to recognize the individual. The reverse is true; it is only through the recognition of personality differences and their cultural origins, participation of each child in shared responsibilities and provisions for operation of the social processes, that each child senses his belonging to the group and finds the status for which he yearns. This inter-relationship is well stated by Jennings:

"The kind of group life in which an individual participates contributes to his personal development. Individuals can fully develop only in interaction with their fellows. The happiness and growth of each individual student depend in large measure on his personal security with his classmates. In a group he also learns to face, to anlayze, and to assess problems in a social context, and to develop ways of solving them with others. In interaction with others, furthermore, the broadening of his personal universe takes place; he gets to know his fellows, their values, and ways, and so gradually extends his sensitivity in human relations. His personal social maturity is also dependent on interaction with others."

The importance of status has been emphasized earlier in the discussion of the development of personality. Teachers have long recognized that students differ markedly in the extent to which they identify themselves with the classroom or school group. They have noted, too, that the larger classroom group divides into smaller groups, each focusing in one or two persons who are popular with the subgroup. But such differences in interpersonal relationships were seldom recognized in terms of their significance in personality development nor where efforts made to direct them.

Within relatively recent years a field of sociological research called "sociometry" has been developed in an effort to determine interpersonal relationships more accurately and to appraise means through which they may be directed. Obviously, this can be done informally through observation, noting the groupings on the playground or in classroom situations or as the children leave for home. But such informal study can scarcely be definitive. It likewise may project more significance into association than exists in the attitudes of the members of the group.

One method of procuring data for a sociometric study is to ask the children to indicate their own preferences of companions. The simplest but not the best way of procuring such information is to ask each child to write the names of the two (or more) children in the room they "like best" in order of preference. Experiments with adding also the one (or more) they "like least" have indicated that this negative emphasis is unwise and the same information is derived from noting the children named least often by their peers.

A more reliable method, using the same general technique, would be to find or create a situation in which it is natural for the class to divide into small groups—for committee work, to sit together, to play games. After deciding on the activity, each child is then asked to write down the names of two (or more) persons, in order of preference, with whom they would like most to associate in the small group.

The lists of names, signed by each pupil, provide the basis for tabulation and for graphic presentation as shown in Figure 9.3. By relating these data to other facts known about each child and the factors affecting interpersonal relations, causal factors begin to emerge. Specific programmes may be planned to influence the indicated grouping, and especially to give status to those who are least chosen. The same questions can be repeated at a later date and the extent to which the programme has affected relationships can be determined. (See Figure 9.4).

The following illustration of the use of sociometry in her class was written by the teacher:

> A class of 25 sixth grade boys and girls, drawn from four different fifth grade rooms, showed during the first three

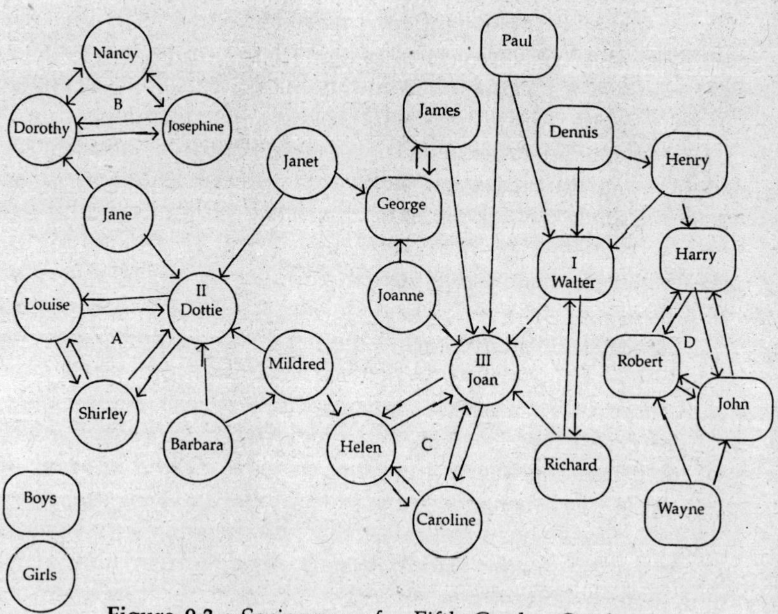

Figure 9.3 : Sociogram of a Fifth Grade—October

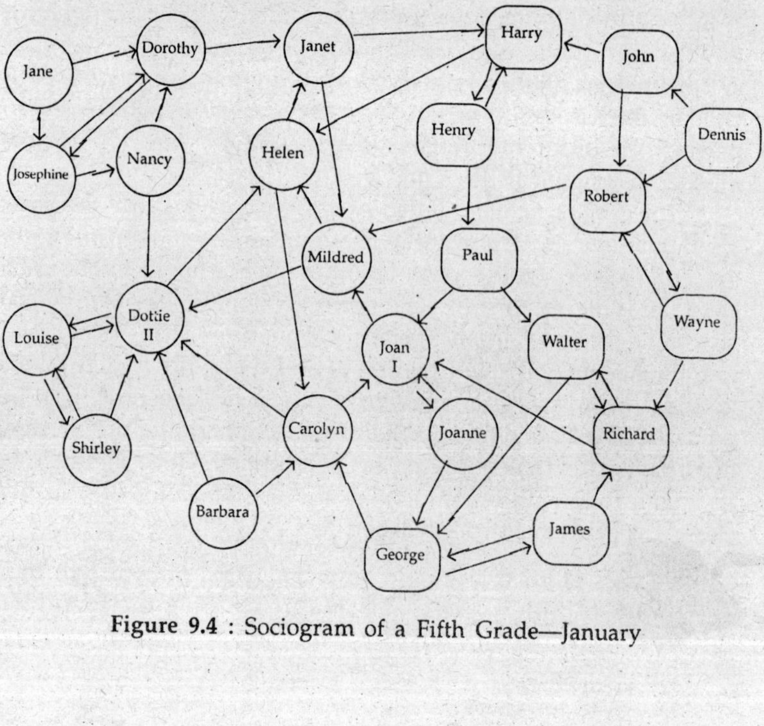

Figure 9.4 : Sociogram of a Fifth Grade—January

weeks of school a tendency to drift into little cliques with a certain amount of friction between them. To further disturb the class organization there seemed to be some undercurrent of unrest among the boys. After allowing three weeks to pass in order to give the pupils a chance to form new friendships, the teacher asked the class to write on a slip of paper the two persons in the class with whom they would like most to work.

This October sociogram Figure 9.3 showed that the class has divided into three groups clustering around Walter, who has been chosen by five of the boys; Dottie, who had been the choice of eight girls; and Joan chosen by four boys and three girls. The most interesting group of choices was that which clustered around Joan, a shy, brown-eyed girl. It seemed a departure, for the average group of sixth grade boys do not express a desire for heterogeneous sex grouping. A study of sub-groups C and D revealed that they had been a carry-over from groupings in the fifth grade, and that of subgroups A and B revealed they were girls riding on the same bus or living in the same neighbourhood. There were thirteen mutual choices, and even pupils were not chosen by any classmate.

Feeling that better social relationships were necessary among the pupils, a definite attempt was made between October and January to achieve this in the following ways:

I. *Pupil-Pupil Relationships:*

1. Desks were arranged in small groups of threes and fours, thus increasing the intimacy possible in the groups and developing more potential leadership in the class.
2. Pupils, who rode on the same bus or lived in the same neighbourhood, were placed in other seating groups.
3. In the seating arrangement and other work groups, "fringers" such as Barbara were placed with one of the class that they had chosen. Later experiments were made of placing groups of "fringers" or near fringers" together but this did not seem to be advantageous.

4. The new pupils were teamed with pupils who were good mixers.
5. The boy-girl relationships in the class were placed on a more satisfactory basis by the organization of mixed team games, folk dancing, class parties and outings, and the study of social etiquette pertinent to this age group.

II. *Pupil-Group Relationships:*

1. Personal guidance was provided by the teacher and guidance director for some such as Dennis and Barbara, in an effort to overcome personality difficulties that tended to make them unacceptable to the class. Attractive clothing from an outside source was given to Jane, in the hope she might become more a part of the group. In the case of Joanne, parent conferences were held in an attempt to solve her own personal problems and to help her develop some worth-while interests.
2. Library books, posters and discussions were used to build certain attitudes and appreciations and to promote a "give and take" spirit among the class.

III. *Group-Pupil Relationships:*

1. A definite change in curriculum and classroom activities was made to provide for the special abilities of the members of the class.
2. A "See Here" chart was posted listing the special talents or abilities of each member of the class with the suggestion that they be encouraged to contribute to classroom activities.
3. Frequent recognition was given to the committee chairman who succeeded in getting the largest number of the class to participate in a class discussion or project.
4. A small red feather was given to those who had made some special contribution. (In some instances, this contribution was contrived by the teacher).

IV. *Total-Group Relationships:*

1. Total-group relationships were improved by special class projects such as publishing a class newspaper, a cafeteria work-project and safety patrol activities.
2. An unusual number of the class had some type of artistic ability, and the class planned and carried through a commendable class art exhibit.

In January, prior to initiating a new group of related activities, the students were again asked to write down the names of the two people with whom they would like most to work. Even within the three months there were marked changes in social relationships. In the January sociogram (Figure 9.4), there were fewer mutual choices than in October and the number who remained isolate dropped from seven to three, Joan and Dottie still held their position as stars. Of the two who entered late in September, Janet had been drawn into the class but Jane was still an isolate.

A kindergarten teacher who had combined activities and sociometry concludes at the end of the year's experiment.

"I hope that the next group of children with whom I am going to work will emerge with the same spirit of co-operation, and consideration for their own needs and the needs of others as well, with the same poise and self-discipline, that I myself had never thought possible in so young a group of children."

Only when these evidences of social interaction are recognised as a typical social pattern can they be guided into a larger pattern of relationships for the group as a whole. The staff of the Commission of Teacher Education summarized the role of the social processes in classroom organization as follows:

"The social cosmos of the school is the children's own world. This working out of social roles, these processes of affiliation, identification, group action, and interaction are among the primary means of social development for all children. The social learning that result from successful group affiliation may include skills in dealing with people, insights into the nature of social process, and sensitiveness to the motives and feelings of others. Such learnings mature children. They produce an evolution of the society that is formed by each new generation entering school from a society of elementary school peers into a society of adolescent peers, and finally into the next generation of adults."

The Role of the Teacher

The teacher is the most important person in determining the extent to which the in-group feeling is developed. It is she who determines whether the classroom is but an assemblage of individuals who obey orders and complete assigned tasks, or whether it is a group earnestly and happily working together for the goods of the group and its members. Through her awareness of student roles and manipulation of the classroom procedures, the teacher can create a competitive attitude dominated by a few students with the rest accepting a passive role, or she can create a lively situation in which all share and participate.

This emphasis has been reflected in the shift from educational psychology and child development exclusively to the addition of educational sociology and a social emphasis. The last decade has witnessed the publication of many books and hundreds of articles for teachers on group dynamics, human relations, and inter group understanding. Experimental centers have been established an extensive research has been conducted. Institutes, workshops and courses emphasizing these social values have multiplied to provide both pre-service and in-service education for teachers.

If the schools are to fulfil the expectations of the society which maintains them and increasingly translate basic principles into effective action, teachers must analyze the culture of the community and relate educational activities to its cultural pattern; must know and evaluate the cultural heritage of students; must record and guide behaviour in social interaction.

The first of these three essentials implies the utilization of new techniques of community analysis, simple enough to be feasible within the time allotted for teaching various subjects and commensurate with other requirements set for the teacher, yet comprehensive enough to provide adequate data for the adaptation of school and class activities.

The second essential—analysis of the cultural heritage of children—implies a personal knowledge of each student. Too often teachers have been satisfied with knowing only Jack's I.Q., and his record with the previous teacher or in other subjects. These may, under certain circumstances be important to know, but may be misleading and injurious in that such information determines the teacher's attitude toward the child in advance of the latter's performance. "Jack's record is poor so he will probably continue as a weak student" is a natural but unwholesome reflection of the average teacher's knowledge of students. The facts that are of very much more importance are: what is his home life like; where does he spend his out-of-school time and with whom; what racial, religious, and economic factors influence his behaviour? These are but a few of the questions for which answers must be sought. Each, in turn, breaks down into many specific questions. The home is the first in-group of the child; it is through the family that original nature first begins to be human nature; interaction with other members of the family group is what determines, to a large extent, the child's status. Consequently, the teacher must know the family, not only in terms of the number of brothers and sisters and the objective factors—neatness, relative income and educational level of parents—but also the more personal relationships: what is the attitude of the parents toward each other and toward the child? If there are brothers or sisters, it is important to know the attitude toward the child in relation to that toward other members of the family. But even this is not enough, for the student's attitude toward property, the rights of others, government, and ethical values is the reflection, often in exact detail, of that of the home.

To gain this type of information will require tact and good judgment, but such information cannot be gotten in detail for every child, nor is it necessary. An observant teacher will know for the guidance of which child such information will be helpful.

To those who would say that this is not the concern of the teacher, the growing record of the satisfactory adjustment of children and young people by teachers who know how to procure and wisely use such information is an effective answer. Frequently, too, the teacher may be of genuine assistance in modifying the home situation, for the interaction of school and home may be made reciprocal through the medium of the child.

The third essential in the role of the teacher—to record and guide behaviour in social interaction—requires a new emphasis in teacher observation and recording of the behaviour of students. It entails a new point of view on the part of school administrators and school boards. Of course it is necessary to report progress in mastery of the subject-matter field; but even in schools in which other types of behaviour are recorded, the teacher's report is in terms of the child's behaviour in relation to her own standards. Such reports are usually confined to generalizations : "lazy," "unattentive," "well behaved," "does not adjust well to school routine," "quarrelsome." School systems that require character ratings are too often content to report abstract qualities such as honesty, diligence, co-operation, or initiative. Such ratings have the merit of calling attention to behaviour as contrasted with subject-matter mastery, but fail to emphasize the causes of such behaviour. It is not enough to know that Betty rates high in honesty but law in helpfulness. It is necessary to go back of the rating and discover why Betty does not co-operate.

The major emphasis in the explanation of behaviour has been psychological. The results of temperament tests, interest analyses, and subjective evaluations of emotional characteristics have been assumed to be sufficient explanations. The school psychologist and the psychoanalyst give only partial answers, since their data are primarily those based on the analysis of the individual. The educational sociologist urges that the causes be pushed farther back to the cultural conditioning of social interaction, not only within the classroom but in the total social milieu of the child.

The sociological approach to reaching is not easy. The pulls and tensions of the day and the necessity of covering essential subject matter makes teaching a demanding task, whether in the kindergarten, the elementary or secondary school, or the college. But the proçurement of such information reveals the very warp and woof ofthe pattern the person's behaviour. Fully known, sympathetically understood, and wisely used, it will do much to believe tensions and stimulate achievement through the identification of each person with the common aspirations of the in-group. Only by meeting this challenge can the teacher fulfil her high calling—that of leading out the child into the larger responsibilities of the adult.

Summary

There are some who have said that the school must be a replica of adult society. This is neither possible nor wish. The processes of adult relationships are inherent in those of the child, but the institutional patterns must remain those of the level of the child's development. To organize a school on the basis of a city government or to do any of the other tricks advocated by their too ardent apostles is to confuse processes with institutions. The importance of the processes of social interaction is forcefully presented in the co-operative study of the Commission on Teacher Education to which reference has previously been made: "Learning to participate in this child society of the school and to adjust effectively to its processes poses for every child some of his most highly motivated and significant developmental tasks. Learning the lore of their peer group is just as important for children as learning the history of our society. . . . The attitudes, values, and ethical code of the group of children with which a child identifies himself seem to have increasing weight with him as he progresses through school. . . . The sanctions that are enforced by his peers and the prestige or recognition accorded him for certain actions are striking in their power to mold a child's behaviour.

"Interaction within and between groups and the differential status and prestige accorded to various roles confront every child daily with avenues to satisfaction or to disappointment. . . . A child's estimation of his own personal worth, his evaluation of his competence, and his sense of personal inferiority or superiority are shaped, often to a critical extent, by the status accorded or refused him by his peers."

It is through these processes of social interaction within the child's own society that the basis is laid for effective participation in the larger groups of the school, the community, the nation, and the world. Meiklejohn has described this larger view as follows : "Learning is not merely the acquiring of mastery over intellectual subject matter. It is, first of all, initiation into many social groups and, ultimately, into one social group. The teacher leads his pupil into active membership in a fraternity to which he himself belongs. The motive force of that fraternity is found in a common devotion to a common, co-operative enterprise. Just as, in the home, each child learns, or should learn, to play his part in the family circle, so, in our schools and colleges, every citizen of the world should become 'at home' in the human 'state.' He should acquire a sense of what humanity is trying to do, and a will to join in doing it.

"The calling of the teacher, as so defined, is one of infinite difficulty. But it is also infinitely significant. He is commissioned to form and fashion both human society as a whole and the individuals of whom that society consists."

The twofold responsibility of the school is clearly pointed out in the above quotation : to understand and give direction to the social interaction of children and youth, and to know what society expects of the school if it is to fulfil its function as an agency of social control. Through the carefully planned development of the in-group these two functions can be simultaneously achieved. Through the in-group they become not antagonistic but complementary.

Topics for Discussion

1. If the data are available, make a study of the holding-power of your own school system, i.e., of each 100 pupils in the fifth grade, how many enter high school; graduate from his school; enter college?
2. What factors have caused the students to leave school?

3. Do you accept the major premise that democracy requires an educated citizenry, and that consequently it is desirable to retain an increasing proportion of young people in school for a greater number of years?
4. Using one subject field, relate the three objectives : learning, self expression, and development of behaviour patterns.
5. Describe specific instances, in your school, of undersirable competition; desirable competition; co-operation.
6. Prepare a sociometric graph of the pupils in one group and interpret the findings. What evidence of domination and isolation does it show? What might be done to improve interpersonal relations within the group?
7. Why has teacher education given increased emphasis to the social development of the child?

10

The School: The Curriculum

Factors which influence the curriculum. Subject matter. Methods. Social measurement of education.

To the educational sociologist, the curriculum is more than the textbook, more than subject matter, more even than a course of study. It is the total situation or group of situations available to the teacher and school administrator through which to make behaviour changes in the endless stream of children and youth who pass through the doors of the schools. This definition implies, first, that situations are directed to achieve predetermined goals and second, that the curriculum includes:

1. subject matter,
2. method, and
3. measurement.

Payne points out: "Applying this conception of the curriculum to a particular school (for it has no meaning aside from its special application), the curriculum of any school consists of all the situations that the school may select and consciously organize for the purpose of developing the personality of its pupils, for making behaviour changes in them. This conception of the curriculum includes whatever means those responsible for the school may decide upon as valuable in producing the educational results desired."

The conception of the school as an agency of social control implies that the curriculum cannot be limited to the child's immediate interests, but must be organized in terms of social values; it must not be exclusively concerned with immediate behaviour changes of individuals but must look also to the long-range behaviour changes of society. This concept lifts the eyes of curriculum makers from the child to see also the adult, and from the immediate situation, to envision the future of man's world. The Thirty-first Yearbook of the American Association of School Administrators forcefully states this point of view : "American education cannot be satisfied with the present and emerging future, but rather it shall give full recognition to the important contributions of the total social heritage. Our scope of vision shall be both national and international." The interest of the educational sociologist in the curriculum is thus twofold : an analysis of the cultural pattern as it influences the curricula of schools and colleges, and the process through which such curricula are determined and continually modified.

Factors which Influence the Curriculum

There are many factors which influence the curriculum of our schools and colleges. In any one community, as will be emphasized in the succeeding chapter, there are local influences that may play a very significant role, since they are frequently reflected in attitudes of the local school board in the selection of administrators and teachers. The degree of initiative and resourcefulness of the staff and their concept of education have a significant bearing on the curriculum. On both the local and national level there are special interest groups that seek to incorporate their specific concern into the teaching materials used by the school.

Thus the curriculum, perhaps more than any other aspect of the school and college, is the result of a complex of forces. At times these influences are in conflict and seldom does the curriculum satisfy all the parents of all the children. But throughout all history, the cultural pattern in the large has determined the goals of education and these, in turn, have significantly influenced not only what the schools have taught and are teaching, but also how it is taught and what standards are used in measuring the effectiveness of the educational process.

Determination of Goals

There have been many statements of the aims of education, from Socrates and Plato, through Locke and Spencer, to the moderns and progressivists. These statements reflect the values of the individual which, in turn, are the product of the cultural values of the individual's we-group. Thus, Plato would have his "guardian of the state to be philosophical, high-spirited, swift-footed, and strong." Locke's emphasis upon "the disciplined and well-ordered mind" reflects the stirrings of the scientific developments of the late seventeenth century. Puritan religion dominated the statement of educational objectives in terms of faith, piety, and duty.

With the development of democracy and its struggling, but never wholly successful, efforts to provide education for "all the children of all the people," the aims of education were correspondingly broadened. Spencer declared that the end of education was "complete living" conceived in adult values; this entailed preparation for self-preservation, earning a living, parenthood, citizenship, and the occupations of leisure. His statements were widely quoted as they challenged much of traditional education and had a profound influence upon the schools both in the United States and in England.

One of the most significant statements of the aims of education in recent decades and one which had very great influence upon the curriculum was that made during World War I by the Commission on the Reorganization of Secondary Education of the National Education Association:

> In order to determine the main objectives that should guide education in a democracy it is necessary to analyze the activities of the individual. Normally he is a member of a family, of a vocational group, and of various civic groups, and by virtue of these relationships he is called upon to engage in activities that enrich the family life, to render important vocational services to his fellows, and to

promote the common welfare. It follows, therefore, that worthy home membership, vocation, and citizenship, demand attention as three of the leading objectives.

Aside from the immediate discharge of these specific duties, every individual should have a margin of time for the cultivation of personal and social interests... Education for the worthy use of leisure is of increasing importance as an objective.

To discharge the duties of life and to benefit from leisure, one must have good health. The health of the individual is essential also to the vitality of the race and to the defence of the Nation. Health education is, therefore, fundamental.

There are various processes, such as reading, writing, arithmetical computations, and oral and written expression, that are needed as tools in the affairs of life. Consequently, command of these fundamental processes, while not an end in itself, is nevertheless an indispensable objective.

And, finally, the realization of the objectives already named is dependent upon ethical character, that is, upon conduct founded upon right principles, clearly perceived and loyally adhered to...

This commission, therefore, regards the following as the main objectives of education:

1. Health.
2. Command of fundamental processes.
3. Worthy home-membership.
4. Vocation.
5. Citizenship.
6. Worthy use of leisure.
7. Ethical character.

The beginning of a shift of emphasis from individual development to societal values is indicates in the following statement of aims as made by the Educational Policies Commission in 1944:

Schools should be dedicated to the proposition that every youth in these United States—regardless of sex, economic status, geographic location, or race—should experience a broad and balanced education which will:

1. equip him to enter an occupation suited to his abilities and offering reasonable opportunity for personal growth and social usefulness;
2. prepare him to assume the full responsibilities of American citizenship;
3. give him a fair chance to exercise his right to the pursuit of happiness.
4. stimulate intellectual curiosity, engender satisfaction in intellectual achievement, and cultivate the ability to think rationally; and
5. help him to develop and appreciation of the ethical values which should undergird all life in a democratic society.

> It is the duty of a democratic society to provide opportunities for such education through it schools. It is the obligation of every youth, as a citizen, to make full use of these opportunities. It is the responsibility of parents to give encouragement and support to both youth and schools.

The further shift to societal needs is indicated in the *Fifty-Second Yearbook* of the National Society for the Study of Education issued in 1953. The 1918 statement of the National Association of Secondary School Principals is based almost exclusively upon the education need of the adolescent, whereas the Yearbook point out the need for a twofold approach : the needs of the child and the needs of adults society which the school must prepare the child to meet. This point of view is based upon there assumptions:

> The purpose of public education in this country is to induct the young into the American democratic culture within the ideological framework of that culture.
>
> Any problem the individual must solve in order to become more effective in furthering democratic ends constitutes a need for him regardless of whether he is now aware of this need or must be helped progressively to became aware of it.
>
> Since American democratic ideology embraces the belief that the individual is of supreme worth and the further belief that the preservation and improvement of society

depend upon the full utilization of his potentialities, the methods employed for inducting him into the culture must neither deny his basic feelings of need nor be limited by his present feelings of need.

The *Yearbook's* statement of the needs of the adolescent varies sharply from the earlier one by the National Association of School Principals. It is quoted at some length:

> The needs which adolescents experiences can be identified as growing out of the disjunction between the behaviour characteristic of their present immaturities and the behaviour which society encouraged them to exhibit. While a complete analysis of the common needs of youth goes far beyond what is possible in the present chapter, an illustration may help to make clear the procedure.
>
> Characteristic of the typical adolescent is his almost slavish conformity to standards of the peer group. It is a matter of prime importance that adolescents dress alike, follow the same hair styles, use the same slang, rave about the same TV shows as others in the group with whom they wish to be identified. Even social behaviour which is condemned by adults may be wholly acceptable to teenagers if it is approved by the peer group. Fear of being called "chicken," for example, may prompt delinquent behaviour if it seems the only means by which the adolescent can be assured recognition by his group. Adolescence is also a period in which differences in race, creed, financial and social status, and even slight discrepancies in physical characteristics may interfere with the individual's feelings of worth. There is nothing quite so disturbing as feeling different.
>
> To equip the adolescent to move toward this desired goal, certain needs now become clear. The adolescent needs to find opportunities in the school to "feel" like others in his age group, to gain reasonable success in his school work, and to participate in school activities on an equal basis with others. He needs to develop the skills and standards of behaviour requisite for group acceptance: ease in conversation, cleanliness and good grooming, reliability, skill in dancing and playing active sports, and

so forth. He needs to understand and accept differences both in himself and in others. He needs to discover and develop his assets to offset physical or other handicaps. He needs to receive understanding guidance if he is using unwise methods to gain approval, such as "buying" acceptance and show-off or anti-social behaviour. He needs to be sensitive to the feelings of others who have difficulty because of social, financial, or physical disadvantage. He needs to learn to take a stand on important issues rather than being unduly swayed by group pressures.

Determining how to meet such relatively broad needs as those stated above necessitates their translation into many specific learning experiences and their allocation to appropriate subject areas. Such an analysis, if performed for every important growth characteristic of normal youth, would take much of the guess work out of a needs formulation by anchoring needs solidly to defined criteria.

Turning to the analysis of societal needs, the *Yearbook* gives the following emphasis:

> *Society as the Genesis of an Analysis of Needs:* A second approach which is useful in identifying the needs of youth is to begin with an analysis of the American scene today—the respects in which society is functioning or failing to function in harmony with the democratic values and ideals we espouse. Just as a description of the typical adolescent tells us the level of maturity which he has already achieved and establishes the point from which he must make progress, so a description of the present state of affairs, so far as our social arrangements are concerned, tells us how far we have already progressed as a group in achieving satisfactory conditions for community living and, thus, where we begin in order to effect social improvement. Such a description of social reality when contrasted with a description of hoped-for social arrangements indicates, as did the preceding analysis, the distance which must be travelled to achieve community goals and thus aids in locating important needs of the individual. As stated in the initial assumptions the individual must be the active agent for perpetuating the durable features of our cultural

heritage and, at the same time, for improving group living through behaviour which harmonizes with our democratic beliefs and values. His needs, then, would involve acquisition of skills, knowledge, habits, and ways of behaving which would move us toward out community goals.

This emphasis upon the school's responsibility to meet the needs of the individual and of society is further illustrated in a recent publication of the National Association of Secondary School Principals. It includes ten statements of "the common and essential needs that all American youth have in a democratic soceity" paralleled by ten statements of "the imperative needs of soceity." The following illustrate one of each of the two sets of statements:

> All youth need to understands the rights and duties of the citizen of a democratic soceity, and to be diligent and competent in the performance of their obligations as members of the community and citizens of the state and nation and to have an understanding of the nations and peoples of the world.
>
> Society needs to develop loyalty to the principles of democracy, to protect individual freedom of thought and expression, to assure justice to all its citizens, and to develop independent people free from harmful propaganda and uniformity.

The following statement developed in 1953 by the administration and faculty of the University of Pittsburgh illustrates the dual emphasis upon the individual and society at the college level:

> The University has the following purposes and aims toward its student body:
>
> To draw out, cultivate excite, and inspire the full development of each student.
>
> To create an atmosphere in which students will learn to think; where faculty and students will be critical enough to be objective and at the same time have faith enough to be constructive—where they will seek truth, solve problems, reason, and develop the power of thought.

> To help students establish values through intimate acquaintance with the humanities, the arts, the natural sciences, the social sciences, and religion.
>
> To develop the character of students—integrity, honesty, judgment, co-operation, friendliness, and good will.
>
> To create a community of scholars where research, curiosity, free inquiry, and discovery advance knowledge.
>
> To provide competent, well-trained professional leadership for one of the world's most important industrial areas.
>
> To prepare men and women for citizenship in a democratic nation where freedom and liberty go hand in hand with law and justice and where responsibility, national and international, is a characteristic of the individual.

The above quotations are only illustrative. They clearly indicate, however, the change that has taken place at all levels of education from the subject-matter-centered curriculum which dominated American education until the turn of this century and the child-centered curriculum which reached it height of dominance during the 1920's, to a reappraisal of the curriculum in the light of the dynamic character of modern society. The results of this shift in emphasis, so continually urged by the educational sociologist, will be shown later in this chapter. Before doing so, it is necessary to make further reference to changes in school and college enrolment, since the change in the school population has significantly modified the curriculum.

Enrolment Trends and Projection

The vast percentage increase in enrolment is shown in Figure 10.1 actual, for the period 1899-1900 to 1952-53; projected, from 1952-53 to 1965-66. The projection is based upon the number of babies born to December 31, 1952; hence, within the time span of the projection, it will not be significantly influenced, except in the lower grades of the elementary school, by later changes in the numbers of annual births.

Changes in enrolment in the elementary school have approximately paralleled those of the total population 5-21 years of age. Secondary enrolment has shown the largest percentage

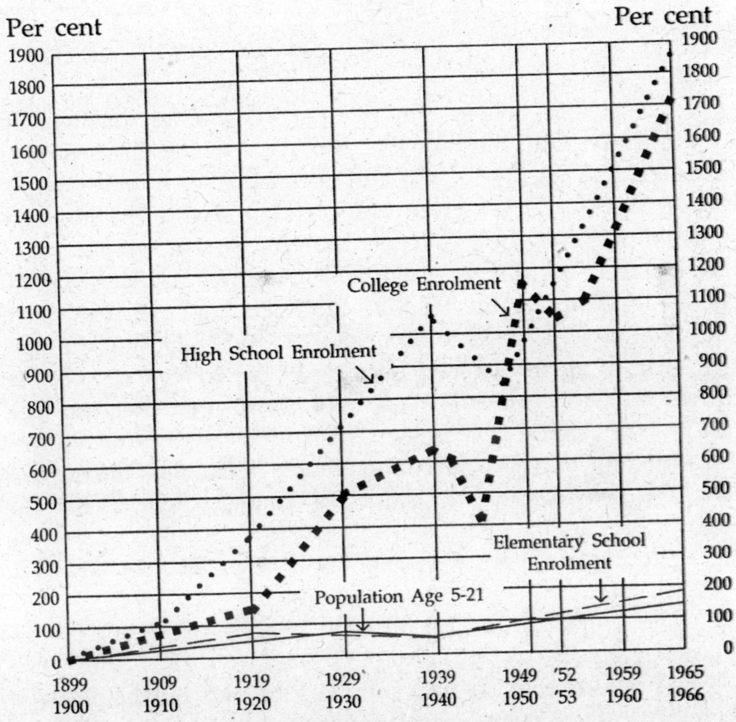

Figure 10.1 : Per Cent Change in Population, Ages 5 to 21 Inclusive, and in Full Time Enrolment in Elementary, Secondary, and Higher Education, Actual; 1899-1900 to 1952-53. Projected; 1953-1954 to 1965-1966.

increase. It approximately doubled each decade form 1900 to 1940 but declined during the period from 1940 to 1947. By 1952-53, enrolment has returned to its former peak and at least until 1965 will rise steadily and rapidly due to the ruse in annual births and the increasing proportion of persons of high school age who continue their education. The latter is forcefully brought home in the following terse comparison : in the 33 years from 1919-20 to 1952-53, the proportion of the population of high school age in high school increased from 32.3 per cent to 82.4 per cent and, on the basis of current trend, will be 91.5 per cent by 1965-1966; the per cent of high school graduates was but 16.3 in 1919, is now 57.7 per cent, and is predicted to be 68.1 per cent in 1965-66.

Changes in college enrolment show even less relationship to population than those of the secondary school. The number increased less rapidly to 1941 and decreased much more sharply during World War II. From 1946 to 1950, due to the numbers who had deferred their college education for war service and to the financial assistance provided to approximately 3,000,000 college students by the GI Bill, enrolment more than doubled from its low in 1944-45 to its peak in 1949-50. During the next two years it again declined because of the Korean conflict but turned upward again in 1952-53 and, short of another war, will continue to increase. The new GI Bill for persons inducted into the armed forces since 1947, although less liberal than the original Bill, will provide very considerable financial help. That the major factor in the increase is motivation is indicated by the fact that the number of women in college also increased in 1952-53.

The projection of college enrolment is borne out by the following summary. During the 33 years from 1919-20 to 1952-53, the proportion of the population of college age who received their first college degree increased from 2.6 per cent to 12.0 per cent and, again based on trends, may be 16.9 per cent in 1965-66. The increase in master's degrees follows much the same pattern from 9.7 per cent of persons in 1919-20 who had earned a bachelor's degree to 17.1 per cent in 1952-53 and 20.0 per cent in 1965-66. The increase in doctoral degrees awarded, based on the number holding bachelor's degrees, was from 1.49 per cent in 1919-20 to 2.09 in 1952-53 and is predicted to be 2.29 in 1965-66.

When these per cents are shown in terms of numbers based upon the increase in actual births to 1953, the needs of education are appalling. In 1943-44 there were 19,892,000 boys and girls enrolled in the elementary schools, an increase of only 3,400,000 over the number in school in 1900. Only 400,000 more were in school in 1949-50, six years later. Within three years, 3,500,000 more children entered the elementary school and the number will continue to increase at approximately 1,000,000 1 year to 1965-66 reaching a total of more than 34,000,000 boys and girls!

In spite of the vast increase in the number in the secondary school, the enrolment of a little over 7,000,000 in 1952-53 will increase to nearly 13,000,000 by 1965-66. College enrolment after its sharp rise from 1,500,000 in 1939-40 (1,155,000 in 1943-44) to 2,700,000 in 1949-50, will again increase. It is estimated

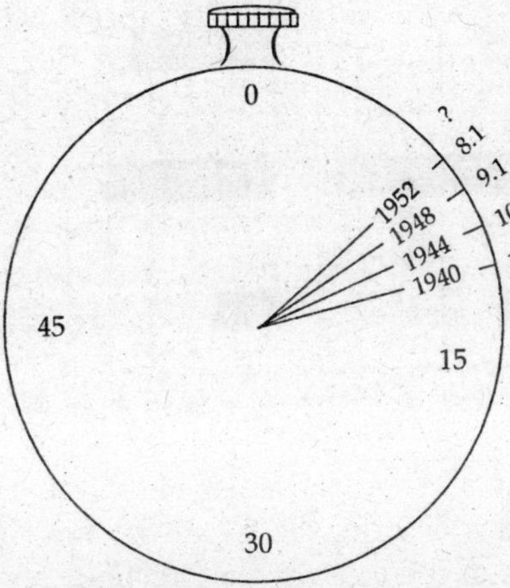

Figure 10.2 : Number of Seconds between Births of Live Babies in the United States, 1940-1952.

that the number will be 3,00,000 by 1957-58 and at least 4,000,000 by 1965-66 with further increases beyond this date! If to these numbers were added the vast increase in part-time enrolment and adult education, the total demands upon education would be even more challenging.

That the projections to 1965-66 may prove conservative and that the trends will continue beyond this date are graphically shown by Figure 10.2. In 1940, one baby was born in the United States every 12.2 seconds; during 1952, a baby was born every 8.1 seconds.

Figure 10.3 is but further verification of the effort to achieve a higher level of education for all. Although the contrasts are only for the decade between the census of 1940 and that of 1950, it actually indicates the changes which occurred in education during the periods 1925-35 and 1900-10. If each age group is compared in terms of the changes in per cent of the

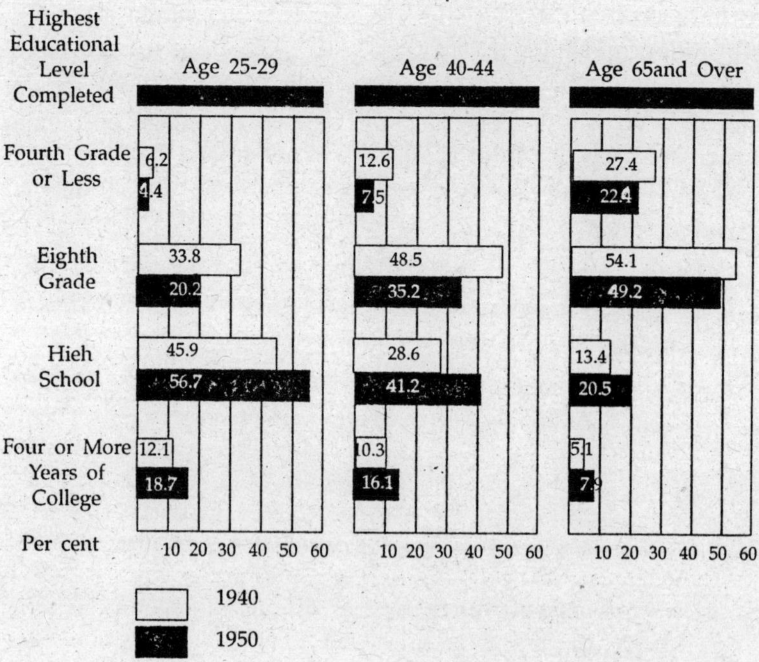

Figure 10.3 : Per Cent of Persons in Each Specified Age-Group Who Had Completed Designated Educational Level in 1940 and in 1950. (From 1950 *Census of Population*, Preliminary Report, May 15, 1952. U.S. Department of Commerce, Bureau of the Census).

population who had completed the levels of education, the per cent is consistently less for those in 1950 who had completed only the fourth grade or less and who had finished no more than the eighth grade, and more for those who had completed high school and four or more years of college.

This basic change in the school population, which reflects changes in the cultural pattern, has had tremendous impact upon the curriculum of our schools and colleges. Adaptations and minor changes have been inadequate. A completely different outlook has been required and, it the predictions indicated are correct, still further drastic changes will be forced upon our institutions of education, especially at the secondary and higher education levels, by the necessity of meeting the needs not only of more student, but of students with a wider range of ability, aptitudes, and interests.

In the field of higher education, in spite of the great increase that has already occurred and the unprecedented expansion especially of the community college, there is still a basic issue which has fundamental implications of the future of our colleges. It is shown by the contrasting statements of two national commissions : the President's Commission on Higher Education and the Commission on Financing Higher Education.

The former, in that section of its report entitled "Equalizing and Expanding Individual Opportunity," stated:

> American colleges and universities must envision a much larger role for higher education in the national life. They can no longer considered themselves merely the instrument for producing an intellectual elite. They must become the means by which every citizen, youth and adult is enabled and encouraged to carry his education, formal and informal, as far as his native capacities permit.
>
> At least 49 per cent of our population has the mental ability to complete fourteen year of schooling with a curriculum of general and vocational studies that should lead either to gainful employment or to further study at a more advanced level. At least 32 per cent of our population has the mental ability to complete and advanced liberal or specialized professional education.

The latter stated:

> American society requires two interrelated but fundamentally different kinds of education. One is common schooling. Its goal is the steady improvement in the literacy and social competence of the individual. The public primary and secondary school is the chief instrument of this purpose, although it has always been accompanied and sometimes stimulated by the private school. The other education goal is the development of the intellectual capacities of those processing unusual talent. This is the special province of higher education.
>
> We believe higher education should accept as its first concern the education of those young people who fall

approximately within the top 25 per cent in intellectual capacity.

The contrasting views indicated in these two statements have not been resolved but they have extremely important implications for college and university curricula. To a greater degree than at the elementary and secondary school level, each institution will determine which of these two goals is in keeping with its own purpose and provide the type of curriculum which best fulfils its goal.

The above discussion appears to be applicable only to secondary and higher education. It is, however, applicable to the elementary school also. The division of education into grades and even levels of education is for administrative convenience. It does not and should not denote sharp differences of emphasis but only the gradual maturing of the individual. Education is a unified and continuous process, not a stratified or compartment alized one. The search for the needs of youth is equally applicable to all levels, and certainly the goals for adult living must guide the very beginning of the educational process in the nursery school and kindergarten.

Research

The goals of education and the population to be served are basic in the determination of the curriculum. But their implications can be translated into the programme of the school and college only by extensive and continuous research.

This emphasis upon research in determining the curriculum is not new. In the 1920's Bobbitt procured from teachers a list of objectives, specific abilities and characteristics which they belived should form the basis for selection of subject matter at the various grade levels. W.W. Charters used the method of job analysis through which he sought to determine abilities required, the traits involved and the knowledge and attitudes essential for success.

Because of the increasing recognition of the social goals of education, research has shifted to involve two basic approaches to the determination of the curriculum: the needs of the individual and the needs of society. The major emphasis is upon the latter, and includes an analysis of the total cultural pattern and the social processes involved in its transmission. This sociological approach entails studies of patterns of behaviour of different age groups, of communities and regions, and of society in the large. It is as important in determining goals to know antisocial behaviour patterns as those socially approved. Several of these studies will be described later in this chapter.

The broad scope of curriculum research, including the study of the needs of the individual child, is well stated in the following quotation:

> By their very nature, needs must always be both personal and social and are best defined as individual wants and desires plus lacks and inadequacies which are expressed in the interaction of the individual with the social environment of which be is a part. Thus, "the need of the student to use his leisure time wisely" refers to a desire or want (a tension which is personal) and the demands or requirements of society (which are *social*), and the two are necessarily interrelated. . . . For curriculum purposes, it is necessary to identify these broad basic needs. Having identified them so that pre-planning can be done, the teacher is then obligated to study the particular group of students with which he is concerned in order that educational experiences may be planned to meet the wants and desires and the lack and inadequacies as they are expressed within the group.

One of the many illustrations of research as the basis for curriculum building is that of the Wisconsin Co-operative Planning Programme. The pages are divided into three parallel columns. In the section dealing with growth problems, the captions are : "Characteristics and Behaviour related to Growth," "Tasks the Pupil Faces," and "What the Schools Can Do"; under "Social Pressures Influencing Junior High School Youth," the heading are: "The Situation We Confront," "What the Pupil Needs and "What the Schools Can Do."

Another approach to subject-matter revision involves analysis of attitudes held by students in relation to optimum attitudes, and of contents of currently used textbooks and other teaching materials which may influence such attitudes. This method was employed by the Committee on the Study of Teaching Materials on Inter-American subjects in its study of American textbooks. The method has definite bearing upon the subject matter of the schools. Having established factual data concerning the history, geography, and culture of Latin America, the research staff made a careful appraisal of all references to Latin-American countries in American textbooks to determine the extent to which such statements were inaccurate or misleading. A similar study has been made of what is said in our textbooks about Canada, and in Canadian texts, concerning the United States. Although a piecemeal type of research, it illustrates the importance of subject matter in the development of social attitudes.

An approach more applicable in the social science fields than in others is that of analyzing cultural change and seeking to adapt the subject matter of the school to such changes.

Subject Matter

"Subject matter" and "curriculum" are frequently assumed to have the same meaning, and the terms are used interchangeably. This confusion of terminology has made the textbook and the school synonymous in the mind of the child and the general public. Subject matter includes all that is embraced within the courses of study—texts, the school library, visual and auditory aids, field trips, and all the other instruments through which a specific field of the cultural heritage is transmitted to students. Subject matter is but one aspect of the total curriculum.

The sociologist's concern with subject matter is twofold: first, that it be selected to accomplish the social purpose of education; and second, that it be so organized and related to method and classroom procedures that it may be an effective instrument in social control.

The possibility exists that the subject matter taught in the schools will be confined exclusively to the materials of formal instruction and that the schools will be isolated from the subject matter of life experience. This has been a constant danger, and especially so amid the swift succession of the epoch-making events described earlier in our discussion. The school, rooted deep in the past, may be the chief agent in creating cultural lag, or it may, with courage and foresight, be the instrument of society to lead the world into the as-yet-unknown vistas of tomorrow.

To some degree, changes in the school have been a natural concomitant of increase in knowledge; it has resulted partly from the efforts of the school to take over functions not adequately developed through other agencies of society. Changes in the school have also been due to changes in our cultural pattern. One example is the current emphasis upon modern language in the elementary school, reflecting America's expanding role in world affairs.

Expansion of Fields of Knowledge

The extent to which change has been in the nature of additions is shown for the elementary school in Table 10.1. Similar contrasts could be drawn for secondary and higher education, but space will not permit. Reports received from State Departments of Education indicate a total of 253 separate subjects were being taught in 1950 in the secondary schools. In one university, for example, a student would need more than the normal life span of three score years and ten to take all of the courses. In the Liberal Arts college alone it would require 22 years of full-time study to take all of the subjects offered. There have been changes other than additions, of course, but reorganization of subject matter has been achieved only against the resistance of vested interests in a subject-matter field and of those who seek to keep the school isolated from the current of social change.

Subject matter of the secondary school was continually challenged during the three decades prior to World War II. But change was uneven. Too many high schools clung to the traditional subject matter, looked backward rather than forward to determine the course of study, resisted new devices of instruction, attempted to force the new generation of youth through the old pattern of required subjects. There were, of course, many leaders in the field who resisted this social lag and sought to keep secondary education abreast of the times.

Table 10.1
Changes in the Subject Matter of the Elementary School
1800, 1850, 1900, 1945

1800	*1850*	*1900*	*1950*
Reading	Reading	Reading	Reading
Spelling	Declamation	Literature	Literature
Writing	Spelling	Spelling	Spelling
Catechism and Bible	Writing	Penmanship system	Printing and script writing
Arithmetic	Manners and Conduct	Conduct	Citizenship
	Mental Arithmetic and chipering	Arithmetic	Arithmetic
			Oral presentations
	Grammar	Oral language	Correct usage
	Geography	Grammar	Geography
	U.S. History	Geography	History
			Local
	Object lessons	U.S. History	National
			Backgrounds
		Constitution	Constitution
		Object lessons	General Science
		Elementary science	Art
		Drawing	Music
		Music	Hygiene
		Physical exercises	Physical education
		Manual training	Vocational education
			Home making
			Foreign language
			Trips and excursions
			Extracurricular activities

Effect of Increased Enrolment

The increase in school population at the secondary level, previously shown (Figure 10.1), was more than an increase in numbers: it changed the entire character of those who were to seek, through the high-school courses, a richer preparation for living. Although no plan for the selection of students, such as that devised by Jefferson, was ever put into operation, the economic status of the family was a highly important selective factor and failures weeded out those who could not master the traditional subjects of the secondary-school curriculum. The purpose of a high-school education was to prepare for college. Those who attended were a relatively homogeneous group.

Such a description is not applicable to the high-school population of the present. The economic factor still prevents some adolescents from attending high school, and opportunity for secondary education is not evenly distributed as between urban and rural, and Negro and white population. But America has moved steadily toward the goal of the minimum of a high-school education for all youth. As stated in the Harvard Report: "Democracy is not only opportunity for the able. It is equally betterment for the average, both the immediate betterment which can be gained in a single generation and the slower ground swell of betterment which works through generations. Hence the task of the high school is not only to speed the bright boy to the top. It is at least as much (as far as numbers are concerned, far more) so to widen the horizons of ordinary students that they and, still more, their children will encounter fewer of the obstacles to that achievement."

The ways in which the secondary schools sought to meet the new demands and more adequately to serve the ever-increasing heterogeneity of its pupils were many and varied, and can be little more than enumerated. The basic method was the system of unit courses, which provided a varying degree of election of areas of study. These courses soon were grouped into programmes with differentiated requirement for graduation. Such terms as "classical," "technical," "vocational," and "general" were used to designate them, the "general" usually being the one in which were placed students who did not give promise of success in any of the other three. In a few communities, for the most part only in the larger cities, this differentiation has been carried to the extent of establishing separate schools somewhat along the line of several European systems. Such separate schools are illustrated by the Chicago Trade School, the Music and Arts high School in New York City, and the establishment of "area vocational schools" in selected consolidated districts. Another method of meeting the wide range of pupil needs was the segregation of students into ability groups, and differentiating courses on the basis of such relative ability.

Three basic criticisms can be levelled at both the course-unit system and that based on ability grouping. Both are divisive influences. Students think of themselves as different from those in another course or group. At a time when the complexities of modern living provide unfortunate divisive forces in the adult population, the school should be a unifying force rather than one which abets social stratification. The second criticism is that the interests of adolescents are constantly changing, and ability to succeed in school is as much a matter of motivation as of the mythical IQ. Yet both methods of organization of subject matter entail the sealing off of the student from access to areas and activities other than those prescribed for him or which he has selected. The third and, from the point of view of the sociologist the most serious criticism, is that both methods are developed only with reference to the individual; neither gives serious recognition to the needs of society nor is developed with reference to social values.

Meeting These New Needs

Critics have urged that the subject matter of the secondary school be reorganized along patterns more nearly adapted to the society which it sought to serve.

A Special Committee of the American Youth Commission carried still further this emphasis upon common elements of subject matter to meet societal needs. The Committee recommended the development of four new types of basic subject matter for the high school: the continuance of reading with stimulation of wide use of libraries, work experience, social studies, and personal problems. These additions, together with changes in the traditional fields to relate them to these basic subjects, would form the subject matter of the secondary school.

While the clouds of World War II were gathering over America, the basic issue of secondary education was the relative importance of general education—that which should be the common heritage of all pupils—and of special education—that which is elective and provides for differentiated subject matter. Much of the argument was based only upon a priori principles, but an increasing body of data, based upon sociological research, was giving new emphasis to subject matter selected to make the school a more effective agent in social control.

Changes in the subject matter of the college have largely paralleled those in the secondary school, preceding or following changes in the secondary school from time to time. The basic pattern, since the introduction of the elective system about the middle of the last century, has been the same—unit courses grouped into organized programmes with a varying number of free electives. The issue is, as in the high school, the extent to which there should be common elements as contrasted with specialized training.

During the two decades before World War II, with the rapid increase in college enrolment (see Figure 10.1), the same conflict arose not only between general and specialized education, but also over ways to meet the needs of a more heterogeneous population. As the professional schools increased their entrance requirements, especially in medicine and dentistry and to a lesser extent in law, these schools reached down and dictated the specialization in the pre-professional level. New professional schools were established in journalism, business. administration, and other fields, each with its own required cluster of subjects. Of the rapidly developing junior colleges, many offered terminal courses that required the selection of the field of specialization in the freshman year. Even the liberal arts course was divided into specified majors and minors from which it become virtually impossible to change without loss of credit even after one year.

Concurrent with increasing specialization was the growing demand for a more prolonged period of general education. The goal of education shifted on up two more years, with the completion of the sophomore year of college or its equivalent being considered the minimum of universal education. The rapid increase in knowledge, and the extension of educational opportunity argued strongly for a general college to include the first two years, with specialization delayed until completion of the general course.

The Emphasis Upon General Education

The rapid expansion of human knowledge was spurred by the vast Federal subsidies for research in both the sociological and natural sciences, begun during World War II and continuing in the post-war period. Selection of subject matter is essential at all levels of education. There can no longer be a Bacon or a Spencer who is an authority in the entire universe of human knowledge. It is difficult for an individual to be an authority on every aspect of even a limited field. The result, as indicated above, has been the continual splintering of courses and the multiplying of areas of specialization.

The basic issue is the extent to which the expansion of knowledge involves greater specialization or an extension of general education. The emphasis, especially in the past decade, has been upon the need to develop more adequate ability in communication, a deeper appreciation of human relationships and values, and a better understanding of social problems, at the community level as well as national and international. The Purdue Opinion Poll of 2,343 high school students throughout the United States in comparison with a Roper Poll of adults indicated significant differences in answer to the question, "Which one of the following do you think is the most important thing young people should get out of high school?" Of the adults, 13.4 per cent thought "academic background" was the important thing; 41.3 per cent, "vocational training"; and 45.3 per cent, "discipline, responsibility, tolerance, personality, etc." Of the high school students 11 per cent put "academic background" first; only 20 per cent, "vocational training"; and 68 per cent, the sociological and personal values. A study at Cornell University of students in institutions of higher education concludes that the shift toward the physical sciences which occurred during World War II has been reversed, and that students in college in 1952-53 show a greater interest in the social sciences and in national and world affairs, "which are seen as a means of getting along with the varied types of people a citizen of today's world encounters." In addition to these broad changes in emphasis, courses in sociology are now offered in 20 per cent of the high school. Educational sociology is considered a basic course in the training of teachers and is given in many other types of institutions.

It has become increasingly apparent that, although specialization is necessary in many fields, there is a broad expanse of knowledge, attitudes, and appreciations that should be common to all. It is further recognized that such subject matter should be related to function in the total cultural pattern. The result has been the reorganization of detailed subjects into related areas. Many terms are used to describe this development such as "life-adjustment," the "core curriculum," and "general education." An elementary school planned its subject matter for the sixth grade around the one theme, "You and Your Community." A high school developed for its twelfth grade a basic course in "Problems in Democratic Living." Including the goals of democracy, human behaviour, family living, vocational life, and beliefs and values. The courses in general education at the college level seek likewise to relate specific fields to such major areas as: the humanities, the world of the physical sciences, human relations, and communication. The following characteristics are suggested:

1. The general education programme is a co-operative faculty venture. The course of study is determined by the entire faculty concerned, and not by the delegation of courses, subjects, and responsibilities to given departments.
2. The programme is self-contained rather than preparation for advanced study. Instruction is justified by what has been done for the student at its conclusion.
3. There is a minimum reliance upon an automatic and general "transfer of training" or "mental discipline" value from the course of study. The education resembles as closely as possible the conditions in which the results of study will be employed.

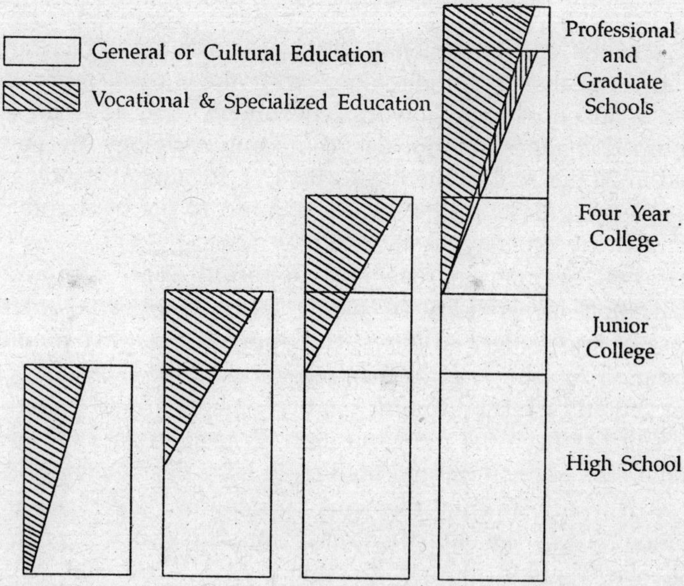

Figure 10.4 : Suggested Proportion of Vocational and Specialized Education and General and Cultural Education for Persons Completing at Each Unit of the Educational System.

4. General education relies more heavily on intrinsic interest and less on intrinsic motivation. This is general education's secret weapon.
5. General education is abidingly philosophical and strives for the unification of knowledge rather than for specialization.
6. General education is presented as an ordered progression, building upon, expanding and applying, at each stage of the work, that which has gone before.
7. General education is concerned with a systematic and continuous investigation of the success of the programme in achieving stated goals.

The point is not that a student should have either general education or vocational and specialized education, but that he should have both, with the emphasis shifting according to the proximity of the student's completing his education. It may be called a shifting hypotenuse pattern, as shown in Figure 10.4. For students who will not go beyond high school, the secondary school programme should involve an increasing proportion of vocational education with a corresponding decrease in general education. For students who continue through only the junior college or the four years, the inclusion of professional education should be postponed until entering college, with a differential in proportion for junior college and four year college students. The programme of students going on to graduate and professional education may well be largely general until the completion of the fourteenth grade. The significance of this concept is that specialization would begin early enough to provide a vocational outlook for each type of student and that some general education would continue to the termination of the education of every student.

Social Processes and Selection of Subject Matter

The social processes of conflict and of co-operation are continually operating in the determination of subject matter of the school and college. There is no uniform pattern of their operation nor should there be. They reflect the local situation, but the social forces involved are of major interest to the educational sociologist.

The writing of a textbook illustrates the operation of the sociological processes. Markedly improved from its predecessors, today's textbook still influences—and too often determines—the subject matter to be taught. Such books can be the basis for regimentation and rote learning or they can be the starting point for significant excursions into the realms of ideas and values. It is the teacher who will largely determine which result is achieved!

That the textbook reflects the cultural pattern is evident from even a cursory glance at textbooks in use in our schools. The moral precepts of the colonial period, the interpretations of slavery and the War between the States, the exclusion or inclusion of sociological issues—these are but a few of the many illustrations. Texts are seldom the product of iconoclastic professors writing in the cloistered atmosphere of their ivy-covered offices. They are increasingly based upon research of at least three types: the maturity of the individual at the grade level for which it is written; the changes in knowledge of the field covered; and, of greatest importance to the educational sociologist, the relevancy of the information to needs in our dynamic sociological structure.

But there are also extraneous sociological forces that influence textbooks and other teaching materials. It is, in one sense, the struggle between reflecting only the dominant cultural pattern and exerting leadership pointing toward desirable social change. In a period of international tension, this conflict is all the more acute.

But in some communities is it more specific. It is a conflict between the professional educator and the groups within the community that seek to dictate the subject matter of the school. Bills have been introduced in state legislative bodies which would exercise control over books in public school and college libraries and over textbooks and other teaching materials. Though few of these bills have been enacted, the fact they have been introduced and promoted by persons who, for the most part, are sincere, has had an indirect influence that cannot be measured. Virgil Hancher, President of the State University of Iowa, stated: "For teachers and students alike the new watchword seems to become 'caution'; teachers were never meant to be cautious."

Fortunately, co-operation also can be illustrated from specific instances in many communities. In Scarsdale, New York, a group of leading citizens, many of them of national reputation, signed the following statement in reply to criticisms levelled at their school:

> We do not minimize the dangers of Communist and fascist indoctrination, but we want to meet these dangers in the American way.
>
> We live in a democratic state. We are the inheritors of a tradition that has encouraged a dynamic development in our intellectual as well as our material life. That tradition has been based on a tolerance that has not feared to permit independent thought. A state that fears to permit the expression of views alternative to those held by the majority is a state that does not trust itself. . . .

> Any sensible person would agree that there are risks involved in allowing young persons relatively free access to a wide range of reading material. Of course there are risks. But we believe there are greater risks in any alternative procedure. Surely we have not, as a people, lost the courage to take the risks that are necessary for the preservation of freedom.

Co-operation is shown also in the participation of pupils, teachers, administrators, and parents in the development of subject matter, using the term in its broader sense. Many co-operative activities are described in an Office of Education report of visitation to school systems throughout the United States. The report concludes:

> This bulletin shows how school systems in various States work to solve some of their problems. The best results are associated with the use of the democratic process at all levels of activity: with primary children, with older children, with teachers' in-service programmes, with parent groups, and with teachers at work with supervisors and administrators. In all instances the problems are of real concern to those involved. Democratic procedures in any group insure the use of the variety of talents and abilities of the members, with each individual feeling that he is a part of the group and that his work and opinion count.

Sociological Principles

From this discussion, certain sociological principles can be established regarding subject matter. It is apparent, first, that change can come only gradually, as it must reflect the basic cultural values of the society it serves yet at the same time be an effective agent in the transmission of the highest values.

Second, the subject matter of the school must be functional in its relation to adult living and, concurrently, be adapted to the level of development of the child. As pointed out in the earlier discussion of objectives, this principle is now increasingly a basis for determination of subject matter.

The third principle is that *subject matter should change continually toward the more effective realization of socially determined objectives.* Research has only begun, but it has already pointed the way to the carrying out of this principle. It is the means through which the school seeks to lay the foundation for the continued improvement of society.

The fourth principle is that *subject matter should be co-operatively determined.* The "expert" still has an important role, but, to assure the effective utilization of the changing subject matter in the classroom, it is essential that students, teachers, administrative officers, and parents have their proportionate responsibility within the range of their experience and ability.

Methods

Although for purposes of analysis, subject matter and method are discussed separately, they cannot be separated in actual practice. The assumption that they can be thus divided is one of the reasons for the wide gulf that still persists between education as a professional field of study and the academic fields, and between teachers colleges and liberal arts institutions. Assertions are still made, "If you know your subject you can teach it to others" and, in opposition, "Teaching is both an art and a science; skill in teaching can be acquired only through professional study." While both statements are true to a degree, neither expresses the whole truth. The unifying factor between these two extreme positions is the emphasis upon the resultant changes in behaviour in students. There can be then no line of cleavage between content and method.

Lock-step Versus Active Participation

In no other field of education has there been such almost revolutionary changes as in both the procedures and the materials of instruction. Contrast the lock-step method of the Lancastrian schools with the active participation of students in the modern classroom, or the forbidding texts of 1900 with the beautifully illustrated books now used!

World War II brought new developments is some methods and accelerated others. The pressure of time made speed of acquisition essential, and the consequences of ignorance or lack of facility in operating an instrument of death provided the necessary motivation. Visual and auditory aids were developed far beyond those that the limited funds for civilian education had previously made possible. Models that simulated actual combat were developed through moving screens, the electric impulse, and numerous other devices. "Mock-ups," models, charts, graphs, posters, cartoons, comic books, recordings for language and other instruction, films—these and many more devices came into common use in military establishments. More important was the fact that the military placed primary emphasis upon learning by doing and upon the use of realistic situations in the learning programme.

Some of the positive methods of the military have carried over to civilian education in the postwar years especially in language teaching and in the physical sciences. But perhaps the most significant change which has occurred in method is the utilization of group interstimulation and interaction. To some degree this was involved in the project method so popular during the 1920's but its major emphasis was the product—making a model of a community, building a school store, or putting on a play. In group dynamics it is the process which is important and through which learning both of subject matter and of behaviour takes place. Although the specific techniques such as "role playing" and "projection" are not equally applicable to all types of subjects, the basic concept is broadly applicable at all grade levels, including adult education.

Utilization of Audio-Visual Material

In the above discussion, little has been said about the vast range of audio-visual aids and of pupil activities which are an integral aspect of subject matter. Motion pictures for instructional use are available through industrial organizations, commercial companies, and through educational film libraries. Pupil activities include filed trips, studies of the community, essays on current issues, literary and dramatic presentations—the list is endless.

The concern of the educational sociologist is not to describe such aids and activities but rather to analyze the processes through which they are selected and carried on. In such analysis there is little need to differentiate one aspect of subject matter from another. In fact, pressures from groups external to the school are greater in relation to the use of such instructional aids than in the more traditional subject matter.

Social Measurement of Education

The importance of measurement and examinations cannot be overemphasized. Not only do they provide a check on the extent of learning that has taken place, but they also, to a large degree, determine both the subject matter and methods of instruction. State board examinations determine the content of professional schools; college entrance examinations dictate the courses of study of the academic high school; the type of tests used by the classroom teacher determine the nature of the material children learn—whether detailed facts, general principles, or data upon which to show relationships and make judgments. Measurement is, then, a vital part of the curriculum.

For the most part, measurements of education have been of the amount and character of learning. The development of standardized tests has tended to crystallize the educative process with its major emphasis upon mastery of subject matter.

The contrast between this traditional emphasis of measurement and that of the educational sociologist is so forcefully stated by Payne, in an unpublished manuscript, that it is quoted at some length:

> The usual principle underlying teaching or method implies three steps:
>
> 1. The discovery of the child's knowledge and interests;
> 2. the teaching of the child on the basis of his knowledge and interests;
> 3. the measurement of the results or his attainment of knowledge.
>
> The principle and its application in practice have notably advanced education along a number of lines. It has led us to ascertain the state of the child's knowledge before beginning the educational process. It has enormously improved the technique of procedure in the educational process itself, and finally it has resulted in very effective

instruments of measurement of the results of education as sought. The achievement along this line represents the most notable progress in the history of education. It represents a definite attempt to make education scientific.

There are, however, from the sociologist's point of view certain weaknesses about this procedure. The sociologist questions the assumption that the acquisition of knowledge is education, although an essential part of the process. He conceives education as a process of making behaviour changes in the individual and in the community, and does not accept the conventional practice as adequate to that end. He regards it as a weak attempt to satisfy certain school objectives which may or may not have social value. Viewed another way, the sociologist looks upon education as a process of developing social controls or controls in the individual over his behaviour in his relationships to the various groups in the social life. He, therefore, regards subject matter as a means to an end, and for that reason will not admit that the three steps in the educational process as they are outlined above are adequate or even significant.

The sociologist, therefore, would state the principle and make its application in another way: He would state the principle somewhat as follows : By adequate survey, measurement, and study, both of the child and the community in which the child lives, find out the character and personality of the child, his social patterns, and his life interests, begin to make changes in his behaviour in line with his social needs, by building upon or modifying his social patterns, his social heritages, his personality and character, and at the end of an instructional period test the child and the community or groups of which he is a part to discover what changes in character, personality, social patterns, and group behaviour have taken place.

This principle like wise involves three steps:

1. the discovery of the personality traits, behaviour patterns, social heritages of the child and the group;
2. the instruction of the child on the basis of these characteristics and interests;

3. and the measurement of the changes in the behaviour of the child and the groups of which he is a part.

The crux of the matter hinges upon the sorts of changes sought through the educational process and the emphasis in the measurement of the results of the educational endeavour. Obviously, we are concerned with functional knowledge and skills, but for them to be functional is not sufficient. What functions do the knowledges and skills serve? The fundamental criterion in determining their value is that they serve the individual in his social relations outside of the schoolroom. Their use in the schoolroom is important only when viewed from the larger social outlook. In other worlds we are interested in the child as a member of a family, a play group, as a citizen, and as an individual that is now functioning in outside-of-school activities ninety per cent of his total time. What the child does in the schoolroom concerns us little except as it rates to his outside activities and changes them. Obviously then the only measurement that is ultimately profitable is the measurement of outside-of-school practices. To be specific, the measurement of the results of education going on in the schoolroom must find application in the behaviour changes of the individual as a social unit.

Although much must yet be done, some illustrations can be given of the application of the principles enunciated by Payne. In the field of safety education, controlled experiments have been conducted, and the results of such instruction measured in terms of the decrease in accident rate. Careful studies, unfortunately limited to a specific practice, the use of a specific commodity, or to a given group, have been made of the extent of changes in home and community diet, measured by consumption, as a result of health instruction in and through the school. Several cities have made extensive studies, by districts, of juvenile delinquency in the effort to determine ways in which the school has changed or may assist in changing antisocial behaviour patterns.

Another illustration is that of the Co-operative Study of Secondary School Standards. The standards originally devised and published in 1939 have been revised and are in use in many schools. It is a self-rating plan and the most fundamental guiding principle of the entire evaluation is that "a school can be studied satisfactorily and judged fairly only in terms of its own philosophy of education, its individually expressed purposes and objectives, the nature of the pupils with whom it has to deal, the needs of the community which its serves, and the nature of the American democracy of which it is a part." Elaborate statistical devices were used as the basis of rating the school on a thermometer scale for each area measured. Reports and judgments by students, teachers, parents, alumni, and visiting committees were utilized. Former students were asked to answer such searching questions as: "To what extent, in your judgment, did your high school education help you in securing or holding your present position? To what extent was your total school experience—scholastic, social, athletic, personal—satisfactory to you?" Table 10.2 presents the rating of 25 secondary schools on the alumni's answers to the question: "To

Table 10.2

Composite Rating of 25 Secondary Schools*

Field	*Very Much*	*Some*	*Very Little*	*None*	*No Reply*
Athletics and sports	9	13	1	2	
Music	8	7	8	2	
Theatres and movies	3	14	7	1	
Use of libraries	15	7	2	1	
Reading books and magazines outside of libraries	13	11	1		
Interest in good health	13	8	3	1	
Religious activities	2	9	10	2	2
Citizenship activities	12	10	2	1	
Social activities	9	12	3	1	
Interest in further formal education	13	9	1	2	
Total	97	100	38	13	2

* Adapted from *Evaluation of Secondary Schools*, page 461. Washington, D.C.: Co-operative Study of Secondary School Standards, 1950.

what extent do you feel that your school course and life developed interest in and appreciation of the following fields and participation in them after you left school?" The low rating given to resulting changes in religious activities, and the scattered effect on music appreciation and the little influence on theatres and movies should be of deep concern to educators at all levels.

This sociological emphasis, supplementing but not supplanting the measurement of subject matter learned and skills acquired, will make education a controlling force in society and will be the basis of evaluating and reconstructing the curriculum of schools and colleges from kindergarten to graduate school.

Summary

The formal and, too often, stereotyped curriculum of earlier years has been challenged at all levels of education. Many factors have brought about this change but two appear to be of primary significance. One, that is as continuous as education, is the changing aim of education. Its results are gradual, as it largely reflects in the United States the changing cultural values; it may be rapid and forced by political changes, as by dictators in totalitarian governments.

The second major factor, which developed largely within this century, is the change in school population. It has influenced the curriculum of secondary and higher education more than that of elementary schools. Some would assert that increased enrolments, present and projected, are the result rather than the cause of curriculum change. There would be reason to accept this point of view were it not for two basic facts in addition to the rise in the number of births: the democratic concept of American education described in the previously and the continually higher level of knowledge, skill, appreciation, and values required for the effective participation of the individual in a dynamic society and of our nation in world affairs.

Many changes in the community have resulted, some involving the establishment of new units of education such as the community college and the separated vocational school and technical institute. Others have resulted in the splintering of subject fields into new fields of specialization. Concurrently, there has been the growing emphasis upon general or cultural education. One fact is obvious: the expansion of knowledge makes selection and reorganization essential.

The educational sociologist is primarily interested in the process through which such issues are appraised and changes are made. Conflict is inevitable as there are few "varieties" and even still relatively little research data. When the conflict is between the school and vested interest groups or self-appointed critics, it may be detrimental to education, when they are the result of sincere differences in judgment they are a constructive force. Co-operation is also a basic proce^s, both among those within the school and between the school and the community.

The task of the school administrator and the teacher will not be easy if these sociological principles are to be translated into effective modification of the entire curriculum—subject matter, methods, school and classroom organization, and measurement. It will entail selection, from the great mass of culture, of those experiences that can be meaningful to the child at his level, that will eliminate or minimize unworthy features from the child's natural environment, and will assure to every person the opportunity to come into living contact with the world of things, of ideas, and of his fellow man.

Topics for Discussion

1. Fill in details, other than those given in he chapter, to show how changes in the aims of education have resulted in changes in the total curriculum. Does the same apply to specific subjects?
2. Do you agree that the changes in the curriculum are the result of the increase in enrolment, especially at the secondary and higher education level, or do you think the reverse is true?
3. Which of the two alternatives in the goal of higher education do you believe is more in the national interest?
4. Review some of the conflicts regarding the curriculum which have resulted from pressure groups. Cite those which you believe have been damaging or those which have been beneficial to education.

5. Is there a danger that the increasing emphasis in social and cultural values will result in too little emphasis upon mastery of content and the development of intellectual ability?
6. If so, what counter influences should be initiated?
7. Describe an instance of the utilization of group dynamics in a classroom situation. To what extent does it differ from earlier concepts of method such as "project" or "problem-solving"?
8. Do you agree with the statement that the instruments of measurement largely determine the curriculum? If so, do present testing programmes exert a wise or unwise influence?
9. To what extent is it possible to measure changes in values and behaviour?

Index